A CRITICAL HISTORY OF

FINANCIAL CRISES

Why Would Politicians and
Regulators Spoil Financial Giants?

A CRITICAL HISTORY OF
FINANCIAL CRISES

Why Would Politicians and Regulators Spoil Financial Giants?

Haim Kedar-Levy

Ben-Gurion University of the Negev, Israel

Imperial College Press

ICP

Published by

Imperial College Press
57 Shelton Street
Covent Garden
London WC2H 9HE

Distributed by

World Scientific Publishing Co. Pte. Ltd.
5 Toh Tuck Link, Singapore 596224
USA office: 27 Warren Street, Suite 401-402, Hackensack, NJ 07601
UK office: 57 Shelton Street, Covent Garden, London WC2H 9HE

Library of Congress Cataloging-in-Publication Data
Kedar-Levy, Haim, author.
    A critical history of financial crises : why would politicians and regulators spoil
financial giants? / Haim Kedar-Levy.
        pages cm
    Includes bibliographical references and index.
    ISBN 978-1-908977-46-5 (alk. paper)
    1. Financial crises--History. 2. Finance--Government policy--History. 3. Financial
institutions--Government policy--History. I. Title.
    HB3722.K43 2015
    338.5'4209--dc23
                            2015021091

British Library Cataloguing-in-Publication Data
A catalogue record for this book is available from the British Library.

In-house Editors: Mary Simpson/Chandrima Maitra

Typeset by Stallion Press
Email: enquiries@stallionpress.com

Printed in Singapore by B & Jo Enterprise Pte Ltd

To Naama, for lifelong love and friendship

Contents

Acknowledgements

I am thankful to Dr. Hagai Boas, editor of the Galai-Tzahal University on Air for many insightful discussions and helpful comments.[1] I thank Prof. Avri Ravid, for inviting me to a sabbatical at Yeshiva University (YU) in New York City, and to the supportive YU faculty and staff, who together allowed me to focus on writing about and teaching financial crises. Many thanks to Dr. Ilanit Madar-Gavious and to CPA Meir Bitan for their helpful comments on accounting issues. I further thank students and colleagues at Ben Gurion University, the Hebrew University in Jerusalem, Ono Academic College, and YU, especially to Gil Elmalem, Orit Milo-Cohen, Benny Naot, and Reuven Ulmansky, for helpful remarks and conversations. From YU, where drafts of this book served as course material on financial crises, I thank Sason Gabay, Ayelet Haymov, Tamar Hochbaum, Judah Isaacs, Desiree Kashizadeh, Shira Leff, Ari Margolin, Akiva Neuman, Aaron Robinow, Penina Rosen, Ilana Schwartz, Dani Weinberger, Michelle Widger, Debbie Wiezman and Aaron Zuckerman. Last but not least, I am indebted to Tamar Lehman and Yaara Levy for outstanding editorial and PowerPoint presentation skills. Thanks to Tamar and Yaara, teachers and students have excellent learning materials.

---

[1] Dr. Boas was the editor of another book of mine: Kedar-Levy, H. *The Major Financial Crises of the Past Century*, Modan Publishing Co., Israel, 2013.

Preface — Regulatory Capture

Modern financial markets and instruments form overly complex economic systems that are interrelated with various media, political, regulatory, social, psychological, and other variables. There is no, and will not be in the foreseeable future, mathematical or statistical model that would account for all those interactions and reasonably *explain*, let alone *predict*, bubbles and financial crises based on observable data.[1,2] Therefore, regulators, politicians, analysts, and the public should always stay on the guard, preparing for the consequences of a crash in asset prices that might lead to a financial crisis.

Given the complexity of modern financial systems, a key question emerges with respect to financial crises: Can one portray, along general lines, the primary causes of financial crises? If so, can particular steps be pointed at in the process that, if adequately modified, could mitigate or evade crises? This book aims to offer the reader a bird's-eye view of the economics and politics behind ten of the most spectacular financial crises of modern times, particularly expanding on the most recent one. The book rarely uses equations, preferring to apply common sense and a chronological description of key facts.

---

[1] On the primary causes of bubbles and crises see, for example, Kaminsky and Reinhart (1996, 1999) and Higgins and Osler (1997).

[2] One reason why mapping those complex interactions cannot yield a reliable predictive model is that unlike physics, the basic elements of econo-social systems are not atoms, but intelligent human beings. While the former react to physical forces in a predictable manner, the latter consider the forces employed on them, and decide how and when to react to those forces.

The financial crisis of September and October 2008 was the largest financial crisis in world history, including the Great Depression of the 1930s.[3] During those months, 12 out of the 13 largest financial firms in the world were on the verge of collapse. Had they gone bankrupt, other financial institutions would have collapsed like a house of cards, innocent depositors would have lost their savings, and real business activity would have shrunk and lead to severe unemployment. Unfortunately, the recent crisis was not the first, and it will not be the last. This book demonstrates that many crises either could have been avoided or mitigated had politicians acted in a timely fashion and empowered regulators to act for the 'taxpayer interest'. Unfortunately, too often politicians and regulators favor the limited interests of the financial sector. More specifically, I show that prior to most crises, *giant financial firms* championed lobbying efforts with politicians and regulators to relax binding regulations. This enabled them to undertake excess risks, which eventually contributed to their collapse. Those financial giants knew they were considered 'to big to fail', thus the bill would be paid by the public. As such, financial giants carry what economists call 'negative externalities', i.e., cost to other firms and members of society. The big question that is asked throughout the book is: Why would politicians and regulators spoil the financial sector?

There is an ongoing debate on the extent of regulation in the financial sector. While in a free-market economy business failures are unavoidable, financial crises are more costly because the financial system is the one that builds and operates the infrastructure that transforms depositors' money into credit to businesses and governments. This function is as vital to economic growth, job creation and prosperity as electrical grids and telecommunications are vital to modern life. For those reasons, the financial sector is, and should be considered as a 'utility', like water supply, power stations and sewer systems. Because most of those utilities are natural monopolies, and hence are regulated, the regulation of most financial institutions is justified as well, whether the industry is dominated by a few giants or many competitive banks.

Surely, financial institutions prefer as weak as possible regulation, while taxpayers prefer a safe and stable financial sector, since the collapse of banks implies using taxpayer money to save those financial institutions that are 'too big to fail'. This tension is expressed in the process of lawmaking where lobbyists propagate their clients' interests in parliament, senate or congress. There is a voluminous research on the 'public interest' theory of

---

[3] Professor Ben Bernanke, see Chapter 15.

regulation, and its implementation,[4] where a key difficulty is identifying the particular segment in the 'public' whose interests should be protected. The identification of 'public' is not clear, and learning about their interests is even tougher. The bottom line is that since there is no way to write the law clear enough to target the specific 'public', legislators leave policy 'slack'. This slack, often denoted 'regulatory slack', allows some leeway to administrators of regulation in fine-tuning the implementation of the law through sets of rules. Essentially, regulators need this slack because they are closer to practice and therefore able to target the specific 'public interest'.

Most economists would agree that monopolistic power should be regulated in favor of the public interest, or else the public will pay higher prices for the particular goods and services. However, Prof. George Stigler argued in 1971 that such regulation would not necessarily work because monopolies have an incentive to 'capture' the regulator by a variety of means, and consequently control it. This result leaves two choices: either tighten regulation and legislation to reduce the costs associated with 'regulatory capture', or give up and pay the high monopolistic prices.

From the economists' perspective on regulatory capture, the interactions between regulators and regulated bodies do not necessarily represent capture.[5] There are a few reasons justifying an alignment of the regulator with regulated firms that do not imply capture. First, the regulator must be familiar with the difficulties of the regulated firms, and has incentives to solve their (real or alleged) problems. Through this interaction, the regulator may adopt the point of view of regulated firms and accept some of their claims. Second, since the public cannot be familiar with the intricate and often complex technical discussions between the regulator and the regulated firms, the public cannot be aware of mistakes that favor with either side. Therefore, the regulator will strive to avoid making mistakes that harm the regulated firms, because they are proficient in the data and will surely fight the mistake. However, the regulator would not be punished if the mistakes harm the public, because the public, in most cases, have no capacity to acknowledge the mistake and act to fix it. Therefore, the regulator may be more tolerant toward making mistakes that favor the regulated firms, at the expense of the public. Third, the regulator may be interested in seeking future employment opportunities in his or her field of expertise, a job that

---

[4] A seminal starting point was Arrow (1951), which has been extended by many, e.g., Levine and Plott (1977) and McCubbins, Noll, and Weingast (1987). A good review is given by Dal Bo (2006).

[5] See Zingales 'Preventing Economists' Capture' in Carpenter and Moss (2013). In this essay Prof. Zingales describes in great details the reasons for capture, irrespective of corruption.

is likely to be offered by a firm the person is regulating at present. Surely, a regulator who is supportive of the needs of the industry is more likely to find a job in the future, thus regulators have incentives to express and implement positive views and actions toward the regulated firms.

Carpenter and Moss (2013, hereafter C&M) offer a 'gold standard' to assess whether capture indeed occurred at given cases. To meet the gold standard, all of the following three parts must be demonstrated:

1. Provide a defeasible model of the public interest.
2. Show that policy was shifted away from the public interest and toward industry interest.
3. Show action and intent by the industry in pursuit of this policy shift sufficiently effective to have plausibly caused an appreciable part of the shift.

The term 'defeasible' means, in C&M's argumentation, that one must show in what ways 'public interest' was hurt, and defend the claim so that future readers and researchers can defy the argument or assess it in an effective way. The terms 'action and intent', in the third point, should not be confused with 'motive', since the latter may prevail without taking any action or having an intent to do harm. For example, a manufacturer usually has an incentive to minimize product cost, but that does not mean that a particular safety incident occurred *because* the manufacturer compromised on safety features of the product, or that there was *intent* to cause harm. Notice that by the second point 'capture' involves shifting policy from the public interest to the firms, and by the third point this shift should be shown to be material enough, and occurred by 'action and intent' of the industry. In Chapter 16 a table is presented, summarizing four cases that meet the gold standard and hence demonstrate that indeed capture occurred prior, and probably led, to major financial crises.

To explore how the above definitions apply to the financial industry, we ask: *Is the financial industry any different from other monopolies?* Seemingly, the financial industry does not reap monopolistic rents because the costs of financial services in most developed countries decline as the financial sector develops new financial instruments. In less developed countries, regulators apply price limits on financial services, which is the easiest regulatory path as prices are observable and comparable. However, financial innovations create value that splits between financial institutions and their clients. Therefore, financial institutions' profits increase, and the question is whether the regulators should intervene. As long as financial innovations merely create value, perhaps existing regulations suffice, but what if financial innovations also increase institutions' risk?

Enter regulatory capture: as you will read throughout the book, prior to many crises and often beneath the surface, the financial industry applied lobbyists' pressure to relax regulation as part of its efforts to tilt policy, or 'regulatory slack' toward its own interests and from the public interest. As long as lobbyists serve one part against another part of the financial sector, then their activities may be considered legitimate. The reason is that the blanket is pooled between those parties, while the public enjoys the good services of a competitive industry (i.e., points 1 and 2 of C&M's golden standard do not apply). However, lobbyists' activities meet both the first and second criteria of C&M if the blanket is pooled away from the public's interest and to the benefit of the financial industry. Some, me included, consider such behavior as *wrong, immoral, and therefore corrupt.*[6] When pooling the blanket to its favor, financial institutions primarily aim at increasing revenues and reducing cost. Among the cost items to be cut one can find quality control on borrowers, and a smaller fraction of equity capital in financing banks; Neither are visible through the prices of financial services, but they increase a bank's risk level (Admati and Hellwig, 2013). When lax regulations pave the way for financial institutions to take more risk, financial crises are bound to follow and reveal the true price of regulatory capture. Because the endgame is that taxpayers pay to rescue financial giants, one must conclude that the financial industry does not differ from other monopolies. The only difference is that the cost of regulatory capture is charged from society in the form of higher than necessary default risks, unemployment, loss of growth and other ill implications of financial crises.

This book will present the different ways regulatory capture precedes financial crises. In all cases the primary motivations to engage in regulatory capture by the financial sector were greed, or 'moral hazard'. Moral hazard is a case where one takes on excessive risk because he or she has insurance against severe losses. Because the financial sector is vital to economic growth, employment and welfare, leaders of the financial industry know that the government will be forced to save the biggest institutions, those that threaten economic and financial stability. Therefore, financial institutions have two incentives that negate the public's interest of competitive free markets: First, they have an incentive to merge and form an oligopolistic industry, as the latter generates higher rents than a competitive environment. Second, knowing that regulators acting on behalf of public interest would limit such

---

[6] The reader may wish to listen to an interview Prof. Russ Roberts conducts with Prof. Luigi Zingales in EconTalk about his 2012 book, including the reference of such capture as corrupt and immoral. This can be found at: http://www.econtalk.org/archives/2012/07/zingales_on_cap.html.

efforts, financial institutions have an incentive to engage actively in regulatory capture, for example, by employing lobbyists toward benefitting the industry at the expense of the public. If successful, politicians and regulators spoil the financial industry by alleviating regulation; financial institutions take higher risks; and once a crisis unfolds, taxpayers pay the bill.

Because financial crises are not frequent, the public tends to forget the lessons of prior crises, turn overconfident and optimistic in times of prosperity, which is the optimal time to relax regulations, until a new crisis hits. When it does, outrage would normally follow, and taxpayers would act on politicians to tighten financial regulation. Therefore, financial regulation is expected to swing like a pendulum: lax before a crisis and tight after a crisis. The last chapter of this book explores the ethical and moral aspects of the interactions between the economics, politics and regulation of the financial system.

So, how may the next crisis look like? The recent global financial crisis forced many governments to increase their debt to other countries, to the International Monetary Fund (IMF), to large banks, to their citizens and others. At the same time, post-crisis regulation was insufficient both in the US, UK, and in the Eurozone. Therefore, the biggest financial systems in the world are still exposed to the high risks that stem from high debt levels, coupled with inadequate regulatory systems. When, eventually, global growth rates increase, the enormous amounts of money that were spent by the US Federal Reserve (the Fed) and European Central Bank (ECB) might cause spending and euphoria. It might create a new asset bubble that will have to crash, and possibly endanger financial stability. Given the poorer ability of indebted governments to cope with collapsing financial institutions, the outcome of the next financial crisis is likely to be more severe than the last one. In fact, as long as key incentive mechanisms in the world financial systems do not change, it is more likely that financial crises will grow more frequent and more severe, than the other way around.

Because financial crises reveal the ultimate cost of financial regulatory capture, and this cost is avoidable, taxpayers should acknowledge the costs and act on legislators to minimize it. Indeed, an important goal for this book is to open those issues to public discourse and facilitate informed discussions on the important roles the financial industry plays in everyone's current and future life. An informed and educated public may play an important role in shaping the scope of financial regulation and avoiding misleading arguments.[7]

---

[7] Admati and Hellwig (2013, 2014) are excellent reads with respect to misleading arguments against increasing the portion of equity capital in bank financing.

Additional Reading

Admati, A.R. and Hellwig, M.F. (2013). *The Bankers' New Clothes: What's Wrong with Banking and What to Do About It.* Princeton, NJ: Princeton University Press.

Admati, A.R. and Hellwig, M.F. (2014). The Parade of the Bankers' New Clothes Continues: 28 Flawed Claims Debunked. Rock Center for Corporate Governance at Stanford University Working Paper No. 143. Available at SSRN: http://ssrn.com/abstract=2292229.

Arrow, K. J. (1951). *Social Choice and Individual Values.* New York: Wiley.

Daniel, C. and Moss, D. (eds) (2013). *Preventing Regulatory Capture: Special Interest Influence and How to Limit it.* The Tobin Project. Cambridge: Cambridge University Press.

Dal Bo, E. (2006). 'Regulatory Capture: A Review,' *Oxford Review of Economic Policy*, 22, 2, 203–225.

Higgins, M. and Osler, C. (1997). 'Asset Market Hangovers and Economic Growth: The OECD During 1984–93,' *Oxford Review of Economic Policy*, 13, 110–134.

Kaminsky, G. and Reinhart, C. (1996). 'Banking and Balance-of-Payments Crises: Models and Evidence.' Working Paper, Board of Governors of the Federal Reserve, Washington, D.C.

Kaminsky, G. and Reinhart C. (1999). 'The Twin Crises: The Causes of Banking and Balance of-Payments Problems,' *American Economic Review*, 89, 473–500.

Levine, M.E. and Plott, C.R. (1977). 'Agenda Influence and Its Implications,' *Virginia Law Review*, 63, 561–604.

McCubbins, M., Noll, R., and Weingast, B. (1987). 'Administrative Procedures as Instruments of Political Control,' *Journal of Law, Economics and Organization*, 3, 2, 243–277.

Zingales, L. (2012). *A Capitalism for the People: Recapturing the Lost Genius of American Prosperity.* New York: Basic Books.

1.

What are Bubbles and Financial Crises?

1.1 Introduction

Financial crises are not new. The first documented ones are the Dutch Tulip Bubble and its painful crash in 1637, and the South Sea Bubble of 1720, when even Sir Isaac Newton lost a fortune. Between the years 1816 and 1866, such crises occurred once every ten years or so.

Although historically each crisis is different, the science of economics seeks to identify lines of similarity between different crises and to formulate a model that describes, albeit in general terms, the different stages along which a typical crisis evolves. This chapter illustrates the key ingredients of a financial crisis by highlighting a few notions of a model developed by Prof. Hyman Minsky. Only financial systems based on free-market principles will be discussed, i.e., crises that have occurred in economies run by a central planner will not be analyzed.

1.2 A Conceptual Framework of Financial Crises

The pace of growth in a market-based economy is often measured as the percentage chance in gross domestic product (GDP). This pace of growth, or 'growth rate', is not fixed but rather cyclical; sometimes rapid, sometimes slow, there might be periods of zero growth, and even negative growth. In other words, the economy expands and shrinks in a process known as the 'business cycle'. In times of rapid economic growth, there is generally a rise in credit, and specifically loans are extended by the banking system to households and firms. On the other hand, when the business cycle is at low tide, a reduction in credit is usually seen. The positive correlation between the credit cycle and the business cycle is an important starting point in Minsky's model.

Hyman Minsky (a Professor of economics at Washington University in St. Louis, 1919–1996) believed that the expansion process of a business cycle is accompanied by optimism among most investors regarding the expected profitability level of enterprises in which they invest. Therefore, they are willing to take out larger loans and invest in more risky enterprises. At the same time, the optimistic atmosphere overtakes lenders who are therefore ready to lend more and finance even riskier enterprises. However, the optimistic phase of the business cycle is ultimately replaced by a pessimistic phase, and the fall in the value of investments gives rise to bankruptcies and a partial loss of previously extended loans. Irving Fisher, one of the most prominent economists of the 20th century, believed that a financial system is liable to significant risk when large borrowers take out particularly large loans to fund purchases of real estate, stocks or other assets *due to speculative motives*. That is to say, the motivation is buying today with the intention of selling the asset later, hopefully reaping a capital gain.

The term 'speculation' will be used frequently throughout this book, with the following definition: The word 'speculation' is derived from the Latin word *specula*, which means 'observation tower'. Just as a watchman in a tower sees further than one on the ground, the speculator similarly presumes to see several moves forward, predicting future prices. The speculator will buy today if the price is expected to rise, and sell today if the price is expected to fall. If they guess correctly, the speculator will benefit from a 'capital gain' (the difference between the selling price and the purchase price). Note that on the other hand, a non-speculative investment is one intended to profit mainly from the yield of a capital asset, i.e., coupon interest on bonds, dividends paid out on stocks, rental revenue from real estate or the utility worth yielded by the apartment one lives in. Nevertheless, if there is no profit but rather a loss, then that large borrower rolls over the losses to the unfortunate lenders and gives them a 'haircut', i.e., he pays back only part of the debt.[1] True, one can get a haircut even when investing in non-speculative bonds, but the risk is lower.

Because asset prices change as new information hits the market — with negative information reducing the price and positive information increasing it — a speculative investment is considered risky. To illustrate, consider a speculator who purchased an asset in anticipation for a price

---

[1]'Haircuts' are often considered as partial payment of debt from a debtor to the lender/s. They occur primarily when the debtor and the lenders understand that forcing bankruptcy on the debtor will result in a lower net income to the lenders.

increase, but a random, unexpected news event reduces the price. This speculator might lose on the transaction, therefore act to immediately sell the asset, further exacerbating the price decline. This implies that while a speculative investment infuses new money into the market so long as prices are rising, it withdraws money from the market when prices fall. Thus, it constitutes a factor that amplifies price fluctuations and contributes to instability.

According to Minsky, the process that leads to a financial crisis (to be called a 'bubble' at this stage and defined later) stems from an external shock to the system sufficiently significant so as to cause at least one sector in the economy to believe that the economic future is positive. Private investors and firms operating in that business sector will take out loans in order to benefit from anticipated growth. These loans will finance what seem to be the most promising enterprises. As excess demand for those enterprises increases, their market value increases. This process may spur optimism into other sectors in the economy, sometimes to the point of generating euphoria.

What may be the nature of Minsky's external shock? In the 19th century it was the success or failure of agricultural crops; in the 1920s it was the development of the car industry and establishment of infrastructures for transportation and industry; in the Japan of the 1980s it was financial liberalization and the rise in value of the Japanese yen; in the second half of the 1990s, it was, globally, the development of the Internet, which ensured (or so people thought) improved profitability of firms to the point of creating a 'new economy'. In other instances it was the start or end of a war.

As one may gather, the causes might be different but the outcome is similar. Time and time again, investors, manufacturers and speculators convince themselves that 'this time is different'. That notion, a repeated and central motif in the long history of financial crises, delivers the sad fact that many of the lessons taught are not learned. And even if they are learned in academic circles, they are not assimilated into the investment community. 'This time is different' is a phrase that Sir John Templeton named 'the four most expensive words in the English language'.

1.3 Bubbles and Models of Bubbles

According to Minsky, financial crises begin with an external shock that results in a bubble; what has not been discussed, however, is why bubbles grow to the proportions that only in retrospect appear insensible. When and why do they collapse, and, generally speaking, how do we define a bubble?

Charles Kindleberger,[2] an important researcher into financial crises, attributes a socio-psychological explanation of a bubble's development in Minsky's model: He contends that private investors and firms who see their neighbors profiting from speculative investments find it hard to remain indifferent, so they too enter the circle of speculators.

Kindleberger coined the expression: 'There is nothing as disturbing to one's well-being and judgment as to see a friend get rich.' In the same vein, banks, too, cannot stand still and watch their competitors increase their market share and profits; therefore they increase loans to interested borrowers, lessen their quality control and expose themselves to increased risk. Thereafter, households and businesses, regularly not part of the circle of speculators, can be swept away into a bubble-producing circle that feeds itself so long as prices rise. Suddenly it seems as if it's exceedingly easy to get rich and risk is perceived as being especially low. If someone acknowledges they are invested in a bubble asset, they are in many cases convinced that they'll be able to sell before the big crash. This is also how numerous other players think, but in the meantime no one is selling because prices keep increasing.

Kindleberger calls this process 'mania' or a 'bubble'. 'Mania' is a word that alludes to irrational behavior while 'bubble' hints at something destined to burst. There are numerous definitions for a bubble, but it seems that most economists would agree on one: a deviation of an asset's market price from its fundamental, basic value. In other words, the size of a bubble is measured by the difference between the asset's market price and its fundamental value, as presented in Figure 1.1.

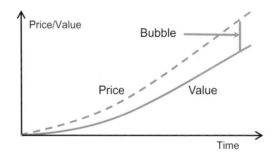

Figure 1.1   Price, value, and bubble

---

[2] Charles P. Kindleberger (1910–2003) was a professor of economics at Massachusetts Institute of Technology (MIT). Considered an important authority on financial crises, he was among the leaders of the post-WWII Marshall Plan.

While an asset's price can be easily observed in the market, its fundamental value cannot be directly observed, but instead is calculated by an economic model. The economic model takes into account anticipated cash flow, risk, liquidity and other factors. Here lies the most problematic aspect of identifying and handling bubbles: Because there is no single agreed-upon model that investors and economists use in evaluating an asset's fundamental value, different analysts will arrive at different values. Therefore, they might not agree on the presence and size of a bubble. A situation may arise in which one analyst concludes that a bubble exists while their colleague, employing a different model may conclude the opposite. The colleague might even employ the same model but make different assumptions regarding the magnitude of specific parameters within that model and conclude that no bubble exists.

Many models attempt to explain bubbles. Most can be segmented into two major categories: rational and behavioral.[3] Rational models can further be segmented into two subcategories. Firstly, 'symmetric information' models where all investors have equal access to information, Secondly, 'asymmetric information' models are those based on differential access to information.

Behavioral bubble models can also be divided into two major categories: 'heterogeneous beliefs' vs. 'limits of arbitrage'. The next four subsections provide more detail on these subcategories.

1.3.1 *Rational models: Symmetric information*

There seems to be agreement among researchers that bubbles cannot evolve in an economy in which prices are determined by rational investors operating in an efficient market[4] under information symmetry, except under very odd conditions. A key reason is 'backward induction', which says that if indeed investors have perfect knowledge of the economy, they must know that a bubble exists, therefore the 'price' must at some point drop to close the gap with the asset's 'value'. But if this drop is expected, say 30 days from today, all

---

[3] Generally speaking, when economists say 'behavioral' they mean to say that economic agents (investors and other decision makers) act in accordance with a psychologically documented pattern.

[4] An efficient market is defined as one that incorporates all relevant information into the asset's price. As such, no investor is able to use new information *in a systematic manner* and reap excess profit on that asset. We highlight 'in a systematic manner' because investors acting in an efficient market may gain on news by chance, but not on a regular basis.

investors know that others will sell it beforehand, perhaps on the 29th day. Because everyone expects a massive sell-off on the 29th day, they will sell on the 28th day, and so on. The end game is that everyone sells the asset today, closing the gap and bursting the bubble immediately. Therefore, rational bubbles under symmetric information are generally ruled out.

1.3.2 *Rational models: Asymmetric information*

The general tone in an asymmetric information model is that not everyone in the economy is aware of the bubble, therefore it may prevail. To understand why, consider an extreme case where although everyone knows that a bubble exists, they are not certain about other people's knowledge. Because people do not know for sure that everyone else knows that a bubble exists, they have an incentive to hold the overpriced asset. They do so because they are hoping to sell, for a profit, to 'a greater fool' (as Kindleberger put it) who is unaware of the bubble.

1.3.3 *Behavioral models: Heterogeneous beliefs*

In these models investors buy an asset because its price increased recently, ignoring its fundamental value. They make this peculiar purchasing decision because of one of the following behavioral patterns:[5]

(1) They may be overconfident in the signals they observe. Overconfidence stems from a number of reasons, among them the freedom to choose, familiarity with the situation, abundant information, emotional involvement and past successes.
(2) If they held the asset before its price increased, and they buy more once it started increasing, they might attribute this good decision to their own judgment, rather than chance. This is called 'self-attribution'.
(3) They may buy the asset because of sentiment.

Either way, rational investors sell the assets to behavioral investors, who end up losing on average. Because neither the rational nor the behavioral investors try to infer the other side's beliefs from market prices, they 'agree to disagree' on the value of the asset, therefore hold heterogeneous beliefs.

---

[5] See Nofsinger's excellent book (2013) on behavioral biases in finance and economics for a broader description of those behavioral effects.

1.3.4 *Behavioral models: Limits of arbitrage*

In these models irrational traders initiate a bubble by buying previously increasing stocks, similar to the behavior in the previous case. However, at the same time arbitrageurs are unable or have no incentive to trade against the bubble. One reason may be the high level of risk that behavioral investors impinge on the stock price. These unpredictable trades make arbitrage too risky, deterring arbitrageurs from attacking the bubble. Another explanation rests with the aversion to high risk that the suppliers of funds to arbitrageurs might exhibit as the bubble grows. A third explanation is that individual arbitrageurs know they cannot burst the bubble with their own funds, therefore they prefer riding it. While they also know that they can burst the bubble by collaborating with other arbitrageurs, they have no incentive to coordinate an attack.

Notice that in both types of behavioral method the investors lose money on average to the more systematic, rational arbitrageurs (professionals call it 'dumb money' vs. 'smart money'). Economists who hold rational arguments maintain that over time either dumb money investors lose all their wealth to smart money investors, or dumb money investors deposit their funds with smart money managers. Either way, prices would eventually be determined by smart money investors, therefore behavioral factors should not have material effects at the aggregate level over the long term.

1.4 Implications of Crashing Bubbles

Why don't bubbles collapse the moment they are exposed? An investor who is certain about the presence of a bubble will prefer selling the asset at its inflated price rather than waiting and taking the risk of losing the bubble component of the price (remember that the inflated price is made of two parts: the fundamental value and the bubble component). This question has several answers, but one of the most convincing maintains that even the largest and most sophisticated investors in the market, namely hedge funds, lack the power to burst the bubble by themselves. True, they could coordinate their actions and burst it with combined forces, but they have no incentive to do so, thus the bubble continues to grow (Abreu and Brunnermeier, 2003).

When a bubble collapses, the first event witnessed is a 'price crisis': asset prices drop sharply. However, not every price crisis leads to a financial crisis, and not every financial crisis leads to a slowdown or recession in the real economy, as measured by declining consumer demand, production and employment. The stages in the evolution of a financial crisis will be described in the next chapter; at this stage it is only mentioned that according to Minsky, a price crisis harms the real economy via the mechanism of 'financial leverage'. Financial leverage refers to financing an investment through debt. As the use of debt increases, it can be said that the firm, the bank, the government or a private investor is more *leveraged*; and with leverage, financial risk increases. In order to illustrate, imagine a firm whose sole asset is a hotel purchased with a loan totaling 90% of the hotel's value. The lender requires a collateral, the hotel, therefore this transaction is a classic mortgage. If a price crisis causes the hotel's value to fall by more than 10%, then the hotel's value becomes lower than the value of debt. In such a situation the lender might force liquidation of the hotel to redeem the loan, forcing the firm into bankruptcy. This will result, among other things, in a loss of jobs and hence to lower purchasing power of the unemployed. True, the firm could try to convince the lender to postpone or reduce loan repayments (the 'haircut') and continue running the hotel toward a better fortune to both the firm and the lender, but that could prove to be impossible.

The credit cycle was especially important to Minsky, mainly the unstable pace in the growth of credit supplied by the banking sector. Before the era of commercial banking, in the 17th and 18th centuries credit was granted based on the private funds of the entrepreneur or the supplier's credit. Therefore, speculative investment was financed by personal capital or suppliers' capital. When commercial banks developed, it was they who brought about an increase in the credit supply, mainly through the banking/money multiplier (expanded on in the next chapter), but it was also caused through the establishment of new banks. New banks sought to increase their market share and thus improved their deposit conditions for the public. Yet the established banks were not happy to give up their market share and consequently supplied more and more credit to their customers. This type of banking competition was witnessed in the 1980s when European banks granted credit to South American countries, primarily Mexico, Brazil and Argentina, while competing with American banks. American banks reacted by providing loans with even more lenient conditions. Thus it happened that banking competition flooded those countries with loans. When Mexico and Argentina ran into trouble, resulting in losses to the banks that extended loans, the banks' financing sources dried up and the two countries were forced to turn to Western governments for assistance. The Europeans passed the hot potato to the US government, which was forced to help. Such being the case, it is seen that the banking credit cycle can range between a surplus of credit supply and a severe credit shortage. This means that the banking/money multiplier can work in reverse! Without credit, numerous business owners are dependent on the good grace of lenders. And if the banking sector doesn't supply the financial resources, then business owners turn to government, which for its part considers economic policy and political restrictions. As history proves, sometimes governments cannot or do not want to help private firms.

One of the important political issues associated with the credit cycle is the question of whether the government or central bank, entrusted with managing the monetary system, must and can supervise the banking credit supply and impose restrictions in order to prevent severe fluctuations in it. More than once, supervisory authorities have imposed restrictions on the ability of banks and other financial institutions to extend credit to all or some of their customers. Occasionally, such a move has been successful, but there are cases in which it has not. For example, in the 1920s, responding to restrictions on credit for stock purchases, banks set up fully owned, unregulated subsidiaries that 'imported' capital from Europe and Japan, thereby supplying credit to speculators. Because these subsidiaries were not supervised, the credit supply grew despite the limiting actions of the central bank.

1.5 International Implications

Before concluding this chapter, it is important to briefly discuss the international aspects of bubbles — in other words, the mechanisms that transfer a bubble from one country to the next. This is often denoted in the financial literature as 'contagion', which is essentially a domino effect. The first linkage mechanism consists of commercial relations. For example, the housing and stock market bubbles in the Japan of the 1980s affected asset prices in South Korea, Taiwan and Hawaii. Why? Because South Korea and Taiwan, once colonies of Japan, supplied it with raw materials and other products, so the economic boom in Japan was beneficial to its two suppliers. Hawaii is a favored vacation spot for many Japanese. As the Japanese grew richer they spent more time in Hawaii and purchased vacation homes there. Japanese entrepreneurs purchased land to build hotels and golf courses, and thus the Japanese bubble led to increased real estate prices in Hawaii.

The second mechanism in the transfer of bubbles between countries is arbitrage. The simplest example to demonstrate the concept of arbitrage would be a situation in the market where a specific asset is traded at two different prices in two different markets. In such a case, investors will purchase the asset in the first market, where it is traded at a cheaper price, and sell it in the market where its price is higher. The investor will indeed profit from the difference, but as such transactions multiply, the cheaper price will rise because of excess demand while the expensive price falls due to excess supply. Ultimately, both prices will even out, therefore the first traders to buy low and sell high will gain the difference. The arbitrage mechanism is what transferred the price of steel, which rose in China due to unprecedented local demand in 2010–2011, to the rest of the world, while causing a wave of rising prices in associated branches.

The third mechanism is the international flow of capital. A boom in a particular country is expressed in high demand for its financial assets, which are perceived as being safer and expected to yield high returns, a process that strengthens the currency. Take, for example, a situation in which the US is considered a stable economy. Foreign countries (such as China) are interested in holding US government bonds, as they are considered very safe. Beyond rising demand for American bonds, which increases their prices, foreign countries must sell their own currency in order to purchase US dollars. This raises the price of the dollar, which becomes a strong currency that makes imports to the US cheaper. Thus an economic boom in the US converts into demand for overseas products, which helps those foreign countries in their growth. Understandably, the strong currency makes it difficult for American exports, thus lowering local production and employment. For example, throughout the 1990s and 2000s many US firms 'solved' this problem by relocating factories to the Far East, generating unemployment in the US and increased employment overseas, i.e., the US exported local jobs.

The fourth and final mechanism is the psychological connection. A sense of euphoria or pessimism in one country spreads to other countries, mainly through the media, and influences investor expectations as well as the tendency to consume or save.

1.6 Conclusion

This introductory chapter concludes by saying that financial crises have always existed and will continue to exist. Their forms may change according to changing economic environments, but they have similar characteristics that are identifiable. Therefore, the next time your taxi driver, barber or cashier asks you if it's the time to enter the market or invest in real estate, be aware that this is the ultimate signal that you are in the midst of the euphoric stage of a bubble. The next chapter will get into more detail and survey the world of investments as well as the banking system at the heart of the financial sector.

Additional Reading

Indispensable and not too formal books on financial crises include:

Kindleberger, C.P. and Aliber, R.Z. (2005). *Manias, Panics, and Crashes: A History of Financial Crises*. 5th edition. New York: John Wiley and Sons.

Krugman, P. (2009). *The Return of Depression Economics and the Crisis of 2008*. New York: W. W. Norton & Company.

Minsky, H.P. (2008). *Stabilizing an Unstable Economy*. New York: McGraw-Hill.

Roubini, N. and Mihm, S. (2010). *Crisis Economics: A Crash Course in the Future of Finance*. New York: Penguin.

A quick read on behavioral effects in finance:

Nofsinger, J.R. (2013). *The Psychology of Investing*. 5th edition. Upper Saddle River, NJ: Prentice Hall.

There is a long list of academic research papers on bubbles and crises. Here are some that discuss key aspects of bubbles.

1. Rational bubbles

Blanchard, O.J. (1979). 'Speculative Bubbles, Crashes and Rational Expectations,' *Economic Letters*, 3, 387–389.

Blanchard, O.J. and Watson, M. (1982). 'Bubbles, Rational Expectations and Financial Markets,' in P. Wachtel (ed.), *Crises in the Economic and Financial Structure*, Lexington, MA: Lexington Books, pp. 295–315.

Burmeister, E., Flood, R. and Garber, P. (1983). 'On the Equivalence of Solutions in Rational Expectations Models,' *Journal of Economic Dynamics and Control*, 5, 311–321.

Flood, R. and Garber, P. (1980). 'Market Fundamentals Versus Price-Level Bubbles: The First Tests,' *Journal of Political Economy*, 88, 745–770.

Santos, M.S. and Woodford, M. (1997). 'Rational Asset Pricing Bubbles,' *Econometrica*, 65, 19–57.

Tirole, J. (1982). 'On the Possibility of Speculation Under Rational Expectations,' *Econometrica*, 50, 1163–1181.

2. Rational bubbles under information asymmetry

Allen, F. and Gale, D. (2000). 'Bubbles and Crises,' *Economic Journal*, 110, 236–255.

Allen, F., Morris, S. and Postlewaite, A. (1993). 'Finite Bubbles with Short Sale Constraints and Asymmetric Information,' *Journal of Economic Theory*, 61, 206–229.

3. Behavioral models of bubbles

Barberis, N., Shleifer, A. and Vishny, R. (1998). 'A Model of Investor Sentiment,' *Journal of Financial Economics*, 49, 307–343.

Daniel, K., Hirshleifer, D. and Subrahmanyam, A. (1998). 'Investor Psychology, and Security Market Under- and Overreactions,' *Journal of Finance*, 53, 1839–1885.

DeBondt, W. and Thaler, R. (1985). 'Does the Stock Market Overreact?' *Journal of Finance*, 40, 793–805.

DeLong, B., Shleifer, A., Summers, L. and Waldmann, R. (1990a). 'Positive Feedback Investment Strategies and Destabilizing Rational Speculation,' *Journal of Finance*, 45, 379–395.

DeLong, B., Shleifer, A., Summers, L. and Waldmann, R. (1990b). 'Noise Trader Risk in Financial Markets,' *Journal of Political Economy*, 98, 703–738.

Scheinkman, J. A. and Xiong, W. (2003). 'Overconfidence and Speculative Bubbles,' *The Journal of Political Economy*, 111, 1183–1219.

4. Why and how do bubbles crash?

Abreu, D. and Brunnermeier, M.K. (2003). 'Bubbles and Crashes,' *Econometrica*, 71, 173–204.

Chen, J., Hong, H. and Stein, J. (2001). 'Forecasting Crashes: Trading Volume, Past Returns, and Conditional Skewness in Stock Prices,' *Journal of Financial Economics*, 61 (3), 345–381.

Hong, H. and Stein, J. (1999). 'A Unified Theory of Underreaction, Momentum trading and Overreaction in Asset Markets,' *The Journal of Finance*, 54, 2143–2184.

Hong, H. and Stein, J. (2003). 'Differences of Opinion, Short-sales Constraints and Market Crashes,' *Review of Financial Studies*, 16, 487–525.

2.

Key Properties of the Financial System and Financial Securities

2.1 Introduction

This chapter describes, along rather general lines, the structure of the economic system and examines the role that the financial system takes within it. It also describes the key attributes of two of the most important financial assets: bonds and stocks. Readers familiar with these basic terms can skip to Chapter 3, which describes the importance of commercial banks within the economic system, and the different types of banking crises.

2.2 Key Players in a Free-Market Economy

Any free-market economy has three key players, or 'agents', as the economists often refer to those groups: households, the private business sector and government (Figure 2.1). Households supply labor services to firms in exchange for 'gross income' (salaries, before tax payment). From those salaries, taxes are paid to the government in return for government services, leaving the household with 'net labor income'.

This remaining net income serves households for two main purposes: consumption and savings (Figure 2.2). Each household decides how much it spends on food, education, communication bills, recreation and other expenditures. The amount left after paying expenses is directed into 'savings'. And what do people do with savings? The principal purpose of savings, other than a cushion for a rainy day, is to finance consumption for the years following retirement, when the monthly flow of labor income stops. Households that do not save might face an unpleasant decline in standards of living after retirement.

Figure 2.1   Interactions between the three key economic agents

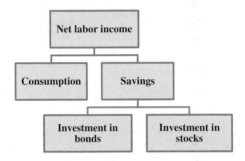

Figure 2.2   A household's income allocation

Most savings are managed by financial institutions such as pension funds, insurance companies or mutual funds. These institutions collect the relatively small amounts that individual households deposit with them, and invest those collective large amounts primarily in bonds and stocks. Obviously, households can and do manage savings on their own, also mostly holding bonds and stocks.

If households and financial institutions hold those assets, then other parties in the economy must have issued them and sold them to the public. The issuers of bonds include business firms, governments and municipalities, while issuers of stocks (equity shares) are business firms only. All security issuers, whether bonds or stocks, issue them in order to finance short- and long-term activities. Businesses need the financing to establish new factories, or to invest in research and development, in building inventories or in marketing campaigns. By doing so the business sector creates new jobs. Governments and municipalities need the financing to establish

and improve societal services like security, road construction and mainte-
nance, education, entertainment and so on. It turns out that households'
savings serve as an important (albeit not single) source of funds for economic growth and employment.

2.3 Key Properties of Bonds

A bond is a loan contract between a lender and a borrower. The terms of the
loan are specified as an integral part of the contract. The lender (for example, a household) gives the borrower (for example, a government or company that has issued the bond) a cash amount today, against the borrower's
promise to pay it back in the future. In many cases the lender receives a flow
of 'coupons' on pre-specified dates, normally at annual or semi-annual inter-
vals, which make a 'cash flow'. The coupon amount is calculated as the product of the 'coupon rate' (measured in percentage terms, and specified in the
bond), by the 'face value' of the bond, i.e., the loan amount (which is specified on the front page of the bond, therefore denoted 'face value').

If, for example, the loan amount is $1,000 and the coupon rate is 4%
paid once a year, then the coupon amount is $1,000 x 0.04 = $40. The bond
also specifies the term of the loan, which may range from less than one day
to many years. Most bonds pay a series of coupons, and pay back the face
value amount together with the last coupon. Therefore, they are called 'coupon bonds'. In order to be entitled to receive this cash flow the bondholder
must pay the bond price, −P, today. If the bond just described 'matures',
(i.e., the loan's term, or ending date), three years from today the bondholder may expect to receive the following cash flow over those three years:

Year	0	1	2	3
Cash flow ($)	−P	+40	+40	+1040

Notice that P has a negative sign in the cash flow because it is an outlay
for the investor, while the other elements are positive because they represent proceeds.

Some bonds do not pay coupons (zero coupon bonds), but rather pay
the face value amount on a pre-specified date. These include, for example,
the US Treasury Bills. A zero coupon bond with a face value of $1,000 that
matures a year from today has this expected cash flow:

Year	0	1
Cash flow ($)	−P	+1000

How is the price 'P' determined? Should the market value of this zero coupon bond today be $1,000? Generally, the answer is 'no', because a prospective buyer of this bond may have an alternative use for their money. If our prospective buyer can earn, say, 3% on a dollar invested today, than a $1,000 investment will be worth $1,030 = $1,000 × (1 + 3%), a year from today, which is more than the zero coupon bond that only pays $1,000. The, $1,030 is said to be the 'future value' of the $1,000 at present. Equivalently, the $1,000 today is the 'present value' of the $1,030 of the future. To covert future cash flows to the present, and present values to future values, we use interest rates that serve as *relevant alternatives* for the investor. This interest rate is known as the 'alternative cost of capital', and it must take into account various factors, primarily the anticipated risk level of the cash flow.

If $1,030 cash flow a year from now is equivalent to $1,000 today, then how much is a $1,000 future cash flow worth today? The answer is $1,000/(1 + 3%) = $970.87. Notice that we convert a present amount to a future value by *multiplying* it by 1 + the relevant interest rate, but we convert a future amount to present value by *dividing* it by 1 + the relevant interest rate. The process of bringing future cash flows to the present is called 'discounting'.

Because the borrower is *obliged* by the contract to pay the interest and face value — whether in a given fiscal year they had a profit or a loss — coupon payments to the bondholder are secured so long as the company, or government, has not gone bankrupt. A bond, then, is considered a relatively safe asset. The lower the bankruptcy risk, the safer the bond and the lower the relevant interest rate. Clearly, the more risk associated with the expected cash flow, the higher the interest rate. It is seen below how important this attribute is in times of financial crises.

When discounting cash flows of periods that are longer or shorter than one year, the discounting procedure must be made by raising the denominator to the power of a number that represents the count of periods until the payment is made. This is mostly denoted by a counter, t. If, for example, we wish to discount $100 that we expect to receive in period $t=2$, and the interest rate is 5%, then it will be discounted by $100/(1 + 5\%)^2 = \$90.70$. This is important because long-term bonds pay the face value and many coupons far into the future, where t is high. Therefore, small changes in interest rates go into high powers and induce large changes in the bond price. This is one reason why long-term bonds are more risky than short-term bonds.

These calculations reveal a very important attribute of bond pricing: *bond prices move in an opposite direction to the change of discount rates*. When discount rates increase at a given amount, bond prices decline, all the more so as the bonds mature far in the future.

This property means, for example, that two bonds offering identical expected cash flows might trade at different prices today (the present value of expected cash flow), which means their cash flows must have been discounted by different discount rates. A general rule (exceptions of course exist) is that higher discount rates represent higher risk, or uncertainty in receiving the expected cash flow of coupon and or face value. Therefore, the cheaper bond between the two identical ones must be riskier. For that reason, as a crisis evolves, and the anticipated risk level of governments and firms increases, their bond prices drop.

Another property that is beyond the scope of this book but deserves a brief description is liquidity. Consider a case where many investors wish to sell or buy together, and there are no buyers or sellers on the other side. In this case a given excess supply will induce a large price drop, while a given excess demand will induce a large price increase. If investors' trades have a substantial impact on the asset's price, we say that this asset is not liquid, or 'illiquid'. Illiquid assets must pay a premium to their holders in order to compensate them for potential losses when buying or selling. This is called the 'illiquidity premium'. In periods of distress in financial markets many investors trade in the same way — they sell or buy the same assets, therefore the illiquidity premium becomes very high and increases the discount rate on (mainly corporate) bonds. As a result, their prices drop even more than the decline that was warranted by the increase in bankruptcy risk. At the same time, investors normally flock to buy government bonds because they are considered safer and more liquid. This 'flight to safety' increases government bond prices, therefore reducing their yields (r, in the cash-flow discounting examples above). As a result, the difference between yield on corporate bonds and government bonds increases. This difference is denoted in the market as 'spread'. It will be seen that, in times of crises, spreads increase rapidly and sharply. Comparing spreads of government bonds sees a similar notion: The spread is often calculated between the yield of any government bond and a comparable one issued by the US government.

2.4 Key Properties of Stocks

Stocks are different from bonds in two key aspects. First, instead of receiving a fixed amount (coupon) periodically, a stock *may* pay an uncertain dividend amount. Second, a stock has no end date at which the invested amount is to be 'paid back' to the investor. Instead, the investor may sell the stock in the stock market (or to another person if the stock is not traded on an exchange), and receive the uncertain price that prevails on that day.

A stock represents partial ownership of the firm that issued it (see Figure 2.3). Today most such firms are 'limited liability' firms, characterized by the fact that the largest possible loss to stockholders is limited to their investment in the firm. As a result, an investor who purchased ten shares for $100 each might lose at most the investment amount, $1,000, and this will occur if the firm goes bankrupt. The firm may or may not have its shares registered for public trading in an exchange. Privately held firms also issue shares and they have stockholders that are exposed to the same risks.

Unlike the contractual obligation to pay coupons on bonds, the firm's management decides if and how much of its net profit it will distribute to shareholders. If a payment is made, a shareholder receives a 'dividend' for each one of the shares held. Notice that there are two conditions for dividend payment: first, the company must show positive net profit; and second, the company management decides whether to pay out a dividend.

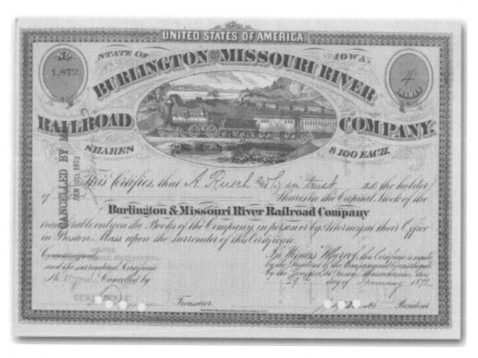

Figure 2.3   A stock certificate for the Burlington and Missouri River Railroad, 1870s

Source: By Burlington and Missouri River Railroad (http://www.stocklobster.com/1064.html) [Public domain], via Wikimedia Commons (accessed 4 November 2014).

Stockholders are not forced to hold their shares forever — they may sell the stock to another investor (obviously, this is relatively easy if the stock is registered for trade in an exchange). The selling price may be higher than the purchasing price if the company value rises. However, if the company's value falls, the stock will be sold at a loss. The difference between the selling price and the purchasing price is denoted as 'capital gain/loss'. In extreme cases, as mentioned above, if a company goes bankrupt the stockholder loses all of their investment; however, no one has the right to touch the investor's other assets such as their home or the remainder of their savings, thanks to the limited liability framework. Because a stock pays an uncertain flow of dividends, and its capital gain might turn into a loss, it is considered rather risky.

Stocks are extremely important for economic growth, employment and technological innovation. Before the creation of limited liability firms in Britain in 1855, wealthy individuals were wary of investing in enterprises for fear that an enterprise's failure would impact their other assets. Limited liability is an extremely important feature, for it allows those with savings to decide how much they are willing to risk from the total assets at their disposal. The senior American economist William Baumol maintains that since Roman times and until the upsurge of the industrial revolution, a period of 1,500 years, economic growth in Europe amounted to approximately zero percent! Among the main reasons was the lack of protection for enterprises and investors, the absence of a limited liability framework and the absence of intellectual property rights. The formation of the limited liability concept and its adoption in France and the US (the two most important trading partners of England at the time) by the year 1860, plus patent protection on inventions, were extremely significant. They contributed to stimulating entrepreneurship and facilitating the sizeable equity raising needed for financing the industrial revolution. This created jobs and extricated millions of people from the circle of poverty.

The valuation of stocks is more complicated than the valuation of bonds because of the risk involved. There are many complex mathematical models that researchers use to determine the value of common stocks, which are beyond the scope of this book. However, a brief description of a simple model will prove to be sufficient for our purposes. This model is known as the 'dividend growth model', with its origins going back to 1934, after the crash of the 1929 bubble.

The patterns by which stock prices fluctuate in financial markets made no sense to traders of the 1920s. The first analytical exploration into stock valuation was made by the legendary investor Benjamin Graham (tutor of

Warren Buffet) together with a Columbia University scholar, David Dodd, in their book *The Memoirs of the Dean of Wall Street* (1996).

Graham and Dodd figured that the sum of all shares that a firm issued, multiplied by their market price must make the value of the firm's business. This business may increase over time if the firm keeps investing and expanding the assets that generate income, be it a factory, real estate, issuing insurance policies or software development. If the business indeed expands, it is expected to generate higher average profits as the years go by. The key point is that if a fraction of the annual profit is distributed to shareholders as dividends, and the remainder is invested in expanding the business, the firm will both expand, and will pay increasing dividends to its shareholders. Before the model was mathematically formalized in 1959 by a scholar named Myron Gordon, some concluded that as long as the firm expands, its stock price should keep increasing. This intuition was shared by many investors and speculators during the roaring twenties and it will be seen how this problematic conclusion contributed to the spread of euphoria before the bubble crashed.

Rather than developing the model here, it is preferable to highlight its key results and implications. The model has two main results that depend on the question of whether the firm retains some of its annual net profit (denoted also as 'Earnings') and therefore grows, or not. Let us consider the no-growth case first. In this case, the firm distributes its entire annual profit to shareholders as dividends. Therefore, there are no additional investments in the business, and the profit remains *constant over time*. It can be shown that the present value of a constant stream of dividends to infinity (unlike bonds, the firm has no maturity date) is simply formalized as:

$$P_0 = \frac{Earnings_1}{k},$$

where P_0 is the stock price today (period 0), $Earnings_1$ is the next period's (period 1) expected dividend per share, and k is the cost of capital which potential investors attribute to this firm. The latter, k, must correspond to the appropriate risk level of the firm ('appropriate' means by comparison to other investment opportunities having the same risk level). Here is a numerical example: Assume that the next year dividend per share (which equals Earning per share) is $3 and that the cost of capital is 12%. The price will therefore be:

$$P_0 = \frac{\$3.00}{0.12} = \$25.$$

This stock price will remain constant as long as the firm's profitability and its level of risk do not change, therefore an investor should not expect this price to appreciate in the future.

The second result of the dividend growth model builds on the assumption that the firm retains a fraction of $b\%$ of its annual net profit to finance expansion of its productive assets. The firm pays out the remainder, $100\% - b\%$, as dividends to its shareholders. This firm will grow because the retained earnings are invested in the firm's assets and yield a constant return on equity (ROE), which will accumulate periodically and result in the firm's growth. It is evident then that the growth rate of the firm is determined by b and *ROE*, and indeed, the model implies that the annual growth rate, denoted by 'g', is simply $g = b \times ROE$. To see how this changes the firm's stock price consider the previous example, but now assume that the firm retains 40% of its annual net profit ($b = 40\%$), and it earns 20% on the installed productive assets ($ROE = 20\%$). This yields $g = 40\% \times 20\% = 8\%$. In this scenario, however, investors do not receive $3 per share, but only 60% of it (because 40% of the profit is retained). A solution of the model shows that in this case the stock price is calculated by the formula:

$$P_0 = \frac{Earnings_1 \times (1 - b)}{k - g} = \frac{\$3 \times (1 - 0.4)}{0.12 - 0.08} = \$45.$$

This price is much higher than the one obtained from the no-growth case. The difference, $45 − $25 = $20 per share is often denoted the 'present value of growth opportunities', because it stems from the addition to present value due to exploitation of growth opportunities by the firm. A key result of the latter result is that the stock's price will rise at an increasing pace as long as the firm maintains this policy. Graphically, it will look like Figure 2.4.

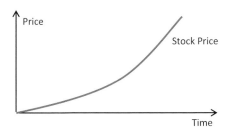

Figure 2.4 Stock price over time for a growing firm

To summarize, note that while this simplistic model ignores many important attributes that were found essential for the pricing of stocks worldwide, it does capture some interesting insight. First, there must be a link between the real profitability of the firm while employing its productive assets and its stock price. Second, firms cannot grow if they do not invest in expanding their productive asset base. Third, firms will grow faster the higher is their ROE, which reflects their productivity rate. Lastly, the higher the firm's risk, the higher the required rate of return (k) by shareholders — which means that the firm's value will decline. This book will show how the dividend growth model helps us understand different bubbles and crises.

2.5 Overview of the Financial System

In most modern economies, regulators assure that most households' savings, which are managed by pension and retirement funds, are invested in safe bonds, with a lesser portion invested in stocks. The reason is a preference for the safety of bonds over the risk of stocks. Still, in most cases it would be unwise to avoid investing in stocks altogether, as they offer an opportunity for higher rates of return at tolerable levels of risk for most investors. In other words, the degree of exposure to stocks depends on the saver's willingness to bear risk.

The financial system creates and defines 'stocks', 'bonds' and other more complex financial assets. It issues these assets to the public and to investors who manage public savings in financial markets. The creation and selling of new assets to the investing public are known as activities of the 'primary market'. That is, a primary market is one where new securities are sold to the public, and the proceeds are paid to the issuing firm (less a commission to the financial intermediary). In this way, the financial system supplies brokerage services that mediate between public savings and the capital needs of business firms and governments.

After such securities are sold to the public, the financial system facilitates ongoing trading of those securities. On each trading day, holders of securities may sell them, while people with disposable savings can invest in securities as they see fit. These trading activities occur at 'secondary markets' — also known as 'exchanges'. Here, securities change hands, but no funds are payable to the issuing firm. A properly functioning financial system facilitates social growth and welfare so long as it efficiently channels public savings into financing *the most profitable and promising enterprises in the business sector*. In a corrupt or ill-functioning economy, public savings are

Figure 2.5   NASDAQ

invested in lower-quality firms, often because of distorted incentives across the financial sector. If public savings finance the most promising enterprises, the business sector develops and creates jobs. If an enterprise fails, jobs are lost, and people with no labor income cannot allow high consumption, which translates to lower demand for other businesses. This is one example of how a dysfunctional financial system imposes indirect costs on society.

From the government's perspective, the higher the number of successful businesses and employees in the economy, the more tax revenues it receives from firms and employees. With higher taxes, the government is able to finance various projects and improve social welfare. Such being the case, it is seen that the more efficiently the financial system operates, the more resources flow from household savings towards business growth and government operations. Failure of the financial system damages economic growth, employment and social welfare.

Together with an overall goal of efficient operation of the financial sector, regulators such as the Central Bank, the Ministry of Finance and the Securities and Exchange Commission must apply an effective supervisory policy on the financial system. This is in order to prevent abuses of the system's capacity and, primarily, to protect public savings from unnecessary risks.

One of the topics that will emerge as a central motif throughout this book is the tension between the desire of players in the financial and business systems to extract a fair profit, and the risks that evolve when the quest for profitability turns into greed and reckless behavior. It will be seen that supervision by investors, the press, government agencies and professionals, headed by accounting firms, is necessary for preventing corruption in the system. Still, an excess of control and restrictions on business firms and financial system also negatively affect growth, employment and welfare. This leaves policy makers and regulators the important and delicate task of letting the financial system operate efficiently, but monitoring it to avoid excess risk taking.

Additional Reading

Bodie, Z., Kane, A. and Marcus, A.J. (2009). *Investments*. 8th edition. New York: McGraw-Hill Irwin.

Gordon, M.J. (1959). 'Dividends, Earnings and Stock Prices,' *Review of Economics and Statistics*, 41(2), 99–105.

Graham, B. and Dodd, D. (2008). *Security Analysis*. 5th edition. New York: McGraw-Hill.

3.

Commercial Banking and Banking Crises

3.1 Prologue

On 15 September 2008, a symbol of the American financial industry, Lehman Brothers, collapsed. The bank, founded in 1850, went bankrupt and caused the largest loss in American history, some $600 billion. This bankruptcy signaled to the entire world that the financial system was in severe crisis. Eventually, the crisis in the American financial system evolved into the most serious one since the 1930s. The US financial earthquake quickly reached the banking system in Europe. Greece, Spain, Ireland, Iceland and other countries found themselves in need of an unprecedented inflow of funds in order to stabilize their economies. The world economy, it seemed, was about to crumble.

This chapter discusses the reasons to fear a bank's collapse. On the one hand, it can be argued that a bank is like any business enterprise, and many enterprises go bankrupt in an economic recession. However, banks have a unique role in the economy. The collapse of a single but large bank can topple additional banks like a set of dominos, potentially dragging the entire economy into recession and high unemployment.

3.2 Commercial Banks and the 'Money Multiplier'

Commercial banks are at the heart of the financial system. One of their primary roles is securing short-term customer deposits in checking accounts and giving long-term loans to business firms. The bank pays low interest on the deposited amount and uses those deposits to extend loans to borrowers. Since the interest it collects from loan recipients is higher than the interest the bank pays out to depositors, the difference constitutes an important income source for the commercial bank. Such banks are very important to the economy because they enable additional players in the system to utilize deposits based on a mechanism known as the 'money multiplier'. The idea is simple. Since most depositors do not need the entire sum of their deposit on a daily basis, a considerable portion of it, say 90%, is extended as a loan. If, for example, the bank receives a deposit of $100 from a depositor, it loans 90 out of the 100 to another individual or business. The loan recipient uses it to purchase something from a seller, who receives the $90 and deposits the money in their commercial bank. The same $90 are registered as a deposit, and now 90% of the $90, i.e., $81, is again used as a source to extend loans. Those loans, too, will ultimately be deposited in a commercial bank, with 90% of this amount becoming other loans. The amount *not* extended as a loan is called the 'reserve'. In our example the reserve is 10% and it is determined by the central bank.

A simple calculation will prove that when the reserve is 10%, commercial banks are able to convert $100 of original deposits into $1,000 in the overall banking system.[1] In other words, for every $100 of original deposits, commercial banks create an additional $900 of deposits and loans via the banking multiplier. Those funds enable a large number of borrowers and depositors to execute economic transactions and enhance economic growth.

3.3 Bank Runs

Now consider the overall commercial banking system. The system remains stable so long as the inflow of deposits to commercial banks and the outflow of withdrawal from deposits more or less offset each other. Imagine, however, what might happen when many depositors wish to withdraw their money at the same time. As aforementioned, for every $1,000 registered as deposits, the cash actually held in bank safes totals $100. Therefore, if for any reason the public fears that a certain bank — or even a number of banks — is about to become bankrupt, then the $100 will be given to the first depositors who show up at the bank and ask to make a withdrawal. The moment that fears of bankruptcy erupt, each depositor will want to be first in line and will therefore 'run' to the bank in order to withdraw the deposit. Only one depositor will be first in line as the others form a long, worried line. This phenomenon is

---

[1] The calculation is $100/0.1 = $1,000. Therefore, if the reserve rate is reduced by the central bank to, say, 8%, an initial deposit of $100 will end up generating $100/0.08 = $1,250.

known as a 'bank run'. When a bank run unfolds, the bank first serves deposi-tors with cash from its safe, but this might not meet the demand. In many cases, the bank is forced to urgently sell some of its assets in order to supply cash to all depositors standing in line. These assets are often pools of loans that the bank made to business firms. They may be 'good' loans, meaning that the likelihood of repayment is high, or they might be 'bad' loans. Anyhow, the fact that the bank must sell those loans urgently implies that it bears losses and might bankrupt. If this happens, the bank must obtain exter-nal infusion of funds in order to keep serving its clients and cool down the panic. The external provider of funds is known as the 'lender of last resort'. It may be a private investor, a partnering bank or the government. Remember, though, that the bank might be under a run because of justified reasons, i.e., it may be ill managed or holding bad business loans. Therefore, the lender of last resort often assumes high risks. This attribute makes funding by other banks or private investors a very difficult task, particularly due to the short time needed to make a decision and act in the market.

3.4 Central Banks as Lenders of Last Resort

The bank run phenomenon led to the collapse of numerous banks centuries ago, though most notably in the 19th century and at the start of the 20th century. Commercial banks sought ways to cope with it and indeed there were some attempts by commercial banks to form a sort of consortium,[2] whereby members may (or may not) wish to help a bank in distress. However, these attempts were not successful, thus came the establishment of *central banks*. A central bank is essentially a governmental agency that provides funds to commercial banks if bank runs evolve. Central banks have operated as far back as 1668 in Sweden, 1694 in England and 1800 in France. In 1913, the US Congress and President Woodrow Wilson passed the Federal Reserve Act, and the US 'Fed' was formed soon afterwards in 1914.[3]

Today, all countries have a central bank, and some countries have a com-mon central bank. Most importantly, the European Central Bank (ECB) serves as the central bank for 17 countries, which means that it has to imple-ment policy tools that affect all member countries. This is a very delicate task because different countries need different monetary tools. For

---

[2]For example, the New York Clearing House, which started as a clearing hub for checks across participating banks, but then expanded to include kind of a lender of last resort function.
[3]For more details on the history of central banks see Bernanke (2013).

example, one country might need an increase in interest rate, while other countries are better off with a decrease. For this, and other reasons, the ECB faces great difficulties in making decisions that are unanimously acceptable by all member countries.

In almost all countries, central banks have two primary goals: first, implement monetary tools[4] in order to achieve macroeconomic stability. This means ensuring stable growth (i.e., avoiding or mitigating recessions, and cooling down an overheated economy), and maintaining low and stable inflation rate. Second, central banks act to maintain financial stability, and this means that policy tools are deployed to avoid or minimize financial panics and crises. One important way of doing so is by acting as a credible and decisive lender of last resort. Credibility is essential since the public must trust that the central bank is capable and willing to save commercial banks when a panic evolves. Decisiveness is important because resources spent on saving the financial system might be needed elsewhere, and therefore opposition should be expected (by politicians or groups of interest). A non-decisive action might hamper the public's trust in the central bank, and exacerbate the panic.

Bank runs still exist, as encountered in 2007 when depositors ran to, amongst others, Northern Rock in England and Wachovia in the US. Nevertheless, the frequency of bank runs lessened in the 20th century thanks to tighter supervision of commercial banks and deposit insurance tools. For example, the US Federal Deposit Insurance Corporation (FDIC) was established in order to moderate the bank run phenomenon. This governmental agency insures sums of up to $100,000 in individual investors' accounts. This safety net reduces the motive to run to the bank, as their deposits will be returned by the FDIC should the bank collapse. Not all countries have instituted deposit insurance, though, partly in order to avoid a firm commitment to depositors, which might be rather expensive.

Before deposit insurance was instituted, many bank runs, in retrospect, proved to be unjustified. In other words, they stemmed from rumor and unfounded fears that caused unnecessary jolts in the financial system. Banks took action in a number of ways in order to prevent rumors of instability. For example, many banks set up multiple service counters in order to avoid the creation of long queues extending outside their doors. They feared that passers-by would see the queues, mistakenly conclude that a bank run was developing, and join the line in order to withdraw their own deposits.

---

[4] Some of the tools that central banks deploy include changing interest rates, printing money, and issuing government bonds or buying them back from the market.

Understandably, the longer the line, the greater the risk that the bank is unable to provide all of the deposit money — thus generating a self-fulfilling prophecy.

3.5 From Bank Runs to Banking Crises

If a bank has successfully proved to its depositors that it is not on the verge of collapse, those who have withdrawn their deposit will redeposit the money as the bank returns to a stable situation. However, if the bank has not succeeded in calming down depositors, it will collapse; and whoever has withdrawn their deposit will place their money in another bank — obviously a bank that succeeds in signaling to the public that it is stable.

So what happens when the public loses confidence not only in one bank, but in a number of banks? Then, numerous other banks are liable to collapse since the public will withdraw its deposits and not rush to reinject those deposits into the banking system. Bear in mind that for each $100 withdrawn from deposits, an additional $900 are erased from other deposits; therefore, numerous households and businesses lose their money. This is how the money multiplier works *in reverse*. A bank run that spreads across a large number of banks is known as 'banking panic'. Banking panic can be prevented or mitigated if the central bank announces that it is ready to supply the necessary amount of cash in order to preserve the stability of the system (this assumes that the public trusts the central bank). This type of action is denoted the 'Bagehot rule', after the British journalist Walter Bagehot, who proposed this central-banking policy in 1873 (Bagehot, 1999). However, knowing they will eventually be saved, bankers might have an incentive to take on excessive risk; this phenomenon is known as 'moral hazard'.[5] To minimize the moral hazard problem Bagehot proposes charging the banks a penalty rate of interest on the loans they receive from the central bank. The loans must be sufficiently large to save the bank, and they must be given against collateral that would be more valuable than the loan once the bank stabilizes.

A central bank that injects liquidity acts as a lender of last resort — it has supplied loans to the banking system just before collapsing. If the public

---

[5] This term was originally used in the insurance industry. It highlights that once a person or business entity has paid for an insurance policy, they have an incentive to engage in more risky (and profitable on average) activities, because someone else eventually pays for the losses, should any be incurred. In the banking case, the insurance policy is implicit by adopting the Bagehot rule.

believes in the central bank's ability to supply the enormous sums needed for this, it is possible for the panic to subside and for stability to return to the system.

If the system does not stabilize then the banking panic spreads, numerous deposit accounts are closed, and many depositors — including businesses — lose cash and lines of credit. Since many businesses cannot continue to function in the absence of bank financing, they near bank-ruptcy. Such bankruptcies give rise to dismissal of employees, so unemploy-ment increases. Workers who have lost their source of income reduce consumption, which in turn leads to wider waves of employee dismissals due to reduced activity of other businesses. In this way, banking panic turns into a 'crisis in the real economy'. A crisis in the real economy is expressed by high unemployment, low growth, reduced tax revenues to government and therefore a cut in government services to the public.

However, this is not the worst scenario — the nightmare scenario is called a 'systemic banking crisis'. In a systemic banking crisis all, or the majority, of commercial banks go bankrupt. Chapter 8 discusses a case such as this that occurred in Israel in 1983. If a systemic banking crisis happens, only the government (through the central bank) is able to save the system, if at all.

According to a study conducted by the International Monetary Fund (IMF), the cost of systemic banking crises documented between 1970 and 2007 amounts to an estimated 6% of gross domestic profit (GDP) injected as capital to banks. Additionally, some 13% of GDP was utilized from gov-ernment budget, and furthermore, there was an average loss of approxi-mately 20% of GDP over the course of four years following a crisis. Finally, on average, the public debt almost doubled. A very high level of govern-ment debt (often measured by ratio to GDP) constitutes a heavy burden on the government budget (as the government must pay perhaps twice the interest on debt than it previously paid); therefore, it must cut other ser-vices the state regularly supplies to its citizens. Overall, systemic banking crises can amount to more than ten years of economic growth. For this reason, it can be seen throughout this book that as a crisis emerges in any part of an economy, the government is deeply concerned that a banking crisis, or even worse, a systemic banking crisis might evolve.

3.6 Basel Accords for Banking Regulation

Being central to economic stability and growth, the financial sector, and par-ticularly commercial banks, came under tight regulation after the 1930s. The regulation process started in the US after a devastating financial crisis and was gradually adopted by most countries, with slight modifications. Chapter 4 presents the principles of the first US regulations and their reasoning, given the preceding financial crisis. Subsequent chapters discuss modifications to the US regulations throughout the 20th century, and their interactions with other financial crises.

An important measure for a bank's ability to cope with risk is the portion of equity capital out of total financing sources, like deposits, short-term debt and long-term debt. If a bank finances its operations based on deposits and debt only (for example, by issuing bonds) than the bank owners have no 'skin in the game'; that is, they will not lose if the bank fails. Having nothing to lose, bank owners might take on excessive risk by lending depositors' money to risky enterprises, expecting high profits if the ventures succeed. If, however, the ventures fail, they will lose nothing — but the bank's depositors and debtors might lose everything. The fraction of equity capital out of all assets at risk is denoted 'capital requirement'. If this ratio, for example, is 8%, it means that a bank has an equity cushion to absorb losses of up to 8% of its assets. As a result, the higher the capital requirement, the safer the bank will be, but this safety serves the needs of depositors and lenders of the bank, not its equity holders. From the equity-holders' point of view, the lower the capital requirement, the less money they put at risk, while reaping higher returns on the equity they invested. Banks argue, correctly, that their assets (primarily long-term loans given to businesses) have different levels of risk, depending on the credit rating of the borrower, with AAA being the best quality (Standard & Poor's [S&P] scale), down to AA+, AA, AA−, BBB+ and so on. To determine the overall level of credit risk, banks need to assess the credit quality of each borrower, and the weight of each rating category is presented in a bank's portfolio of risky assets. Reasonably, the weighted average of risk exposure should be related to the level of equity requirement. This was the general notion that resulted in the Basel Accords by the Basel Committee on Bank Supervision (BCBS).

The Basel Accords for banking regulations took a center-stage role in cross-country financial regulations. The need for a multinational perspective on financial regulations stems from the fact that global financial firms (with subsidiaries in many countries) face different and sometimes contradictory regulations and capital requirements. The first Basel Accord, Basel I, of 1988 presented a limited and perhaps flawed scope of regulations and rules (see Crouhy *et al.*, 2013). It addressed credit risk only, and required a minimum of 8% capital requirement based on risk-weighted assets. For example, it considered cash and government bonds (very safe assets) as receiving 0% weight in the calculation of risky assets, but stated 50% for residential mortgages.

The recommendations of Basel II in 2004 materially expanded the scope of risk measurement and eventually risk management. By expanding the scope, Basel II accounted for a variety of sources of risk in addition to credit risk, primarily operating risks and market risks. With respect to minimum capital requirement, it proposed an internationally standardized way to calculate regulatory capital. The significance here is the ways that credit risk is measured. Without going into fine detail, there are three levels of sophistication in calculating credit risk, all built on credit ratings, where the biggest institutions may implement their *internal credit rating*. By doing so, BCBS gave big financial institutions an incentive to report higher ratings for assets than objectively warranted. Indeed, academic research found evidence that big financial institutions manipulated the risk weights, particularly throughout the years preceding the financial crisis of 2008 (see Mariathasan and Merrouche, 2014).

In 2009, as evidence amounted regarding the severe impact of system-wide shocks on individual bank stability, the first version of Basel III was published. Basel III primarily expands the Basel II recommendations toward improving the banking sector's ability to cope with system-wide shocks. As such, Basel III aims to reduce systemic risk of the entire financial sector to allow better transparency for more effective regulation.

3.7 Epilogue

If government is not interested in the banking system's collapse, then why did the Bush administration abstain from saving Lehman Brothers? The short answer is that American supervisory agencies did not have sufficient data on the activities of this investment bank in commercial banking. Moreover, information on Lehman's exposure to other institutions around the globe, via derivative contracts, was rather obscure. Its full scale would only be revealed after the bank collapsed. This lack of information was due to loose regulation, loopholes in reporting requirements and an incentive system that promoted high risk-taking in the short term. As a response to the loose regulations before the crisis, which were partly loosened due to the financial sector's lobbying activity, Basel III accord focused diminishing systemic risk.

Future chapters will expand on this matter, but first, as aforementioned, Chapter 4 will describe the way in which one of the most destructive bubbles of the world economy developed during the 1920s. The chapter will show

how avarice and greed on the parts of the public and investment managers, combined with inadequate supervision over the financial system, led to the bubble that preceded the largest economic depression of the 20th century. This is comparative to the factors that brought down Lehman Brothers — it seems as though many of the lessons of the Great Depression were forgotten after 70 years.

Additional Reading

There are many introductory textbooks on macroeconomics that can shed more detailed light on the description provided in this chapter. A very good book is:

Mankiw Gregory, N. (2011). *Principles of Economics.* 6th edition. Mason, OH: Thomson South-Western.

A rather simple read on the history and function of central banks in general, and the actions of the Fed during the 2008–2010 financial crisis is:

Bernanke, B.S. (2013). *The Federal Reserve and the Financial Crisis.* Princeton, NJ: Princeton University Press.

Other useful works are:

Bagehot, W. (1999). *Lombard Street: A Description of the Money Market.* New York: Wiley.
Michel, C., Galai, D. and Mark, R. (2014). *The Essentials of Risk Management,* Second Edition, New York: McGraw-Hill.
Mariathasan, M. and Merrouche, O. (2014). 'The Manipulation of Basel Risk-weights,' *Journal of Financial Intermediation*, 23 (3), 300–321.

4.

The Roaring Twenties
and the US Bubble of 1929

4.1 From Recession to Expansion

As World War I ended in 1918, the US economy, like others, was in deep recession, as evidenced by its high unemployment, floundering businesses and sparse activity in the capital market. In 1921 the Dow Jones Index, which measures the average price of the 30 leading stocks traded on the New York Stock Exchange (NYSE), stood at 64 points. Remember that number, 64, because it will be referred to later. Notwithstanding the above, a number of factors combined to create a sense of optimism. These included the peace following the end of the war, young people returning home and technological innovations such as the establishment of power stations, deployment of electricity lines and development of the auto industry and radio industry. These generated numerous jobs and helped the economy gradually emerge from its recession. The preferred investment asset for most savers during that time consisted of bonds because, among other things, the stock market had experienced several bubbles and crashes, which deterred investors from entering the stock market. One of the worst crashes occurred in the summer of 1914, with the outbreak of World War I in Europe. As events unfolded, the most important capital markets were paralyzed, stock prices plunged and stock and bond exchanges in Europe and New York closed down for several months. The NYSE opened for trading after five months, and then only in bonds. Stock trading resumed eight months later.

An additional factor that deterred investors from purchasing stocks was the public sense that trading on the stock exchange was much like casino betting. During that time stock trading was not supervised and there were almost no regulations in place to protect investors. In the absence of regulations, various phenomena such as price run-ups,[1] insider trading and rumor spreading became a matter of routine. Small stock traders, as opposed to the more reputable investment firms, were thought to be dubious types. Even the most highly regarded newspapers such as *The Wall Street Journal* and *The New York Times* were found guilty of publishing reports aimed to inflate the prices of specific stocks in exchange for bribes totaling hundreds of thousands of dollars.

One of the first stock analysts and certainly the most famous one, Benjamin Graham, wrote in his memoirs that almost all stock traders referred to themselves as 'speculators'. As defined in Chapter 1, the term 'speculation' serves to describe short-term trading behavior intended for extracting profits based on the speculator's expectations; for example, by riding a trend of rising prices. Such being the case, speculative trading behavior infuses additional money into a rising market and withdraws money from the market when in decline; thus it amplifies price fluctuations.

The absence of regulations, laws and standards had additional implications. The NYSE did not require its listed firms to provide detailed information on their profitability, but rather general information only. For example, firms were required to present a balance sheet at least once a year but there was no requirement for quarterly reporting as there is today. Most firms did the minimum and provided investors with a profit and loss statement. But since there was no specific reporting requirement in place, many firms simply reported the amount of profit or loss without a detailed profit and loss statement (not to mention a report audited by an accountant). A true description of a firm's business including its fields of activity, progress in projects it invested in and so forth was considered valuable information, almost like inside information, which, ironically, was not included among the required reporting items to the public.

Having said that, it is important to note that not all firms and brokers that adopted poor reporting practices were fraudulent or corrupt. In the 1920s many firms, mainly the large industrial ones, paid dividends in both good and bad years. A lot of firms faithfully reported on their business achievements and maintained a respectful attitude towards their shareholders. Yet the generally negative atmosphere vis-à-vis the stock market also affected the prices of 'good stocks', and many of those were traded at low

---

[1] A price run-up occurs when a manipulator bids up prices to induce naïve investors to join the ride, effectively generating a bubble in the particular stock. See the discussion on behavioral bubbles in Sections 1.3.3 and 1.3.4.

prices. So when the market started recovering, the good stocks were first to rise.

4.2 Back into the Stock Market

In order to attract investors to invest in stocks, investment houses offered loans intended solely for purchasing stocks. This type of investment is known as 'buying on margin'. For example, an investor who wishes to purchase shares of a specific firm in the amount of $10,000 asks his broker for a loan. If the broker is willing to grant a loan of, say, 60% of the value of the purchase ($6,000), the investor has to come up with his own capital of $4,000. As a result, the investor is able to profit from an investment of $10,000 for an out-of-pocket outlay of only $4,000. In fact, the client is risking his broker's money in the stock market. And from where does the broker get the money he lends to the client? In many cases he takes out a commercial bank loan. Thus, commercial bank deposits are rolled over into the stock market.

Since during that time there were no restrictive regulations in place and brokers fiercely competed for clients' money, the loans they offered were extremely generous. Numerous investors received loans of 80 to 90% of the value of their purchases; in other words, an investor had to come up with only 10% to 20% of his own capital. Why do we need to understand this mechanism? Because it works for everyone's benefit so long as stock prices rise, but it is dangerous when prices fall. The broker who owes money to the bank under no circumstances wishes to lose it in the stock market. Consider an investor who has invested $10,000 in a stock, of which $9,000 is a loan from the broker. When the price of the stock falls by 10%, the investor's personal stake of capital (their equity) is erased altogether. The investment in the stock is now worth $9,000, exactly the size of the debt. Obviously if the investment value falls even further, say to $8,000, the broker may call the investor and ask them to infuse funds into the account; however, the investor might not pick up the phone. In such a situation, the broker cannot fully repay the loan to the bank. In order to protect him against these losses, the broker will require the investor to add his own money to the account *before* the stock's value goes down to $9,000, for instance when the value reaches $9,500. This call for equity infusion is known as a 'margin call'. If the investor refuses, the broker sells the stock and returns the $9,000 loan to the bank. The important notion here is to recognize that a mere 5% fall in value is enough to lead the broker to issue a 'sell' order almost automatically. The higher the size of the loan relative to the total investment (the 'leverage', a term that will be used frequently here), the smaller the fall in price needed to start the selling-off process. That selling, in turn, is liable to exacerbate the trend of a falling price. The more investors use margin trading and the higher the leverage, the greater the likelihood of this scenario, making the market more volatile. Between the end of 1927 and October 1929, loans extended by brokers increased by 92%, almost doubling, and intensified the pace of falling prices.

Occasionally the public increases its appetite for holding stocks. This happens mainly when there is an expectation for particularly high profits from stocks, when the risk of investing in stocks is perceived as particularly low, and/or when the return on bonds is unusually low. Note the difference between these three factors. The first, an expectation of high profitability, expresses optimistic beliefs, which may be justified but often stem from euphoria. The same is true with the second reason, a perception of low risk that might be influenced by mood and irrational ignorance of reality. The third, the low-interest factor, highlights the lack of an attractive investment alternative. For all these reasons the public turns to investing in stocks.

When the public and/or its investment managers shift savings into stocks at the expense of bonds, excess demand might lead to stock overpricing. As explained when bubbles were described in Chapter 1, overpricing occurs when the market price is higher than the value implied from the expected stream of dividend. The emergence of a bubble in specific stocks encourages additional investors to join the circle of buyers. Prices continue to rise, which might result in a price-increase cycle that feeds into itself (positive feedback). When increased demand for good stocks raises their price, they become less of a 'bargain'. For that reason, money diverted to the stock market seeks other stocks whose prices have not yet increased, and therefore seem attractive. Subsequently, a rumor or positive trend in a stock's price, a run-up, is sufficient to draw investors' money into dubious stocks.

4.3 The 'New Economy' of the Roaring Twenties

One of the prominent economists of the 20th century, John Kenneth Galbraith, analyzed the events of the 1920s in a book published in 1954, *The Great Crash of 1929*. He concluded that the lack of rationality among investors was among the main causes in the bubble's development. In this book, Galbraith contends that people believed they were simply destined to be rich and thus didn't allow reality to spoil their party. In 1934, Graham and Dodd wrote in *Security Analysis* (see 2008 edition) that many investors during the 1920s believed there was no need to analyze the economic value of a firm's business. The belief was that firms of the 'new economy' were rapidly growing, therefore investors needed to purchase stocks of firms that showed high growth rates, *irrespective of their current prices.* The logic was that the stock price would continue to rise so long as the firm remained profitable.

Why a new economy? Because the feeling in the public was that the old laws of economics were no longer valid and that new industrial developments justified high stock prices. Investors had some tangible examples they could refer to. For example, between 1915 and 1926, the profits of the Computing Tabulating Recording Company, which later changed its name to International Business Machines (IBM), grew from $0.7 million to $3.7 million per year, a five-fold increase. The dividend that was paid out tripled and its price rose similarly. Consumers concluded that they could afford spending money and buying without restraint since future profits from stocks would cover all debts. The general public, in effect, was behaving like an irrational speculator; euphoria spread all over.

Taken together, the factors described above amounted to the start of a trend of rising prices. Between 1921 and 1925, the Dow Jones Average rose by 100%. After a respite in 1926, the index once again rose rapidly and on 3 September 1929 reached 381 points. Remember that in 1921 the index stood at 64 points. Now, eight years later, the index had risen by 500%.

As stock prices increased, so did the appetite of investors for more and more stocks as the positive atmosphere swept over the masses. Republican US President Calvin Coolidge said in December 1928, less than a year before the crash: 'Americans can regard the present with satisfaction and anticipate the future with optimism.'

Until that time, the major banks were the guardians of the financial system against fraudulent actions, headed by large and respectful banks such as J.P. Morgan and the National City Company (later known as Citibank). These reputable banks at first refused to provide underwriting services to doubtful firms, despite rising demand for stocks, due to genuine concern for their own reputation. However, facing the huge demand for stocks, a plethora of dealers could be found who were less stringent about quality and credibility and who supplied the goods to the masses. As the price bubble continued to develop, even the reputable banks lowered their standards and participated in the party. The punchbowl was the huge profits due to the rising wave of stock issues. For example, Goldman Sachs established a mutual investment trust fund, which, in light of the limited supply of stocks in the market, purchased other mutual funds that invested in stocks. Thus, a sort of stock investment pyramid was created. According to conventional present-day laws, this type of action would constitute a serious crime in any modern financial market.

The number of trust funds rose from 40 in 1921 to 750 in 1929. The Central Bank was aware that the market was 'overheating' and imposed restrictions on credit, mainly for transactions involving margin purchases on stock. However, commercial banks bypassed those restrictions by setting up subsidiaries for investing in the capital market that were outside the scope of the Fed's monitoring of commercial banks. The number of such firms grew from 10 in 1922 to 114 in 1931. Those investment firms channeled money from Europe and Japan and invested it in US equities; therefore, despite the actions of the Fed, money continued to flow into the stock market.

As aforementioned, the name of the game was to show high rates of growth of companies traded on the stock exchange. In order to present a rosy picture of sustained and rapid growth to the public, accountants often employed dubious practices, such as transferring losses from the traded company to related companies not traded on the exchange. As another trick, accountants transferred assets from non-traded companies and presented them as profit for the exchange-traded company. Or, they classified expenses such as advertising and marketing as 'investment in brand name' (a fixed asset) so as to reduce expenses, i.e., to inflate profits. Naturally there were other such 'creative accounting' practices. The expanding bubble blinded many, leading them to believe that stock prices had only one direction — up and up, and risk-free. Unfortunately, the fate of every bubble is collapse, and that is what indeed happened on 'Black Tuesday', 29 October 1929.

4.4 The Crash

At the beginning of October 1929, stock prices had somewhat eroded. Eight days before the crash, on 21 October 1929, *The Wall Street Journal* wrote: 'Thousands of investors were waiting for those price drops in order to purchase more stock.' Five days before the crash, on 24 October 1929, trading opened on the NYSE and stock prices quickly fell by 15% to 25%. The NYSE closed its doors to worried and angry investors, for fear of riots.

In order to curb the panic of Black Thursday, J.P. Morgan, Jr. organized a group of distinguished bankers who raised $130 million and purchased stocks of the larger companies so as to support and increase prices. This exercise only helped temporarily. Indeed, the trading session closed with only a moderate drop, but fear was already in the air. One day before the crash, on 28 October, the index fell some 13%, but *The New York Times* wrote: 'Investors can buy the stock of good companies with full confidence.'

Figure 4.1   Wall Street on Black Thursday

However, no individual, no banker, no group of bankers or even the government was able to stop the crash of 'Black Tuesday', 29 October, when the index fell 11.5%. Panic gripped everyone: Private investors, who sold assets such as homes and land and invested the proceeds in seemingly promising stocks, lost all of their property. Brokers, who extended loans to their clients with margins of 80 to 90% for the purchase of stocks rushed to sell everything they could in order to cut losses. But too few buyers could be found amid the flood of supply. The losses of brokers due to margin purchases of stock carried over to the commercial banks, which fell into a state of distress. On the same day some 16 million shares were traded, more than triple the daily average up to then (and even many years thereafter).

From the beginning of October until mid-November, the Dow Jones average fell by approximately 50%. During the spring of 1930 the market rose, but the stock exchange crisis quickly extended into a credit crisis, when banks closed their lines of credit and loans to companies that had run into difficulties. Forty percent of commercial banks, approximately eleven thousand, went bankrupt due, among other things, to numerous bank runs. Evidently, banks' collapse intensified the credit crunch. The price drop in the stock exchange thus turned into a banking crisis, which in turn caused a crisis in the real economy because companies were unable to continue routine activity without bank financing sources.

The somber atmosphere that spread throughout the US led the public to reduce consumption and other purchases. Reduced purchases by households reduced demand for consumer goods. Factories were forced to close down production lines and fire workers as the wave of bankruptcies intensified. There were cases of suicide among capital market players and managers of companies that collapsed. Remember, the Dow Jones index stood at 64 points in 1921. In June 1932, it fell to 41 points, (a 36% drop), and the lowest level since 1897.

Later chapters will show how the factors described in the evolution of the 1929 bubble repeated themselves, with some variations, in other crises. Chapter 5 will review the social and economic costs of the bubble, and further explore the ways in which the US economic leadership dealt with the crisis and what actions were taken in order to increase supervision and bring sanity back to the unfettered dealings of the financial sector.

Additional Reading

Berenson, A. (2004). The Number: How the Drive for Quarterly Earnings Corrupted Wall Street and Corporate America. New York: Random House.

Books on the history of the US economy and its financial system:

Galbraith, J.K. (1954). The Great Crash of 1929. New York: Penguin.
Galbraith, J.K. (1994). The World Economy Since the Wars: A Personal View. London: Sinclair-Stevenson.

5.

The 'Great Depression' in the US

5.1 Introduction

The 1929 stock market crash in the New York Stock Exchange (NYSE) shocked the American economy and severely affected all of America's overseas trading partners. This chapter will describe the factors in play as this crisis deteriorated into the most severe economic slowdown of modern times, often denoted the 'Great Depression'. Similarities with the real estate crisis of 2007–2008 and the financial crisis of 2008–2009 will be examined in subsequent chapters, but it is possible to read between the lines here and note the many points of comparison. In particular, note how the lack of effective regulations, laws and accounting standards enabled excessive risk taking by financial institutions; and also the reckless investment practices by traders and private investors, as well as corruption and greed.

5.2 Rage

The burst of the stock market bubble evaporated the imaginary wealth that numerous investors thought they had, and presented them with a grim reality. Normally, people happily change status from 'poor' to 'rich', but when they switch the other way around it is painful and frustrating. People's rage was directed at the political system and those who ran the system, as well as at the leaders of Wall Street. The 'Occupy Wall Street' protest movement of the late 2000s was not new: it happened before, in the 1930s.

The sense of public rage against the financiers of Wall Street continued to grow in the face of what seemed to be a ruin of the economy due to the greed of speculators and stock traders. The public believed that

Wall Street traders and executives profited big time, not only from the expansion of the bubble but also from its collapse — through 'short' transactions.[1] The response of financial leaders was cynical and patronizing, a tone that increased the public's sense of alienation from this industry. In April 1932, the Senate opened an investigation (the Pecora Commission) into the causes of the crash, and investigated leaders of the financial system. Among them was Richard Whitney, President of the NYSE, who insisted on defining the stock market he headed as 'a perfect institution'. Like many others, he speculated in the stock market and lost a fortune. To conceal his financial difficulties and maintain his extravagant standard of living he borrowed heavily from Morgan Bank, where his brother served as a Vice President. But that was not enough for him; he embezzled funds from the New York Yacht Club (where he served as treasurer), and from his father-in-law. Whitney would stand trial and be found guilty of embezzling, on top of the above, more than a million dollars from the NYSE. He was sent to Sing Sing Correctional Facility for five years (Goldston, 1985, pp. 39–40).

Whitney attended the Senate hearings with another important figure, J.P. Morgan Jr., who at the time was considered the indisputable leader of America's reputable bankers.[2] Morgan's testimony in 1933 drew great attention from the press because it exposed numerous acts of corruption. For example, he testified that he and many of his partners did not pay taxes in 1931–1932, a time when one out of four people in the labor market could not find a job and when farmers were penniless. He also confessed that during the bubble, the company he headed sold shares of an attractive company to government officials at prices below market price.

Scan to watch 'The Crash of 1929' in YouTube

---

[1] 'Short' transactions are essentially an arrangement that enables an investor who believes that an asset's price is expected to decline, to sell it today, and buy it after the price has declined. Because this is a speculative transaction, the investor bears a risk that the asset's price will increase, and they might lose.

[2] Remember from Chapter 4 that J.P. Morgan Jr., arranged a pool of investors to support the crumbling stock prices on Black Thursday? Well, it was Whitney whom the pool sent to the exchange in order to bid up prices. Whitney came in at 13:30 and started shouting as he submitted aggressive 'buy' orders for shares of the biggest firms. The crowd followed him and the Dow Jones rebounded.

5.3 New Rules

The Senate hearings resulted in three laws that changed the face of the American investment system for decades. Those laws also shaped financial systems in many other countries. This was the beginning of the most meaningful regulation of the financial industry. The system was broken, and it had to be fixed. Later chapters of this book will show how in the 1990s a relatively fixed system was broken again because of narrow interests, corrupt politicians and heavy lobbying pressure on the financial industry. The laws gave government considerable power in supervising financial firms, primarily those dealing with the stock exchange. Here is a brief description of the three laws.

1. The Glass–Steagall Act, 1934, obliged banking institutions to choose one of two banking activities — commercial banking (e.g., administering deposits and extending loans) or investment banking (e.g., executing commercial securities transactions on behalf of customers, matching investors with companies that seek investments, etc.). The reason for the separation was to prevent conflicts of interest between commercial banking activity and investment banking; for example, the fear that bank deposits might be used as collateral for stock investments.
2. The Securities and Exchange Act, 1934, established a Federal authority, the Securities and Exchange Commission (SEC), to supervise the trade and offering of securities to the public. In fact, the SEC was supposed to replace some of the roles that banks and accounting firms had played as the 'watch dog' of the investment and trading system.
3. The Securities Act, 1933, obliged companies to submit a prospectus for approval by the SEC prior to issuing securities to the public. According to the law, all those involved in the issue of financial securities to the public — primarily company managers, accountants and investment bankers associated with the issue — all bear responsibility for the correctness and completeness of information contained in the prospectus. Notwithstanding, the law limits the obligation of those parties to *present* the information; investors are supposed to be responsible for *processing* the information and making investment decisions.

The Securities Act increased the demand for the professional services of accountants. Eight large accounting firms were formed and provided auditing services for most of the companies traded on the NYSE. Although the Securities Act granted formal authority to the SEC for supervising security dealings, persistent struggles by heads of the banking system, auditors and their close associates (mainly politicians hungry for contributions) shifted a portion of supervisory authorities to parties outside the SEC, mainly auditors. In other words, the force of crony capitalism acted over the years to weaken government regulatory power and magnify the power and revenue of auditing firms. Chapter 6 will expand on these complex interactions.

Until the eruption of the real estate crisis and the subsequent credit crisis in 2007–2010, the economic depression of the 1930s had been considered the most important event in American economic history.

5.4 The Political System

The economic depression of the 1930s affected tens of millions of people and led to the bankruptcy of numerous banks, factories and farms. This crisis changed American politics in that it led to a considerable increase in the government's intervention with economic and social affairs. The government was forced to stabilize the economy and reduce the suffering of the population. In 1932, the Republican Party lost power to the Democratic Party, and Franklin D. Roosevelt instituted his broad economic plan known as the New Deal. While key concepts of the deal were devised before the elections, President Herbert Hoover was unwilling to execute them. President Roosevelt said the program should make 'use of the authority of government as an

Figure 5.1   Franklin D. Roosevelt

Source: By the U.S. National Archives and Records Administration [Public domain], via Wikimedia Commons (accessed 9 November 2014).

organized form of self-help for all classes and groups and sections of our country'. He also said the deal is aimed to help the 'forgotten man at the bottom of the economic pyramid'.

Under the New Deal, social support systems were established, including Social Security, unemployment insurance and Federal assistance for families in need. This plan was, if you will, the first American version of the welfare state.

The scope of the Great Depression was overwhelming. For almost a full decade, between 1930–1939, the average US unemployment rate was 18.2%, reaching a peak of 25% in 1933. Between 1929 and 1933, gross national product (GNP) fell by 30% and returned to its 1929 level only ten years later in 1939. Prices of most commodities fell by tens of percent. For example, prices of agricultural products fell by 51% between 1929 and 1933, which explains farmers' difficulties in earning a living and working their land. During that time the agricultural sector was relatively large, thus the effect was extensive. World trade shrunk by 65% in dollar terms and by 25% in unit terms. This led to exporting the crisis to many countries. For example, in 1932 the UK unemployment rate reached 7.2%, while in Germany the depression generated severe resentment that accelerated Adolf Hitler's rise to power.

5.5 The Gold Standard

An important factor that worsened the situation was the 'gold standard'. The gold standard served as the basis for the quantity of money in the economy. Although most money in the economy was made out of paper, as it is today, there was a law in effect (in countries that adopted the gold standard) stating that any citizen interested in doing so could exchange paper bills for gold bullion held in Central Bank repositories. On average, against each paper dollar some 40 cents in gold was actually held. This fixed exchange rate created a boundary on the amount of paper money the government was allowed to issue. The more the crisis deepened, the more governments feared that their gold reserves would be depleted. The reason was that people might lose confidence in the value of paper money (due to devaluation, for example), and 'run' on the central bank demanding gold. Such runs had happened before and governments were thus concerned. To mitigate the probability of gold runs, governments raised interest rates and reduced lines of credit. The reasoning for the latter action was that so long as interest rates were high, it was less attractive for people to withdraw money and exchange it for gold, which earns no interest. At the same time, the danger of an outbreak of inflation was lessened. The outcome was that numerous businesses that needed credit and low interest rates could not repay their debts, went bankrupt and fired workers. Today it is clear to most economists that what was needed was to lower interest rates and open up lines of credit, even at the cost of severing the linkage to gold quantities.

5.6 Economic Policy

An additional factor working in the background was the lack of clear economic policy, or of any policy. This stemmed from the fact that the science of macroeconomics was in its infancy and the relationship between important economic variables was unclear. The general feeling was that the government was unable to act effectively against crises of this scale. President Hoover strongly opposed many ideas of Roosevelt's New Deal, arguing that it would lead to severe government deficits. Moreover, many viewed the crisis as a sort of Darwinian event that strengthens the strong and eliminates the weak; therefore, the expectation was that the crisis would pass on its own accord. The treasury secretary in President Hoover's Republican administration said at the beginning of the Depression: 'enterprising people will pick up from less competent people.' Even today crises are indeed considered as Darwinian events; however, the need is clear for providing liquidity and supporting those businesses that, in a stable situation, could continue to sustain themselves. This could happen if employee salaries and interest rates fell sufficiently low to allow businesses to be profitable again.

One of the exceptions to government passivity was the central bank. As described in Chapter 3, the US central bank, the Federal Reserve (the 'Fed'), was established in 1913 with one of its declared objectives being the provision of emergency financing to commercial banks. The rationale was to prevent collapse in the event of a bank run and banking panic. Indeed, the Fed adopted a 'contractionary monetary policy' in order to curb rising stock prices in 1928 and the beginning of 1929; but as described in Chapter 4, commercial banks found overseas sources of capital in order to circumvent restrictions. As the crisis unfolded, the Fed made generous loans to banks at the beginning of the collapse to enable them to endure the loans extended for margin purchases of securities. The Fed lowered the rate of interest on loans given to banks (the 'discount rate') from 6% in October 1929 to 2.5% in June 1930. However, starting in 1931, the Fed ceased acting as the lender of last resort and stopped saving commercial banks from collapse. This led to the bankruptcy of thousands of banks, which in turn led to a further reduction of credit and to the bankruptcy of numerous businesses and households whose savings were wiped out.

An important question is whether it was possible to do something in order to quickly stop the worsening crisis. Monetarist economists such as Milton Friedman and Ana Schwartz have argued that the Fed could have prevented the collapse of many banks if it had loaned to distressed banks and acted in the open market by purchasing government bonds. This way it would have infused the system with liquidity and slowed down, if not stopped, the worsening crisis. Friedman and Schwarz maintain that had the Fed continued to be managed by a decisive governor like Benjamin Strong (who died in 1928), a significant portion of the crisis would have been avoided. However, after Strong's death, the Fed's administration fell into the hands of Washington technocrats, who seem to have avoided making courageous decisions.

5.7 Global Effects

In contrast to Milton and Schwarz, other economists such as Kindleberger view the crisis as a global event stemming from a lack of global leadership. The starting point of this approach is that Britain was the global leader before World War I. It facilitated world trade while leaving its market open to the world, enabled international investments and prevented financial crises by granting loans in emergency situations. Following World War II, the US filled the role of global leader. However, between the two world wars no global leader existed, therefore no one country did enough in order to curb banking crises. One of the reasons for this was the lack of trust between the dominant countries following World War I.

In 1931, American banks began withdrawing funds from banks in Europe, causing the collapse of many European banks and eroding the value of European currency. An eroded currency generates incentive for cutting away from the gold standard. Thus, the moment fears arose that a specific country was intending to split itself from the gold standard, speculators and depositors immediately converted local currency into gold or a negotiable currency such as US dollars or pounds sterling. The withdrawal of deposits, as noted in previous chapters, generated panic and reduced credit according to the money multiplier. That was the trigger for many countries to cut away from the gold standard until it was totally abandoned and world trade significantly decreased.

The decrease in world trade grew more severe when countries adopted the policy of protecting local industry by raising trade barriers, such as increased customs on imports. For example, in 1930 President Hoover signed a bill that allowed a 52% duty increase on a variety of products.

In response, countries that traded with the US raised their customs duties in order to protect their own domestic production. This policy restrained world trade when it was needed more than ever. Kindleberger ties the lowered price of products to the collapse of the stock market. Since foreign banks and companies were the source of numerous loans extended for margin purchases of stock, those lenders demanded their money back when stock prices collapsed. In order to protect themselves, American banks cut back on loans given to traders in general including importers of raw materials such as rubber, cacao and coffee. Since exporters of raw materials, many in South American countries and primarily Mexico and Argentina, found themselves facing low demand, their income declined. Because their income brings dollars and other negotiable currencies to their home countries, these countries were not able to purchase industrial products from industrialized countries, a process that further affected world trade.

Today, economists see a degree of justness in both the monetarist approach and the global explanation. Whoever has followed the handling of the crises of 2008 in Europe and the US will have seen that many of the lessons were indeed applied.

5.8 Could the Government Do Better?

Another important question is whether the actions of the administration helped in resolving the crisis. In 1933, Democratic President Roosevelt presented his New Deal immediately after being elected and thus stimulated an optimistic spirit. When it offered government assistance programs for those hurt by the crisis the plan constituted a change from the extreme capitalistic policy of President Hoover. When Roosevelt started his first term, he enacted a number of reforms and new laws, some in his first 100 days in office. Here are some examples (United States History, n.d.2):

- The Emergency Banking Act provided the president with the means to *reopen* and *regulate* banks. Aid was granted to banks that proved they were immune to bankruptcy.
- The Agricultural Adjustment Act (AAA) established the Agricultural Adjustment Administration to *decrease crop surpluses* by subsidizing farmers who voluntarily cut back on production.
- The Thomas Amendment to the Agricultural Adjustment Act permitted the president to *inflate the currency*.

In addition, the Federal Deposit Insurance Corporation (FDIC) was established and supplied banking insurance to cover sums of up to $5,000. This move reduced public fears over a banking collapse and thus considerably reduced the bank run phenomenon.

The New Deal was made possible because during a crisis it is easier for an administration to change the economic order; without such a crisis, many long years would be required in order to implement such dramatic changes. However, many of the reforms were hastily formulated and implemented in a negligent manner; some even contradicted each other. In one of the new laws, manufacturers that operated in related areas were allowed to coordinate prices, wages and working hours in order to avoid what was called 'damaging competition'. Naturally, poor competition works against consumers, and the law was abolished in 1935 when it was found to be anti-constitutional. Since these reforms and laws concerned the welfare of all citizens, the public's interest in the economic behavior of government grew and with it, so did public criticism.

Of special interest is the case of the agricultural sector. The prevailing perception in those days was that government supervision and regulation had to increase in order to solve various problems. As noted above, in 1933 Congress passed the AAA for assisting farmers. One of the law's main clauses consisted of a plan for raising prices of agricultural crops by reducing harvests. Farmers received money in order to grow less produce based on the perception that higher prices would leave them with higher profits and thus improve their financial situations. By the time the law was passed, crops had already been planted and were growing, so the administration actually paid farmers to uproot and destroy crops and slaughter pigs. Thus, the supply of agricultural products diminished at a time when many were hungry, an event that stimulated bitter public criticism. The law was abolished in 1936.

Economists consider 1939 as the end of the Great Depression, when World War II erupted and industrial output thus grew.

5.9 The Dust Bowl

Between the years 1932 and 1935, farm revenues increased by 50%. However, this was not thanks to government reforms — a severe drought struck the Great Plains, which reduced agricultural output. Throughout the 1930s, strong winds and sandstorms assaulted the southern states in what was known as the 'Dust Bowl' (Figure 5.2).

Figure 5.2   A dust storm in Stratford, Texas, 18 April 1935
Source: By NOAA George E. Marsh Album, original upload 7 March 2005 (accessed 9 November 2014).

The Dust Bowl was particularly severe from 1935 to 1938, when some 800,000 inhabitants left Arkansas, Texas, Missouri and Oklahoma, many of them traveling westward for the illusion of economic security in California. It is estimated that about 2.5 million people lost their homes. When the immigrants arrived in California, they found it to be different from what they had dreamed of. In 1938 John Steinbeck published his classic book, *The Grapes of Wrath*, which describes the life of a farming family uprooted from their land by a bank, the land seized after its owners could not meet their debt payments.[3]

Another classic of the Great Depression is a song performed by Bing Crosby with lyrics written by Yip Harbur and music by Jay Gorney. The song tells the story of a proud American worker who has lost his job and is forced to beg for a dime (Box 5.1).

Box 5.1   'Brother, Can You Spare a Dime?'

---

[3]This book is highly recommended to those interested in grasping the true meaning of the Great Depression.

Additional Reading

Berenson, A. (2004). *The Number: How the Drive for Quarterly Earnings Corrupted Wall Street and Corporate America.* New York: Random House.

Galbraith, J.K. (1954). *The Great Crash of 1929.* New York: Penguin.

Galbraith, J.K. (1994). *The World Economy Since the Wars: A Personal View.* London: Sinclair-Stevenson.

Goldston, R.C. (1981). *The Great Depression: The United States in the Thirties.* New York: Fawcett Books.

6.

The Crisis of Confidence in Corporate America, 2001–2004

6.1 Introduction

At the turn of the new millennium, the most prestigious US firms, known as 'Corporate America', encountered a major shock, both to their stability and to their reputation. Between 2001 and 2004 dozens of accounting scandals astounded investors worldwide, costing these investors approximately 1.8 trillion US dollars (Weiss, 2002, p. 4). There were a variety of reasons behind this disastrous stretch, which will be discussed in detail below, but one element was consistent throughout nearly all cases of fraud during this time: Accounting firms, who positioned themselves as the 'watchdogs' of business firms, had signed off on their audit duties without issuing a going concern warning about these companies. According to Weiss (2002), of the 33 companies found to have accounting irregularities in 2002, 31 (or 94%) of them had been issued a clean report from accounting firms. Even more alarming to investors was the fact that all but one of these companies was audited by what was known as the 'Big Five' audit firms (KPMG; Deloitte & Touche; Ernst & Young; PricewaterhouseCoopers; Arthur Andersen [now defunct]) (Weiss, 2002, pp. 3–5). These five companies audited a significant portion of the market share and their collective failures reverberated throughout the economy. A crisis of confidence developed, as the public became distrustful of Wall Street, the biggest US corporations and the auditing process in general. This led to investors' reluctance to invest in the stock market based on information presented in the possibly manipulated financial statements. These scandals forced the hand of Congress and after years of deliberating and stalling, significant legislation was passed to help better regulate auditing firms so they can catch fraudulent activities more effectively.

While this chapter does not describe a financial crisis along the general properties described in the previous chapters (i.e., the collapse of a bubble that leads to a banking crisis and to a real-economy slowdown), here stock prices collapsed due to a crisis of confidence. As shall be seen, this crisis also stemmed from a prolonged erosion of regulations, accounting standards and accounting ethics. As such, it represents the cost of a widespread regulatory capture.

6.2 Background

As seen in Chapter 2, Benjamin Graham and David Dodd concluded as early as 1934, in the first book ever published on stock valuation, that it was essential to correctly evaluate 'earnings per share' (EPS) in order to evaluate a stock. Remember that EPS is simply calculated as the total company earnings divided by the number of shares that its shareholders hold. The resulting number tells the investor what profit the company is expected to generate for each share, so that this piece of information can be compared with the price of the stock. Section 2.4 showed that the dividend growth model converts the EPS to the stock's price by discounting all expected cash flows. However, it was also emphasized in Chapter 2 that the resulting stock price, and hence the valuation of shareholders' equity, is highly sensitive to the three parameters that enter into the pricing formula: the appropriate discount rate, the expected growth rate of the firm's earning and the EPS. This chapter will continue by highlighting the motivation that different parties have in manipulating the EPS, the devastating consequences of manipulated EPS, and why it changed the way corporate America is managed.

6.3 Destructive Symbiosis between Managers, Politicians and Auditors

In order to evaluate the EPS adequately and allow investors to compare between different stocks, it is necessary for auditors — those entrusted with reviewing a company's books — to work according to relatively uniform and binding guidelines. Up to the 1930s, many of the rules were neither uniform nor binding. Moreover, auditors did not see themselves as inspecting a company's books for the sake of the investment community. An example that could have been funny if it weren't real is a case from the 1930s where a police investigation disclosed that managers of a particular drug company had fabricated a division and stolen monies that were transferred to that division by manipulating the accounting records, some $18 million. The company's auditors, Price Waterhouse, claimed that their audit was not intended for discovering the non-existence of a division. Police uncovered the embezzlement when they found a document pertaining to a purported shipment transported from Canada to Australia — by truck.

This case aroused a public furor and led to an investigation by the Securities Exchange Commission (SEC). One of the main reasons for the public's outrage and for the investigation was that Price Waterhouse had been considered a high quality, if not the highest quality, auditing firm. The extensive media coverage at the time generated an atmosphere of inquiry and criticism of auditing firms. For their part, the firms argued that an audit does not need, for example, to certify that everything listed as inventory is actually physically located in company warehouses. The public and the SEC thought otherwise. They maintained that if an auditor signs a financial statement, then investors and stockholders should be convinced that the accountant has indeed verified that all figures in the financial statements correctly and genuinely represent the state of the firm. The SEC's review obliged auditors to adopt new auditing standards, which were indeed adopted in 1939. During that same period, the SEC enjoyed broad government and public support and it inspected auditors frequently.

As World War II raged during the first half of the 1940s, many companies did not want to appear as being too profitable, so auditors used the flexibility at their disposal in order to play down profits. The public, still in trauma from the 1929 crisis and the Great Depression, flinched from investing in the stock market; thus, US stocks at the end of the 1940s were extremely cheap. Note that the post-crash multiplier (the ratio P/EPS)[1] was less than ten and the dividend yield rate was about 7%. Long-term interest rates were at a record low, to be broken only after the crisis of 2008. Stock prices could not remain so cheap for so long, and indeed, starting in mid-1949, prices began to rise. In 1954 the Dow Jones Average reached the level

---

[1] The multiplier, calculated by dividing the stock price, P, by the EPS (i.e., Multiplier = P/EPS) gives a rough estimate on the number of years the investor needs to wait until the price he paid for the stock is paid back by receiving the annual EPS. A multiplier of 6 implies six years, where the US historical average is about 15. There are several versions of calculating the multiplier, depending on the definitions of what earnings constitute, and whether these are past or future earnings.

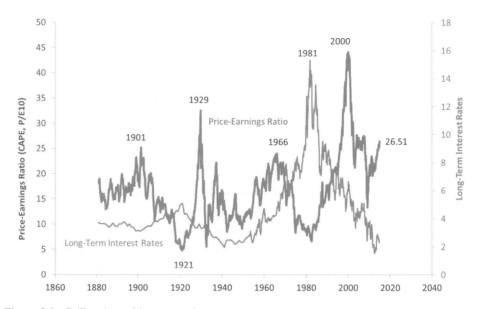

Figure 6.1 P/E ratio and long-term interest rates

Source: Prof. Shiller data: http://www.econ.yale.edu/~shiller/data.htm (accessed 8 November 2014).

Figure 6.2 The Big Eight

it had been prior to the 1929 crash. The public once again invested in stocks and the market of stock issues stirred up.

Due to growth in the number of public companies and rising demand for the services of large auditing firms, such firms grew extremely rapidly. If in 1945 there were approximately 9,500 listed members in the American Accounting Association, in 1980 there were some 150,000 members. This increase was more rapid than the rate of growth in the number of lawyers or physicians in the US. In the 1980s, almost all public companies in the US, i.e., those traded on stock exchanges, received their auditing services exclusively from the eight largest auditing firms, the 'Big Eight'. Some 95% of American public company earnings were audited by the Big Eight, a statistic signifying that the US stock market was under the supervision of what may seem like a cartel.

During that time, the auditing firms abstained from competing over customers and intentionally limited competition-generating activities such as advertising, wooing customers from other firms, price reductions, etc. For example, it has been estimated that the big accounting firms increased annual advertising spending from $4 million in the early 1980s, to more than $100 million in the 2000s (Breton, 2003). In 1977, the Federal administration initiated an examination of whether the behavior of the Big Eight constituted a violation of fair competition rules. The firms didn't wait until the end of the inquiry and immediately removed many of the prohibitions they imposed upon themselves and on other auditors. This move led to increased competition expressed by lowered prices, customers changing companies and an atmosphere that changed from being gentlemanly (characteristic of the profession up to that time) to combative.

A number of academics and professionals warned that the erosion of profitability of accounting firms would ultimately roll over to the small investor, because the quality of auditing would be impacted. Countering this claim, many auditors argued that low auditing fees would not affect the quality of audits, because an *auditor is committed to quality* and would be uncompromising. But economic reality proved otherwise: in light of lowered revenues from auditing activity, the firms began to supply more and more *consulting services* to the audited companies. Demand for consulting reports prepared by auditors emerged from the managerial echelon, for it was easy for a manager to approve a proposal with an auditor's report — supposedly objective and prepared by a respected auditor — resting on their desk. Moreover, the existence of a supporting document to a manager's decision supplied him or her with protection against plausible accusations or even legal claims over decisions that, retrospectively, might turn out to be mistaken. The fact that the manager was the one signing on the accountant's paycheck rendered implicit, if not explicit, power on the content. The result was that company managers tended to be fond of advisory reports prepared by auditors and paid for them generously. This created ill symbiosis: An auditor holding a profitable consultancy contract and discovering a problem during their (unprofitable) audit might be overly forgiving of it. Even worse, they might legitimize an irregularity due to being restrained by conflict of interest.

6.4 The Politics

A Senate committee that examined the behavior of auditors was aware of this problem and indicated it in its report of 1976. The committee wrote:

> The traditional public image of The Big Eight accounting firms as impartial and objective experts is not founded on fact [...] as political partisans and purveyors of nonaccounting services, they became loyal agents of the clients which employ their services [...]. It appears that The Big Eight are more concerned with serving the interests of corporate managers who select them and authorize their fees than with protecting the interests of the public. (Stevens, 1981, p. 134)

In the background of events was a hopeless struggle between the American Institute of Certified Public Accountants (AICPA), representing all accountants and supported to a certain extent by the SEC, and the Big Eight. In 1974 the AICPA set up a commission headed by former SEC chairman Manuel Cohen (1912–1977) with a mandate to examine whether investors and auditors saw eye to eye on the functions of an accounting audit. The commission published its report in 1978, in which it blamed auditors for neglecting their primary role, which was none other than auditing a company's books (The Commission on Auditors' Responsibilities, 1978). For example, the commission found that in 58% of audits, financial statements were signed without undergoing all of the necessary checks as to the reliability of information contained in the statements.

That same year, Congressman (Democrat) John E. Moss, chairman of the Subcommittee on Commerce and Finance inspecting the US securities industry, submitted a bill for the supervision of auditors. But his bill never even made it to discussion, exactly as the recommendations of the Cohen Commission were never implemented, perhaps because the leaders of the Big Eight cartel wielded strong political influence in order to safeguard their standing (these firms were among the largest donors to important politicians from both parties, with a strong leaning towards the Republicans).

In 1979, the SEC issued a call to the Big Eight to abstain from certain consultancy projects, without exercising any sanctions. The absence of

Figure 6.3 The Big Six

sanctions signaled to the Big Eight that there was no real impediment to them to entering the consultancy market, which started the onslaught: At the beginning of the 1980s, only 10% of Big Eight revenue derived from consultancy; in 1986 that figure reached 20%. Subsequently, in 1994, Andersen, the most aggressive of the firms, posted a record 50% of revenues originating from consultancy.

In 1989, the Restrictive Trade Practices Commission allowed the merger of Ernst & Whinney with Arthur Young & Co. (resulting in Ernst & Young), and the merger of Deloitte Haskins & Sells with Touche Ross (forming Deloitte & Touche). Thus, the Big Eight became the Big Six (Figure 6.3).

Shortly afterwards the first signals started to hit the market over the deteriorating quality of accounting audits. Between 1977 and 1989, an annual average of only 13 companies re-stated their earnings (i.e., explained that mistakes had crept into previous calculations of earnings, therefore they were recalculated and re-presented); in 1997 that number reached about 90. In April 1998, Cendant, a large franchising company, admitted that it had evaluated its earnings between 1995 and 1997 to be $640 million *higher* than they actually were. The company collapsed, causing losses of $14 billion to investors, the largest loss due to accounting fraud up to that time.

At the same time, other cases of accounting fraud were discovered, and surprisingly, the findings did not emerge from auditing activity of accountants, but rather from employees and internal audit. The accounting firms argued, justifiably, that no one had ever proved a connection between revenue from consulting services and a flimsy audit. At the same time, accounting firms continued to repel the demands of the SEC to separate between consulting activity and auditing activity. To the contrary, argued the firms, our familiarity with the functioning of a company, gained during the course of consulting, helps us in executing an effective audit.

In 1997, SEC Chairman Arthur Levitt established an independent committee to examine whether auditors needed to comply with precautionary rules even more stringent than those in existence. Let us recall that the Cohen Committee had already examined this issue some 20 years earlier in 1978, although its conclusions were not implemented. The problem Levitt had was that the SEC appointed four members of the commission but accounting firms appointed the four remaining members. Thus, the commission's discussions lingered and yielded no significant results.

In September 1998 Levitt delivered a speech to the New York University Center for Law and Business entitled 'The Numbers Game'. In this speech, Mr. Levitt described publically the various ways accounting firms manipulated their clients' financial records. One by one he described (using the politically correct terms) how accountants provide 'earning management' services to meet the needs of the same management that hired them and paid their salaries. He said, 'Managing may be giving way to manipulation; integrity may be losing out to illusion.'[2]

Levitt also outlined ways in which these issues could be resolved in what he called his 'nine-point action plan'. The plan would improve the accounting framework, the role of the outside auditor in the reporting process and the role of the audit committee. Toward the end of the speech, Mr. Levitt highlights the need for a cultural change:

> Finally, I'm challenging corporate management and Wall Street to re-examine our current environment. I believe we need to embrace nothing less than a cultural change. For corporate managers, remember, the integrity of the numbers in the financial reporting system is directly related to the long-term interests of a corporation. While the temptations are great, and the pressures strong, illusions in numbers are only that — ephemeral, and ultimately self-destructive.
>
> To Wall Street, I say, look beyond the latest quarter. Punish those who rely on deception, rather than the practice of openness and transparency.

In the last chapter of this book, the non-politically correct terms will be used to describe the ethical aspects that lay behind many financial crises, and the cultural contexts of lying and manipulation.

---

[2] The text of the speech can be found in many websites. This one is from The CPA Journal: http://www.nysscpa.org/cpajournal/1998/1298/Features/F141298.html.

Figure 6.4   Arthur Levitt, SEC Chair, 1993–2001

Source: By Financial Times photos [CC-BY-2.0 (http://creativecommons.org/licenses/by/2.0)], via Wikimedia Commons (accessed 9 November 2014).

Figure 6.5   The Big Five

In 1999, Price Waterhouse and Coopers & Lybrand merged, thus the auditing cartel grew stronger and became the Big Five (Figure 6.5).

In June 2000, Levitt once again decided to tackle the Big Five head-on, arguing that they must be prevented from providing technological consulting services to companies on which they performed audits. An aggressive meeting was held between Levitt and the directors of KPMG, Deloitte & Touche and Andersen, the three firms most opposed to the move. In the meeting, as recounted by Levitt, and Dwyer (2002), following his retirement, the Andersen chief executive officer (CEO) said to him: 'If you go ahead with this, your' going to have war.' Indeed, Levitt felt the winds of war begin to blow. The presidential election was approaching, and the Big Five speculated that if George W. Bush were elected, Levitt would resign his position. The Big Five were among the Republican Party's largest contributors — PricewaterhouseCoopers was the fourth largest contributor to the 2000 Bush campaign and Andersen was the fifth.

Levitt understood that time was working against him; therefore, he issued his proposal publicly. In a September 2000 lecture to the National Association of State Boards of Accountancy (NASBA) in Boston, Massachusetts, Mr. Levitt supported NASBA's cooperation with the Independence Standards Board, and attacked the existence of 'a stonewall by some of the profession's leadership to prevent truly independent over-sight' (Levitt, 2000). In response, the Big Five pressured members of Congress from both parties to cut the SEC budget, which was already beaten down. When the moment of confrontation arrived, Levitt found himself facing a hostile Congress and mass media that had no interest in 'technical accounting issues'. Apparently, Levitt had no choice and retired while the SEC's chair desk was loaded with important tasks.

6.5 The Price

The price to investors and the American public due to auditing omissions and manipulations has been revealed among the largest and most reputable firms in a series of scandals and bankruptcies of unprecedented magnitude. The most well-known case is that of Enron. Enron was founded by its chairman Kenneth Lay in 1985 as a result of a merger between two large energy firms. After several years, Jeffrey Skilling was recruited to serve as CEO and opera-tions director and he recruited part of the firms senior tier of management. Working together with the Chief Financial Officer (CFO; Andrew Fastow), company management abusively exploited loopholes in standard accounting regulations and established 'special purpose entities' (SPEs) as sorts of sub-sidiaries in which billions of dollars of debt and losses from failed projects were hidden. Fastow and other managers concealed these accounting 'stunts', genteelly referred to as 'creative accounting', in order to conceal information from the eyes of the company board and audit committee.[3] They

---

[3] In Levitt's September 1998 speech, 'The Numbers Game', he highlighted a number of accounting maneuvers, one of them being SPEs. He was later blamed by some for not being more aggressive on those maneuvers.

even pressured auditors Arthur Andersen to ignore the matter; obviously, Arthur Andersen agreed (remember, they earned their living from consulting, not auditing activity). In October 2001, the extent of the company's actual debt was discovered, when Arthur Andersen maintained that the company should account for a portion of the SPEs' losses as an integral part of its consolidated financial statements. The consolidation of the SPEs with Enron's balance sheet erased about a billion dollars of company capital, leading to a loss of $618 million in the third quarter of 2001. Enron's stock price fell from a record $90 in mid-2000 to less than one dollar. The public lost some $63 billion through its direct holdings of the stock and through the stock holdings of pension funds and mutual funds. Enron employees lost their jobs as well as some of their pension savings. Approximately 20,000 people found themselves unemployed.

The next large accounting scandal, one year later, involved WorldCom, which engaged in corruption *per se*. Bernard Ebbers (the CEO) accumulated immense wealth from the company's rising stock price in the stock exchange. However, in 2000, as part of the collapse of the dot-com bubble, WorldCom's stock price fell quickly. Ebbers, who had taken out loans against WorldCom stock (a situation previously described as buying 'on margin'), received a margin call from his brokers to deposit money into his margin account; or else, they threatened, they would sell off his stock (the 'margin call'). Ebbers asked the board of directors for a loan and guarantee of $400 million after persuading them that it was preferable not to sell the stock for fear of causing a further drop in price. The board consented, but the plan was unsuccessful, and in April 2002 Ebbers was fired from his position as CEO.

Back in 1999, Ebbers and his co-managers had begun employing accounting tricks in order to paint a rosier picture of the company's financial statement; their motivation was to 'support' (i.e., manipulate) the company's stock price. The company inflated its profits by $9 billion in the years 1999 to 2002 via irregular accounting practices. Additionally, media/communication expenses were entered as an investment in fixed assets, an entry that reduces expenses and thus increases reported profit (EPS). In 2002, a secret team of internal auditors, led by Cynthia Cooper, discovered these deceitful practices. They alerted their audit committee, as well as their current auditors, KPMG, who had replaced Arthur Andersen earlier that year. Upon announcing this mistake, WorldCom's stock plummeted and the company eventually was forced to file for bankruptcy, costing employees upwards of thirty thousand jobs. An investigation of the matter revealed that WorldCom executives knew about this manipulation as early as 2000, yet

neither their outside or internal auditors had discovered this ploy until over
a year later. Arthur Andersen had claimed that they were not notified that
these media/communication expenses were being capitalized and had they
known they would have stopped it. However, the investigators determined
that their job was to detect frauds of this magnitude and charges were
brought up against Arthur Andersen.

Another example: Global Crossing (a communication company) collapsed after it had inflated profits via transactions for 'capacity exchange' of
communication lines with other communication companies — a practice
that turned out to be common among both communication companies and
energy companies.

The auditing failures of Arthur Andersen, the auditor for Enron,
WorldCom and Global Cruising, led to the firm's collapse; 113,000
employees lost their jobs, and only four firms remain out of the Big Five
(Figure 6.6).

While Arthur Andersen's faults may have grabbed the largest headlines, each of the Big Five auditing firms had been implicated in some sort
of accounting failure during the early 2000s. Here are a few examples:
Ernst & Young had been the auditor for AOL, when they had inflated
sales in anticipation of a merger with Time Warner. Deloitte had been in
charge of Adelphia's audit when in 2002 it was revealed that the founding
Rigas family had collected $3.1 billion in off-balance-sheet loans (SEC,
2005). PricewaterhouseCoopers had been the auditor in charge of Bristol-
Myers Squibb when it was revealed that they had inflated revenue by
$1.5 billion by 'channel stuffing' (forcing wholesalers to accept more
inventory than they could sell), and improperly recognizing revenues
from those sales (SEC, 2004). KPMG had been in charge of the audit of
Mirant, when in 2002 it was discovered that they had inflated various

Figure 6.6   The Big Four

revenue accounts for an increase of $1.1 billion of income (Patsuris, 2002). Overall, there were more than fifty companies found to have had accounting irregularities during this period. The Big Five audited most of those companies.

6.6 Legal Response and the Need for Better Regulations

President Bush spoke in a forceful tone in July 2002 when he referred to the repeatedly emerging accounting scandals, but he finished off with a demand to merely strengthen the implementation of regulations and the existing laws. There was no call for reform. Public rage over the failure of auditing and against large companies' CEOs led to two developments. First, investors distanced themselves from stock investments in light of the severe crisis of confidence in corporate America. Second, a new law was passed at the initiative of Democrat Paul Sarbanes and Republican Michael Oxley, to clarify and elaborate the responsibility of CEOs and auditors in the dealings of public companies. The Sarbanes–Oxley Act, known in short as SOX, authorizes the SEC to supervise companies, and indeed, SEC chairman Harvey Pitt adopted dozens of laws for the application of SOX. This move strengthens the SEC to a certain extent vs. the Big Four, whose prestige deteriorated following the scandals.

The first order of business created by SOX was to establish the Public Company Accounting Oversight Board (PCAOB). The PCAOB was charged with four main responsibilities:[4] registering accounting firms that audit public companies trading in US securities markets; inspecting registered accounting firms; establishing standards for auditing, quality control, ethics and independence for registered accounting firms; and investigating and disciplining registered accounting firms and the people associated with them for violations of law or professional standards. The PCAOB would stand as the guardian over the public's interest and would be able to bring charges to any firm that they believed violated any of their laws or accounting laws in general. Some of the major provisions included CEO certification of all released financial statements; making CEOs and CFOs personally liable for any errors; prohibition of any personal loans to directors or executives; and making it illegal to destroy any document that could be used in legal proceedings. The act itself also

---

[4] See the PCAOB website for a full list of their standards: http://pcaobus.org/standards/Pages/default.aspx (accessed 3 October 2013).

placed requirements and prohibitions on accounting firms. The auditing firms were required to create their own auditing committees and report any changes in accounting policies or financial condition of their clients immediately.

Most importantly, the act had a provision that protected any whistle-blowers from any legal action, in an attempt to encourage people to alert about fraudulent activities. There also is a rule mandating that a person cannot be the lead partner on an audit for more than five years, as familiarity and comfort is usually the first step in a plan to commit fraud.

Finally, and most importantly, companies were no longer allowed to audit and consult for the same client on the same job. In fact, only Deloitte chose to keep their consulting firm under the same name after Sarbanes–Oxley. Recently, the European Union (EU) has begun the process of trying to force a mandatory firm rotation policy, which would force a firm to change auditors every five years in an effort to increase competition and reliability, and discourage familiarity. It has yet to pass, and has not been put on the agenda for United States companies to this point.

6.7 Was the Enron Regulator Captured?

Washington Post staff writer David S. Hilzenrath published on 19 October 2010 the following story (Hilzenrath, 2010; see also 'Regulatory capture' on Wikipedia). One of the two administrative law judges presiding over investor complaints at the Commodity Futures Trading Commission (CFTC), George H. Painter, was in the retirement process. According to Hilzenrath, Painter requested in writing that his cases not be assigned to the other judge, Bruce C. Levine. According to Painter, Levine had a secret agreement with a former Republican chairwoman of the agency, Wendy Gramm, to stand in the way of investors filing complaints with the agency. Painter wrote: 'On Judge Levine's first week on the job, nearly twenty years ago, he came into my office and stated that he had promised Wendy Gramm, then Chairwoman of the Commission, that we would never rule in a complainant's favor' (Hilzenrath, 2010). Painter continued: 'Judge Levine, in the cynical guise of enforcing the rules, forces pro se complainants to run a hostile procedural gauntlet until they lose hope, and either withdraw their complaint or settle for a pittance, regardless of the merits of the case.' Moreover: 'A review of his rulings will confirm that he fulfilled his vow.' It turns out that Wendy Gramm is the wife of former Senator Phil Gramm, who was accused of helping Goldman Sachs, Enron and other large firms gain influence over the commodity markets. After leaving the CFTC, Wendy

Gramm *joined the board of Enron.* In Section 12.3 is a box dedicated to the additional 'contributions' of Mr. Phil Gramm in relaxing regulations of the US financial industry.

An important thing to take away from this chapter is the linkage found between the erosion of regulations, laws and accounting standards, and the increased financial risks for public firms. The motivation for accountants to erode binding rules stems from their desire to increase corporate earnings, maintain a big client and perhaps, personal gain. The incentives for corporate managers to erode the same rules are job security, reduced uncertainty in reported financial statements and again, personal gain. To mitigate the erosion of regulations and rules, power must be given to external rule-makers, i.e., governmental agencies like the SEC. In a summary table in Chapter 16 I show that the interactions between accounting firms, top managers, and regulators described in this chapter meet the 'gold standard' of regulatory capture as defined by Carpenter and Moss (2013).

6.8 Social Response

Social response echoed widely in popular media coverage and songs. One example refers ironically to the Sarbanes–Oxley Act and the accounting deeds of the CEOs of Enron, WorldCom and others. It is titled 'Happy Birthday to Sarbanes–Oxley', and performed by an accountant, Steven Zelin. The song was composed to mark the law's fifth anniversary (http://www.youtube.com/watch?v=n2ylBKOURtw).

Another example is a 2002 song entitled 'Corporate America' by the rock band 'Boston'.

Chapter 7 will show how corruptive, symbiotic interactions between company CEOs, auditors and analysts, contributed to the expansion of the Internet bubble in the late 1990s and its collapse in 2000.

Additional Reading

Berenson, A. (2004). *The Number: How the Drive for Quarterly Earnings Corrupted Wall Street and Corporate America.* New York: Random House.

Levitt, A. (1998). 'The Numbers Game.' Speech delivered at NYU Center for Law and Business, 28 September, New York.

Levitt, A. and Dwyer, P. (2002). *Take On the Street: What Wall Street and Corporate America Don't Want You to Know. What You Can Do to Fight Back.* New York: Random House.

7.

The Internet Bubble

7.1 A 'New Economy', Again

The Internet stock price bubble, known also as the 'dot-com bubble' or the 'technology bubble', erupted in the US market around 1995, reaching its peak on 10 March 2000. The bubble received those tags because many young technology firms adopted names that referred to information technology (IT) — such as the ending '.com' or the prefix 'e', like Pets.com or e-Digital. One may wonder what the reason was for this colorful naming fashion to develop. It turns out that those companies with names hinting at a connection with information technologies benefited from huge demand for their stocks. Stock prices would shoot up quickly once offered to the public, generating immediate profits for anyone purchasing them at the beginning of the process. In the case of the stocks of young companies, the process began on or before the day of a company's initial public offering (IPO). Many view the IPO of Netscape on 9 August 1995 as the forerunner of a wave of IT IPOs that swept the financial market. For example, on 31 March 2003, *Time* magazine considered this day as one of the 1990s' 'most crucial events in the history of the world' (Cramer, 2003).

Netscape gave the world its first Internet browser, Navigator, which enabled the public to view website content stored on servers of the then-young Internet network. People were able for the first time in history to make secure online credit card purchases, learn about the profiles of firms, their products and services. This represented a paradigm shift in the way businesses and customers learned about each other and conducted economic transactions. For those who were active in the field the business potential of the Internet, and of software that enabled search and transactions, was

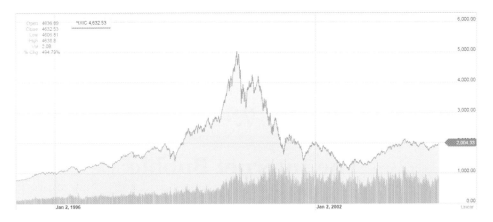

Figure 7.1   Dot-com bubble — NASDAQ composite index
Source: Wikimedia Commons, the free media repository. Public domain.

immense. This optimistic view of the future soon translated into strong demand for businesses in the field. Notice that this technological change is consistent with Minsky's explanation as one of the reasons for increased optimism, as presented in Chapter 1.

7.2 Vague Valuations

The original plan for the Netscape IPO, jointly formulated by the company and Morgan Stanley, the underwriting firm that led the issue, was to sell 3.5 million shares for $14 per share. Such numbers would reflect a company value of $507 million.[1] In the half-year that preceded the issue, Netscape sales totaled $16.6 million and the company registered a loss in its financial statements. So why the $507 million valuation?

Admittedly, the valuation of a new technology firm is extremely complex and subjective since many of those companies are 'one of a kind', i.e., such companies cannot be compared to others, and comparison to other firms serves as an important benchmark in valuation practices. Moreover, Netscape operated in an entirely new technological field, and no one could have had a clue as to the extent of its profitability in the future. The reason is that not only the mere existence of the proposed technological path the company is offering is questionable, but also its size, profitability,

---

[1] Note that not all shares of the company were sold to the public. The valuation of the company for its shareholders is the product of the share price by all outstanding shares, those issued and those that were not. The non-issued shares amounted to 32,764 million.

competitive environment and many other factors are vague. Lastly, Netscape showed no profit therefore it was impossible to calculate the value produced by the sales it generated on an ongoing basis.

Despite the vagueness surrounding the company's valuation, the interest Netscape sparked and its potentially high future profits generated unprecedented demand. In light of that demand Morgan Stanley and the company decided to increase the number of shares offered from 3.5 million to 5 million, and to double the stock price for anyone ordering before the IPO date from $14 to $28. According to the company, against the supply of 5 million shares, the day of the issue witnessed demand on an unprecedented scale, for some 100 million shares!

Trading opened at $71, reached a peak of $75, and ended its first day at $58.25 per share. At this price, the company valuation in the market was in excess of $2 billion. Recall that according to estimates of the highly professional and knowledgeable Morgan Stanley and company executives a short time beforehand, Netscape's value was only half a billion dollars; and even that was based on meager sales and a bottom-line loss. In other words, the market estimated the company four times greater than what its management thought, in full agreement with experts who had examined the company. How, therefore, can one explain such a huge gap between the company's valuation and its market price? In an interview with *The Wall Street Journal* on 8 August 1995, one day before the IPO, Lise Buyer, an analyst who was involved Netscape's valuation, said:

> Everyone is using their own set of growth rates based on current net-related products and a little crystal-ball gazing and fairy dust [...] I don't know how to put a value on it — you pick a price you're willing to pay and you find a way to rationalize it.

Buyer's rare sincerity stimulated a lively discussion in the press and it evoked two quandaries. First, a person untrained in company valuation could wonder how is it possible for different economists to accept such significant differences. Second, if analysts and evaluators are capable of finding a way to justify any figure they choose, do they have incentives to prefer certain valuations? If, for example, their profits increase as valuations rise, is it possible they would tend to exaggerate upwards?

Think of the dividend growth model as if it were the tool to evaluate the value of each stock, and hence, the value of the entire equity of the firm

(by multiplying the price per share by the number of outstanding shares).
Remember that the model is overly simplistic:

$$P_0 = \frac{E_1}{k-g}.$$

That is, the expected profit (earnings per share [EPS]) is divided by the
appropriate rate of return on equity, k, minus the expected growth rate, g.
A simple model is advantageous as is captures the essence of the problem
with just a few parameters. Simplicity, of course, comes at a cost — the
model ignores many important factors that affect a stock's risk and return.
But beyond that, an important problem with this model is that the result,
the stock's price, is dependent on three numbers that must be *estimated*: the
most likely EPS in the upcoming year, the rate of return on equity capital
(which can be described as a sort of interest rate adjusted to company's
risk), and the dividend growth rate.

Anyone experienced in calculating a stock's price based on this model
knows that the result is extremely sensitive to small changes in the parameters; thus with a bit of talent and resourcefulness, *one can justify almost any
price* observed in the market. Of course, with the development of financial
theory, additional models and techniques were developed for company
valuation. However, for analysts, the case of a brand-new technology — not
being able to compare a company with similar companies and lacking
fundamental information in the financial statements — leaves one without
points of reference upon which to base the company's valuation.
Therefore, a gap might result between a company's fundamental value
and its market value. In previous chapters, this gap has been defined as a
'bubble'.

Assuming that data exists and it is quality data, and if all investors use
the same data and the same model to calculate stock price, then no bubble
should emerge. The reason is that in such a situation, all investors will agree
on a uniform price, and no one would be willing to pay more than that
price. On the other hand, everyone will rush in to purchase the stock if its
price goes lower than this price. In the case of the IT firms, or any new
technology firm, the fundamental price is nothing but a phantom.

7.3 Financial Analysts: Roles and Incentives

Now to turn to the second issue suggested by Lise Buyer: Do analysts have an
interest in devising especially high valuations prior to a company's public

stock issue? Let us elaborate on this question. Analysts are busy with many activities such as reviewing companies and issuing reports to the public of their conclusions concerning company strength and value after a stock has been issued, as a matter of a routine. One of the most important activities they engage in is estimating EPS for the upcoming quarter (period) so that investors can map out their strategy. The question, therefore, is: Should we be suspicious of analysts' bias in their reports? Studies by Womack (1996) and others on the US evidence revealed that approximately 75% of all analysts' reports are positive with 'buy' recommendations, about 22% neutral reports with 'hold' recommendations and only 3% conclude a 'sell' recommendation. A more or less similar distribution was found in other countries. Is it possible that, in a consistent manner, the majority of companies in the economy improve from quarter to quarter? Or might there be another factor that influences analysts' recommendations?

Here is some brief background on analysts. Analysts were held in high regard in the 1970s and until the beginning of the 1980s as they performed thorough research studies, mainly on industrial companies. They examined the specific industrial branch, competition, products, strategy and financial strength of a given company and ultimately published their evaluation in a report. All reports were written by analysts who worked for one of two sides of a transaction: investors who purchased a company ('buy-side analysts') or investment banks that sold it ('sell-side analysts'). High-quality reports were valuable because they facilitated transactions that generated value to both sides of the deal, and high commissions for investment banks, thus the banks were willing to subsidize research departments.

During those same years about a third of investment bank revenue flowed from securities trading. However, in the 1980s, following a regulatory change that reduced trading commissions, that source of financing dried up. Investment banks sought alternative business opportunities and, not surprisingly, found them. The main portion of investment-bank revenue now came from consulting on mergers and acquisitions. At the beginning of the 1990s, regulatory changes stimulated competition in lowering the price of analyst reports; as a result, lowered prices reduced the quality of the reports. For example, a company requesting a report for the purpose of entering into a merger transaction with another company would turn to an investment banker who would appoint an analyst to prepare a report. No one had to say it outright, but the analyst understood that if they wrote a report that did not serve the goals of the company, that company would turn to another investment banker who would make sure to produce a more complimentary report. Since analysts were restrained by conflict of interest — their salaries were paid, even if indirectly, by the company they were analyzing — their reports became more and more positive, even enthusiastic, over the company, whether it was a quality company or not.

An additional and important source of demand for analysts' services was the media, which, in light of increasing demand supplied the public's need for analyzing economic information. The demand primarily stemmed from private investors who could not afford to buy analysts' reports, or could not digest their content. The multiplicity of analyst evaluations regarding expected EPS of various companies led to the creation in 1985 of an average called the 'consensus estimate'. This number became important to investors, the media and the analysts themselves because it represented an average of all analysts' estimates. By averaging the estimates of many analysts on the expected EPS of a particular firm, the investing public received a single, summarizing number, instead of browsing numerous sources.

The reason why the 'consensus estimate' gained not only popularity but also importance was that one might ignore the estimate of a specific analyst, but ignoring a number that represents the average opinion of all analysts who reviewed a company means swimming against the flow. In financial markets, this strategy is highly risky — it may either generate high gains or high losses. The number thus became a reference point for companies that were reluctant to end the quarter with an EPS lower than consensus estimate, for if that happened then the stock price would drop sharply. The consensus estimate also became important for the analysts themselves who, in a herd mentality, didn't want to present an estimate far off from the consensus. Analysts who published EPS estimates that were far from the consensus, either above or below it, lost credit among peers, and sometimes lost their jobs and ruined their reputation. Naturally, the consensus estimate influenced the investment decisions of investors in the market.

Such an incentive structure, for the companies and for the analysts, generated a basis for cooperation. In order to produce a forecast that served the interests of the company and the analysts, the two sides conferred with each other. After all, one cannot dispute the analyst's need to delve into the activities and financial records of the firm, often by meeting with top management, and particularly with the CFO. Thus, the analysts learned of the expectations of company management and subsequently often published biased projections. Since management conveys a similar message to all analysts, each one of them is close to the consensus and both sides are happy. But this symbiotic relationship created a number of problems. Here are three of the more important ones:

1. Analysts who in the past had performed independent and comprehensive studies were now receiving only the information that the company *wanted* them to receive. Thus, analysts provided information with little value added, and that information was in most part biased towards the needs of the company.
2. Companies began operating according to short-term quarterly earnings targets, mainly in order to publish EPS figures *not lower* than the analyst consensus. Therefore, management was strained to ever increase its EPS, which is simply impossible in real business life, and it focused on *short-term accounting performance.* This focus on the short term came at the expense of essential *long-term* business vision, expressed in product development, market development, organizational changes and the like.
3. The focus on the consensus of analysts' forecast of EPS generated pressure on auditors. If there was a need to create additional revenue for a quarter that didn't look so good, or to conceal expenses, then creative accounting was harnessed. So long as it is several millions of dollars, which accountants transfer from one quarter to another, the effect on a company's business activity is negligible. Nevertheless, if a dynamic evolves whereby it is necessary to increase EPS from one quarter to the next, and the company's ongoing business activity makes this impossible, that is another story. Analysts will then pressure management, who in turn will pressure accountants to find ways of concealing expenses or increasing revenue on a continuous basis. As we learned from the cases of Enron, WorldCom and other American corporations, sustained creative accounting ends up in a distorted representation of the companies' true financial standing, including its profitability, assets and liabilities. This is why 'creative accounting' and flexible accounting rules played an important role in the over-valuation of corporations. By relaxing their own binding regulations accounting firms created false value, just like a bubble, which had to crash when faced with reality.

7.4 Stock Options

In the mid-1980s, an incentive evolved for US corporate managers to continually increase their firm's stock price in the exchange. This stemmed from 'options', which were generously distributed to top management and members on the board of directors. But why would 'the company', i.e., its shareholders, be willing to give shares to managers? After all, the more shares distributed to managers, the lower the fraction of ownership the original shareholders retain.

Consider, for example, a company that has 1,000,000 shares to begin with, out of which Mrs. Smith holds 10,000. Mrs. Smith's proportional holding is 10,000/1,000,000 = 1% of the firm, therefore she is entitled to 1% of all dividends and 1% of the amount that remains should the firm be liquidated. Now, assume that the board of directors recruits Mr. Manger to run the company. Mr. Manger's goals are not necessarily aligned with those of the shareholders: While shareholders want the firm to earn high profits and grow in value, Mr. Manger may seek job security and refrain from adopting new technologies. Alternatively, Mr. Manger may wish to 'show off' in the executive clubs and build an empire within the firm. For example, he may acquire unnecessary divisions from other companies, buy a helicopter taxi, buy expensive dinners and wine, and so on. These phenomena are known as the 'principal–agent conflict'. To mitigate the conflicts the principal (shareholders) makes the agent (the manager) a shareholder too. This way, theory says, Mr. Manger will more likely act to fulfill the goals of shareholders.

To understand why options created an incentive to inflate stock prices, let us review briefly their key attributes. An option is a financial asset whose value depends on another financial asset, an index of assets, interest rate, inflation or the exchange rate between two currencies. Options for managers are a version[2] of a certain type of options, known as 'call options'. Like other options, their value depends on the stock price of the company that they manage (the underlying asset) and they work in the following way: In order to incentivize a manager to increase company value, the company (i.e., the shareholders, who are represented by the board of directors) grants the manager the right to purchase a predetermined number of shares at a predetermined price. Assume that Mr. Manger was granted the right to purchase ten shares at $5 per share. This right, the option, is limited in time. Assume that Mr. Manger's option to buy the shares for $5 each is one year from the date of issuance. Some options allow the option holder to exercise them throughout the year (American options) and some allow exercise only on the last day of the period (European options). The term

---

[2] This version is denoted 'Warrants' and it differs from standard call options in one simple attribute: If the manager exercises an option, he buys new shares that the firm is issuing to him or to her, rather than receiving them from the option writer.

'option' refers to the most important attribute of this contract: In a year's time Mr. Manger is *allowed*, but not *obliged*, to purchase any number of the shares (up to ten) for $5 each. If Mr. Manger decides that he wants to pay $5 for each share he is effectively 'exercising the option', and holds the number of shares he decided to buy. Once Mr. Manger holds the company's shares he is free to sell them in the stock market.

Now consider the decision that Mr. Manger needs to make: he has a limited time frame to exercise the option, while observing the market price of the stock. As long as the market price of the stock is less than $5, there is no reason for him to pay $5 for it and exercise the option. He can buy it for less in the stock market. But here comes a day where the market price of the stock is above $5, say $8. Mr. Manger pays $5 for each share and sells it for $8 in the market, leaving him with $3 profit per share.

Well, options are granted generously to top managers, and the game is not about ten shares, but rather hundreds of thousands if not millions. If, for example, Mr. Manger exercises an option for a million shares, he receives an income of $3 million that same day. As aforementioned, such compensation is meant to incentivize the manager to increase the firm's value, as reflected in high stock price in the market.

Now consider this thought that passes through the manager's mind: he knows that he earns a great deal of money from the increased stock price in the market; moreover, he knows that he is able to influence analysts and accountants to present rising EPS each quarter. If the manager is not an honest man, he might exploit his status in order to unjustifiably inflate the stock price in the market.

Notice that any time the firm is issuing shares to its managers it dilutes the proportional holdings of all existing shareholders. If, continuing our example, Mr. Manger receives 10,000 shares, Mrs. Smith now holds 10,000 out of 1,010,000 shares, or $10/1,010,000 = 0.99\%$. This might seem a small change, only 0.01%, but it causes a shift of wealth from existing shareholders to a small group of managers, who become very rich and thereby increase the inequality of income distribution across citizens. Is it bad? Well, a certain level of inequality acts as a positive force by stimulating low-income members of society to work harder, educate themselves and their siblings, be entrepreneurs, and act as a vital force in the economy. However, extreme inequality renders those efforts hopeless, and people might turn bitter and promote social unrest. We have seen the bitterness and anger erupting after the crash of 1929, and we will meet it again in the US and in other countries, primarily after the 2008 financial crisis, with the Occupy Wall Street protest movement.

7.5 The Mania

So how does this all relate to the Internet bubble? Well, consider analysts' inability to estimate the fundamental value of IT companies coupled with the incentive managers and analysts had to boost EPS (or since many of those firms had no earnings, 'guesstimate' an *expected* EPS). This led analysts and managers to overestimate company valuation at the time of IPO. Anyone accompanying the IPO, including the investment bankers, accountants and lawyers, could not contradict the analysts' and managements' estimates. One may suspect that since they all had a common interest in large issues yielding huge revenues they wouldn't make special efforts to curb this tendency. In light of the lesson from the stock issues of Netscape and other companies, it seemed that the potential revenue from burgeoning Internet-based information technology was inexhaustible. Headlines in financial newspapers heralded a 'new economy', exactly as had happened in the 1920s bubble. When Yahoo issued its stock in April 1996, the stock price shot up from $13 to $33 on the first day. Qualcomm generated a return of 2600% in 1996. In the parlance of Kindleberger, euphoria evolved into mania and it became obvious to Internet investors that they were destined to get rich very quick. Madness swept not only the layman, but also pension funds, insurance companies and other solid institutions.

The euphoria and rapid price increases of IT stocks affected 'old economy' stocks as well. The Standard & Poor's (S&P) 500 index, which measures the average value of the largest 500 American companies, climbed rapidly. Analysts and managers explained that innovations in IT would improve profitability of traditional businesses, thus justifying the continuing rise in expected EPS.

7.6 Where Were the Regulators?

At the same time, the Securities and Exchange Commission (SEC) was receiving budgets much lower than its needs and could not afford to pay competitive salaries to its employees. Why? Because of the reasons described in the Chapter 6: the big accounting firms applied political pressure to cut SEC budgets, striving to maintain their own. *Regulatory capture par excellence.* As a result, many of those employees opted to work in the booming financial industry, which paid high salaries to various professionals (SEC, 2001, p. 24). The SEC could only inspect less than 20% of annual reports and only a small portion of other reports submitted to it. The SEC's Division of Enforcement dealt with a doubled amount of claims in 2000 as compared to 1991, but the numbers in its workforce grew by only 16% in that same period (SEC, 2002, p. 19). The SEC had no labor force to check prospectuses and in many cases approved IPOs without a thorough examination of the securities being offered. This is an indirect, ill outcome of regulatory capture.

Federal Reserve chair Alan Greenspan hinted in a speech on 5 December 1996 that prices might be too high (Greenspan, 1996; emphases added):

> What about futures prices or more importantly prices of claims on future goods and services, like equities, real estate, or other earning assets? Are stability of these prices essential to the stability of the economy?
>
> Clearly […] lower risk premiums imply higher prices of stocks and other earning assets. We can see that in the inverse relationship exhibited by price/earnings ratios and the rate of inflation in the past. But how do we know when *irrational exuberance* has unduly escalated asset values, which then become subject to unexpected and prolonged contractions as they have in Japan over the past decade? And how do we factor that assessment into monetary policy? *We as central bankers need not be concerned if a collapsing financial asset bubble does not threaten to impair the real economy*, its production, jobs, and price stability. Indeed, the sharp stock market break of 1987 had few negative consequences for the economy. *But we should not underestimate* or become complacent about the complexity of *the interactions of asset markets and the economy*. Thus, evaluating shifts in balance sheets generally, and in asset prices particularly, must be an integral part of the development of monetary policy.

Notice that Prof. Greenspan discusses the conditions under which the central bank should and should not intervene with the formation of bubbles. He concludes that as long as the collapse of bubbles does not impair the real economy, central bankers need not intervene. However, in the last two sentences Greenspan mentions to central bankers that the complex interactions between the asset markets and the real economy must not be underestimated. In hindsight, those complex interactions were ignored not only during the 1990s as the Internet bubble evolved, but also in the 2000s, when the housing bubble grew. This was a *bubble of real assets*; it swept rich and poor in the US, Europe and many other international markets. Notice that in the first sentence Prof. Greenspan bundles 'equities, real estate, or other earning assets' together, a notion that may explain why he did not act not only on the Internet bubble, but also on the housing bubble of the 2000s. Apparently, he did not think that the collapse of a housing bubble, which would be considered real assets by many, would affect the real economy.

The fact that Greenspan did not increase interest rates, which serve as a key tool for the central bank to implement its policy, was probably interpreted by investors that the Fed does not think that a crash will hurt the real economy. And if the Fed is not worried, why should the investors abstain from the party?

It was only in early 1999 that Greenspan started to raise the interest rate, and he did so six consecutive times until the beginning of 2000, presumably in order to reduce the bubble's intensity and cool down the economy. In March 2000, prices of IT stock began to fall, dropping by about 75% by year's end. Price drops also swept stocks of larger companies in the S&P 500 and continued into 2002. By 2004, 50% of dot-com companies were erased from trading, causing a loss of approximately $5 trillion (Goldfarb *et al.*, 2007).

The Twin Towers disaster of 11 September 2001 and the discovery of corporate corruption in large firms like Enron and WorldCom resulted in a crisis of public trust in the financial system. As a result, Fed Chairman Allan Greenspan lowered the interest rate after identifying signs of recession. This low interest rate was among the reasons for the development of the real estate bubble and the credit crisis, which will be discuss in the upcoming chapters.

Additional Reading

Goldfarb, B., Kirscha, D. and Millerb, D.A. (2007). 'Was there too little entry during the DotComEra?' *Journal of Financial Economics*, 86(1), 100–144.

Jensen, M.C. and Fuller, J. (2002). 'Just Say No to Wall Street: Courageous CEOs Are Putting a Stop to the Earnings Game and We Will All Be Better Off for It,' *Journal of Applied Corporate Finance*, 14(4), 41–46.

SEC (2001). 'Human Capital Challenges Require Management Attention (GAO-01-947)', September. Available at: http://www.gao.gov/products/GAO-01-947 (accessed 14 October 2014).

SEC (2002). SEC Operations: Increased Workload Creates Challenges (GAO-02-302)'. March. Available at: http://www.gao.gov/products/GAO-02-302 (accessed 14 October 2014).

8.

When Banks Manipulate their Stock Prices: Israel's Systemic Banking Crisis

8.1 Background

On 6 October 1983, the Tel Aviv Stock Exchange (TASE) ceased operations for two weeks following a crash in stock prices of Israel's largest and most important commercial banks.[1] Recall that Chapter 3 described the different severity levels of financial crises and expanded on the importance of the commercial banking system. The chapter distinguished between a 'bank run', which can topple one or several banks, and the more serious phenomenon of 'banking panic'; however, Chapter 3 concluded that the most serious phenomenon of all was a 'systemic banking crisis'. In such a crisis all or most of a country's commercial banks go bankrupt, depositors lose much of their savings and the availability of credit shrinks, leading to financial distress in many non-financial firms, which if bankrupt, lay off employees. This chain of events began in Israel on 6 October 1983 and obstructed economic growth for a number of years.

When a systemic banking crisis hits an economy, the government is expected to serve as the lender of last resort. Only the government has the power to rescue the financial system from collapse, and it has an important interest in doing so: should most commercial banks actually collapse, the public might lose most of its bank deposits (remember the role of the banking multiplier in creating deposits), an event that will post a heavy political

---

[1] The list included Bank Leumi, Bank Hapoalim, Bank Discount, HaMizrachi Bank, Bank Igud, Finance and Trade Bank, and Bank Clali.

toll on every government. The Israeli government devised a rescue plan during those two weeks of market closure, and effectively took ownership on most of the banking sector. In late 1984, the Office of the State Comptroller submitted its inquiry report on the events that led to the crisis; however, the report did not refer to banks, the stock exchange or securities dealers because those entities were not within the purview of the state comptroller. One week later an independent inquiry commission was appointed to investigate the stock-price manipulation that commercial banks conducted, headed by Supreme Court judge Dr. Moshe Beisky. The commission published its conclusions in April 1986 in what was known as the Beisky Commission report. Most of the information and data presented in this chapter is based on that report.

8.2 An Economy in Transition

In order to understand how the financial crisis evolved it is necessary to present some background information and data. The TASE was established in September 1953 as an initiative of the leading commercial banks and several companies that specialized in securities trading. The banks' representatives constituted a majority of members of the TASE's board and various committees. Therefore, the banks bought themselves *de facto* control in determining trading methods, the extent and content of transactions reporting, and, practically speaking, all the important decisions and operations of the TASE. Surely, the rules they approved favored with the banks, and away from public interest. *This was built-in regulatory capture!* In 1961, the Joint Investment Trust Law was approved by the parliament, enabling the establishment of mutual funds. In 1968 the Israeli Securities Authority was established, for the purpose of preserving the interests of the investing public, much in the spirit of the US Securities and Exchange Act of the 1930s, with proper adjustments.

Since the foundation of the state in 1948 and until the beginning of the 1960s, most TASEe activity was under government auspices. The government virtually 'sucked' the vast majority of public savings in order to finance its activities. As discussed in Chapter 2, households' savings are the source of long-term financing for both the government and the private business sector. In those years the government had high deficits, which it financed by issuing government bonds and paying high and safe interest rates. Had the riskier, private business sector wanted to compete with those terms, it had to offer higher returns to investors (due to the higher risk of its bonds), but such high rates are not sustainable as they leave low profit margins for most firms. As a result, the Israeli government left scant financing sources for the private sector.

The beginning of the 1970s witnessed a boom in stock market activity where both commercial banks and non-financial sectors in the economy raised funds from the public by issuing equity shares. The non-financial sector stocks were denoted the 'free stocks', as their prices were allowed to vary more freely throughout the trading day than banks' share prices. As a result, they were also considered more risky.

8.3 The Motivation and Practice

A generally accepted market practice indicates that public offering of stock issues is much easier after stock prices have risen over the preceding several months. Once the positive trend has been substantiated, in light of an apparent market boom, companies prepare prospectuses and offer their shares to the public. Since the process of preparing a prospectus takes several months, a situation may develop in which a company invests considerable funds and managerial effort, but by the time the prospectus is ready and approved, the market, once booming, might have begun to ebb. Raising capital then becomes difficult if not impossible.

The Beisky Commission found that this connection — between rising stock prices and the feasibility of actual stock issues — was among the factors that stimulated the manipulation of bank stock prices. According to the Commission's findings, Bank Hapoalim, the biggest by all means at the time, apparently began manipulating its shares in the 1960s; later, the second largest Bank Leumi and the third, Discount Bank, were also drawn in. During the 1970s, these three major banks intervened in a progressively serious manner in setting their own stock prices so as to facilitate stock issues, *even during market downturns.* In 1974, issues of banks shares constituted 94% of all stock issues, a record that remained unbroken until the crisis of October 1983.

It is important to understand how practically the banks manipulated their stock prices. The method for determining stock prices in the TASE at that time was known as the 'auction' method. In this method, the auctioneer receives trading orders from all members of the stock exchange, which specify, for each and every stock separately, demand and supply quantities and prices. Those trading amounts represent the net supply or demand for each stock by all clients of the member of the exchange (headed by the commercial banks). If, for example, there is excess demand, the auctioneer declares gradually rising prices. As prices rise, demand falls and supply increases, thus excess demand gets smaller and smaller. If, however, there is excess supply, the auctioneer lowers the price gradually, thus demand increases and supply gets smaller. The price at which demand is equal to supply is announced as the settlement price for the specific stock on that day and is the formal price by which all transactions clear. Under this method only one price is determined for each stock in a trading day (unlike modern systems in many countries where stocks are traded continuously, therefore many prices prevail during the day).

As mentioned, representatives of the banks constituted the majority of board members of the TASE, therefore their traders were also the majority among those who sat around the auctioneer; the rest were members who represented smaller securities trading companies. The document through which members of the TASE conveyed their trading preferences to the auctioneer was known as the 'leader'. This document listed excess demand or excess supply based on the requested transactions of all customers of the specific stock exchange member. Therefore, because of their relatively high market share, the banks could estimate the market trend. In other words, each member of the TASE knew the buy and sell orders of its own customers, and could use this information to estimate the aggregate supply or demand by other members.

At this particular phase the bank representative on the exchange could manipulate prices — they could interfere with their own bank's demand (or supply) by placing *their own orders*. Assuming they wished to make sure the stock price would not decline, they would estimate the aggregate excess demand or supply by all leaders of all members of the exchange. If they concluded that there was *excess supply* for their own bank, they would amend their leader form with a sufficiently large 'buy' order just before submitting it to the auctioneer. This order had to be large enough to turn the excess supply into excess demand, and the auctioneer would then have to increase the stock price in order to close the gap. Notice that although the bank representative was *capable* of intervening in quantities amended on the leader form, he was *forbidden* from doing so. The Beisky Commission concluded that both the bank's representative on the exchange and all bank managers knew that these activities are illegal, and it was found that bank managers had instructed their representatives to conceal the deeds.

Where did the money bank representatives added to the leaders in the form of buy orders come from? Well, the heads of the banks knew that supplying credit or loans to a body that manipulates their stock prices via the leader form was illegal. Therefore, they avoided overt actions and adopted roundabout methods. One of the methods used by Bank Leumi and Discount

Bank was to establish a subsidiary whose main business was to purchase and sell the bank's shares. This is somewhat comparable to the way American banks bypassed the prohibition on securities trading in the 1920s. Another method was to take out loans from pension funds associated with the banks. Thus the savings of pension fund members were used for financing illegal speculation (see how important keeping pension funds and other savings institutions at arm's length from security dealers is). The third method necessitated inter-bank cooperation: for example, the security trading companies owned by Leumi and Discount Banks sold each other stocks that were in their inventories in an action known as 'stock swaps'. Finally, to raise funds to finance those almost daily stock purchases the banks also adopted an aggressive marketing policy of their stocks. Here again, see the similarity to American banks during the roaring twenties. The banks extended loans to their customers, where the loan amount was used to purchase the same bank's shares, and the shares were used as security for the loan. This is nothing but a non-regulated path to provide margin loans to the public, again, resembling the roaring twenties in the US. Note that in a transaction such as this, the bank profits three times: from interest on the loan amount, from the fact that the customer is purchasing bank shares and thereby assisting its manipulation (higher demand for the bank's stock), and from transferring risk to the customer who must pay back the loan even if stock value decreases.

It is important to emphasize that one way or another the banks themselves were the ones supplying the funding for price manipulation. From a quantitative perspective, most of the manipulation funding was raised by the banks through public stock issues. If funding for manipulation had come from sources external to the banks, the Beisky Commission concluded, banks would not have been hampered and no reason would have emerged for them to manipulate their share prices.

8.4 The Macroeconomic Environment

In June 1977, a new government was elected and the Israeli Liberal Party's Mr. Simha Ehrlich was appointed minister of finance. Based on his recommendation, the government implemented an 'economic reform' plan, a component of which was liberalization in foreign currency policy. This liberalization program affected not only the business sector, but also all Israeli residents who were permitted henceforth to hold US dollars in a bank deposit. Such deposits, actually a local currency deposit indexed to the US dollar exchange rate, opened a new investment channel for investors and had two important advantages. First, it constituted an alternative to other investment channels, which at the time consisted only of Israeli bonds and stocks. Second, it enabled Israeli citizens to hedge against inflation, which began to rise rapidly, reaching 'only' 43% in 1977 but much more in the following years. The opening of the dollar investment channel coupled with a sizeable devaluation generated expectations for high inflation; thus, many investors sold stock and purchased index-linked bonds. The selling of stocks was expressed in a 25% decrease in prices of bank shares in December 1977 and a 37% drop in prices of the 'free stocks'.

In 1977–1978 there was a significant increase in the extent of stock issues and trading, which obliged the banks to infuse more and more funds into financing the manipulation regime. In light of substantial stock price drops at the end of 1977, the banks found themselves at a crossroads: Should they continue or cease the ever-growing stock issues for the purpose of financing the manipulation regime? The importance of the decision to continue manipulating their stock prices should have been clear to the bank managers. It means that events on the December 1977 scale might recur; worse, should a prolonged decline in the stock market evolve, it would be impossible for the banks to raise capital through new stock issues. If that indeed happened the banks would be unable to support their stock prices, which would be expected to collapse sharply. In a fateful decision, the bank managers opted to continue the manipulation policy; thus, at the end of 1978, the three largest banks, Hapoalim, Leumi and Discount, came out with new stock issues.

In 1979, in a quantum leap, inflation surged to 111%. The three major banks and, starting that year, Bank HaMizrachi, manipulated their share prices aggressively. To pay positive real returns, assets must yield more than 111%, and indeed, year-end figures for 1979 showed a negative real return of 3% for bank shares at a time when consumer price index (CPI)-linked government bonds fell behind 12% on average and prices of the free stocks plummeted 50% in real terms.

The year 1980 was one of sharp increases in the stock market. Free stocks raised 100% on average, often through speculative stock run-ups and rumor spreading, rendering the TASE the 'national casino'. Bank stock rose 'only' by 40% in real terms. The banks continued issuing shares; the market value of bank shares increased and was comparable to the market value of all government bonds. At the end of 1980, the shares of the handful of banks traded on the TASE constituted approximately 30% of the value of all traded financial assets held by the public. This rate highlights the high risk that savers in the economy were exposed to, whether they held bank shares directly or indirectly via pension funds or mutual funds. The market value of bank shares was 1.8 times the adjusted value of their book capital; compared to a nearly 1:1 ratio in regular times. In other words the prices of bank shares were about 80% higher than reasonable.

In 1981, manipulation activity became more serious as the banks purchased hundreds of millions of dollars of their shares following sharp price drops in January and February. At this stage the manipulation regime entered its most blatantly illogical stage when the banks committed publicly for *daily increases* in the price of their shares throughout 1982 and up to the collapse in October 1983. Remember Kindleberger's mania (see Section 1.2)? It seems to have caught bank managers at that stage because the endgame was clear. The banks were marketing their stocks to the public as if they were 'super securities'. This term, coined by the late Prof. Marshall Sarnat, a member of the Beisky Commission, illustrates how the banks marketed their stocks as if they could generate high returns, while at the same time be safe as if they were government bonds. And indeed banks presented their shares to investors (and depositors) as if they were preferable to investing in government bonds.

8.5 The Crash Unfolds

In January 1983, the Ronit Mutual Fund, managed by two renowned financiers, collapsed, setting into motion a free-fall in the free stocks. This drop continued throughout 1983 and beyond. The commercial banks continued their manipulation policy and emerged from the stock crisis almost unharmed, although Bank HaMizrachi, rumored to be connected with the Ronit Fund, was on the verge of collapse.

At the beginning of October 1983, expectations rose for a major devaluation of the local currency against the US dollar. This sparked massive selling of stocks in order to buy foreign currency or dollar-linked assets. This stock selling forced the banks to infuse great sums of foreign capital into Israel (through their overseas subsidiaries) in order to continue supporting the price of their shares. However, this time the extent of selling was much more significant and bank share prices began to plummet. The government, which saw the financial system collapsing before its eyes, halted trading on the stock exchange for 18 days during which the 'Bank Shares Arrangement' was hammered out. Under the arrangement, bank shares would be converted into dollar-linked bonds based on their value on the arrangement date. The cost of the arrangement totaled approximately seven billion dollars in direct monetary expense, this aside from indirect damages which are difficult to estimate, such as a decline in real investment and slow growth over multiple years.

The economy spiraled. In 1984 inflation shot up to 445% per year; the local currency was devaluated against the dollar by approximately 500%; the budget deficit reached a level of 16% of gross domestic profit (GDP); the public debt reached a level of 171% of GDP. In 1985 a stabilization plan for the economy was implemented: inflation fell from its three-figure level and government deficits began to decrease.

In April 1986, the Beisky Commission's report was publicized and contained recommendations for significant structural reforms in the Israeli capital markets. The report highlighted the need to separate commercial banking, i.e., the management of deposits and current accounts and extension of credit, from investment banking, which is concerned with trading and investment transactions in the capital market. This was similar to the reform in the US following the 1929 crisis. One of the more important issues was the separation of pension and mutual funds ownership from the banks. However, the years passed without any practical steps taken to implement substantial reforms in the capital market. This was because those regulators who were supposed to promote the reforms were 'captured'. They were captured either because politicians prevented them from extracting value from party-related banks, or because they speculated that better jobs await them after ending their civil service.

In 1993, ten years after the collapse, when Mr. Yitzhak Rabin was serving as prime minister on behalf of the Labor Party, the state comptroller published a special report criticizing the fact that banks' shares held by the government under the Bank Shares Arrangement, were not sold back to the public, and/or to large shareholders. In fact, the legislative process to allow that was not ready at this time. The report addressed the Ministry of Finance's opposition to implementing significant reform measures due to the 'economies of scale of the banking industry'. Instead of separating the banks, pension funds and mutual funds, the ministry proposed erecting regulatory 'Chinese Walls' between pension fund managers and bank managers. In response, Prof. Marshal Sarnat wrote an opinion article titled 'If Chinese Walls, Then Why Made Out of Swiss Cheese?' In the article, Sarnat described a great number of problems in the Ministry of Finance's approach. Only in 1996 was legislation completed and from that time, the funds were managed by the commercial banks, while presumably preventing conflicts of interest. This continued up to the time that the Bachar Reform, approved in 2005, eventually separated the ownership of pension funds and mutual funds from the commercial banks. This example shows how regulatory capture might impose heavy costs, for very long time, on the entire economy. It took nearly 20 years until a reasonable, not 'good', reform was implemented. And why can this reform only be considered as 'reasonable'? Because giant insurance and investment firms purchased the pension funds and mutual funds from the commercial banks, therefore switching from one oligopolistic structure to another. Why was there not a better reform? Because of the heavy pressure that the financial sector and politicians implemented throughout the process on committee members. Again: *regulatory capture.*

8.6 Ineffective Regulation

An important question is 'Where were the regulators during all these years?' What did directors of the TASE, the Israel Securities Authority, the Bank of Israel and the Ministry of Finance know; and if they knew something, what did they do to curb the manipulation?

To clarify at the outset, the Beisky Commission found that at the beginning of the process, the banks concealed their manipulative trades. Later on, however, when the banks were forced to obtain assistance from the Ministry of Finance in order to continue manipulating their stock prices and prevent their collapse, it became an open secret that many avoided dealing with. Regulation was captured by fear of alleged necessity, although everyone involved should have figured out that early termination of the manipulation process implied smaller damages.

The Beisky Commission imposed personal liability on the managers of all banks that participated in the manipulation regime and called on them to resign, which they did. Moreover the Commission called on the governor of the Bank of Israel and the minister of finance to resign. However, no personal conclusions were drawn against Dr. Heth (chairman of TASE), Galia Maor (supervisor of banks) or the chairman of the Israel Securities Authority who had entered his post just prior to the collapse. This was also true for others who had left their positions in various supervisory bodies prior to the crisis. Four findings of the Commission are described below.

First, what did the management of the stock exchange know? According to the Beisky Commission, Dr. Heth was aware of the damage of price manipulation and proposed setting clear-cut rules for distinguishing between manipulation and seemingly legitimate intervention in prices. Dr. Heth told the Commission that the fact that the banks' controlled the board of directors of the exchange prevented him from passing decisions to prevent or reduce the use of 'leaders' for the purpose of manipulation. In other words, the exchange, which was captured from its inception by the banks, was paralyzed. In spite of the efforts of Dr. Heth, the taxpayers experienced a *massive loss of value.*

Second, the Israel Securities Authority, whose main function is to safeguard the interests of investors in the capital market, was aware of the manipulation as early as 1979; but aside from blocking one particularly big issue of Bank Hapoalim it did not intervene or act to stop the process. True, it did demand that the banks reveal some facts concerning the manipulation in their prospectuses, but the banks opposed it arguing that: 'The public will notice that the king is naked.'

Third, the Beisky Commission determined that up to 1980, the Bank of Israel (the central bank) took no action against the manipulation regime despite the fact that the supervisor of banks had known about it since 1978. The reason: The supervisor of banks felt the manipulation regime (which he considered a legitimate price adjustment) had positive effects because it helped the banks to maintain the required capital adequacy ratio, an argument that the Commission proved as baseless. The Bank of Israel's governor thought that the manipulation wasn't harmful since it stabilized 'random fluctuations' in prices rather than setting prices. Supervisory activity by the central bank did not prevent the extension of bank credit for the purchase of shares, the use of pension funds for stock purchase and other phenomena.

Fourth, the Beisky Commission found that the Treasury (the Ministry of Finance) dealt with the manipulative activities only from 1981. This was because the public abandoned government bonds in favor of bank shares, which were marketed as a high-yield and fully secure alternative. The Commission found that in 1980, the Ministry of Finance had approved 12 stock issues and therefore was supposed to understand the risk entailed by the manipulation activities and the necessity to act against them. The Treasury argued that it did not act against the manipulation because there would be implications for exchange rates, which would affect many variables in the macroeconomic environment, and it would have necessitated a severe budget cut. Obviously, no politician would embrace those acts.

The (in)action of the Ministry of Finance throughout most of the period highlights an interesting aspect of regulatory capture: The Ministry of Finance seems to have been *captured by its own concepts.* As long as there was probably a way to stop the manipulation at lower costs, between 1977 and 1980 the Ministry turned a blind eye to the problem. In 1981, when the problem grew so severe that it affected the Ministry's ability to issue government debt, they monitored and measured the issue, but did not take real and meaningful actions. An argument is that by this time no minister of finance or key regulator had any incentive to pop the bubble and pay the political or personal bill that comes with a crash. They were captured, and while watching the problem growing, they had all the incentive to let the bubble crash and clean up the mess later on. In the summary table of Chapter 16 I argue that the 'gold standard' of regulatory capture, as defined by Carpenter and Moss (2013) applies for this case.

Before summarizing, it is important to highlight an often misunderstood issue pertaining to the interaction between inflation and banks' capital adequacy. There are a number of ratios that serve to measure capital adequacy in commercial banking. The relevant one for this case is the ratio of $\frac{\text{Equity capital}}{\text{Assets at risk}}$. This ratio is calculated for commercial banks and financial institutions around the world as a measure of a bank's ability to absorb losses that stem from risky assets. For example, if a bank has $100 million of risky assets, of which it loses $2 million, than the bank will remain solvent if it has equity capital that exceeds the value of $2 million. Therefore, in a fundamental way, equity capital serves as a cushion against unpredictable losses. Moreover, because equity holders are first to lose, they have an incentive to avoid excess risk taking, for the benefit of depositors and other stakeholders.[2]

The primary reasoning that Israeli bank managers presented to the Beisky Commission as a justification for the manipulation was based on the argument that inflation eroded the capital adequacy ratio. As a result, they claimed, they were forced to issue new equity capital frequently or their ratio would decline and present them as less solid and safe than they actually were. A high enough ratio was important since they had to present it to foreign banks, mainly from Europe, who considered it before making transactions with the Israeli banks.

The Beisky Commission rejected this argument for a number of reasons. First, the capital adequacy problem was primarily a reporting and recording issue, not a fundamental solvency issue. The reason is that inflation affected the ratio as reported in the financial statements, but not on the bank's ability to cope with losses. Had the banks reported this ratio through inflation-adjusted financial statements, this issue would have disappeared. Second, the ratio of the Israeli banks in 1982 was about 1.9%, not materially lower than the ratio of large banks in Holland (2.54%), Germany (2.73%) and Italy (2.87%). Moreover, the ratio that was calculated in countries where the

---

[2] Readers interested in delving further into this issue may find Admati and Hellwig (2013) an excellent read.

banking system received government backup or was nationalized (like France and Portugal), and was lower than 2%. Therefore, the Commission concluded that the Israeli ratio, in spite of the inflation distortion, was not materially lower than comparable big European banks, and surely did not justify the manipulation. Third, inflation distorted the financial statements of many local firms in those years, and in many cases caused real losses. Exporters, for example, suffered significant losses as their payroll and local raw material prices increased with the pace of inflation; but devaluations, that increased their income, often occurred at a later stage. The Commission concluded that the banks could have protected themselves from inflation, but chose not to do so. As a result, they had no right to compensate themselves by manipulating their stock prices.

8.7 The End

On the evening of Thursday 6 October 1986, a meeting was held between the minister of finance and the representatives of two banks (one of them, The First International Bank, did not take part of the manipulation activities). At the meeting, it was decided that in light of the dramatic collapse of bank share prices, the TASE would be closed and an arrangement hammered out

Source: By Morshem (Own work) [GFDL (http://www.gnu.org/copyleft/fdl.html) or CC-BY-SA-4.0-3.0-2.5-2.0-1.0 (http://creativecommons.org/licenses/by-sa/4.0-3.0-2.5-2.0-1.0)], via Wikimedia Commons (accessed 18 November 2014).

in order to prevent the collapse of the entire banking system. As noted, this arrangement forced the government to nationalize most of the commercial banks in the country and hold on to them for decades.

That same evening, the minister of finance gave an interview to the (one and only at the time) primetime news program, publicly announcing the closing of the stock exchange. The ensuing public sense of rage and frustration was given superb expression in the protest song of Shalom Chanoch, 'Waiting for Messiah' (http://www.youtube.com/watch?v=-0i3mev5EvQ). The record cover pictured an ashtray, which resembles the tense and uncertain period when people were waiting for the government decision on the value and future of their savings.

Additional Reading

Admati, A. and Hellwig, M. (2013). *The Bankers' New Clothes: What's Wrong with Banking and What to Do About It.* Princeton, NJ: Princeton University Press.

Blass, A.A. and Grossman, R. (2001). 'Assessing Damages: The 1983 Israeli Bank Share Crisis,' *Contemporary Economic Policy*, 19, 1, 49–58.

Sarnat, M. (ed.) (1991). *Capital Market Reform in Israel.* Jerusalem, Israel: The Floersheimer Institute for Policy Studies.

9.

The Tequila Crisis and its Hangover

9.1 Introduction

Up to the end of the 19th century, the economic systems in many South American countries such as Mexico, Chile, Argentina and parts of Brazil was based on the haciendas, or estates. The estate owner, the *patrón*, employed many laborers, or peones, to work in plantation crops, develop mines or industrial plants, and sometimes various combinations of these activities. Supposedly, the aim of the haciendas was to supply the needs of the owners and laborers, avoiding ostentatious luxury goods, but the division of wealth was highly unequal (Mörner, 1973). This chapter describes the upheaval that accompanied the economic development of two important countries in South America, Mexico and Argentina, until their economic state relatively stabilized, rather recently. Since a major part of these countries' troubles emerged from their foreign trade policies, it is important to review briefly some key notions of international trade. Understanding those interactions will prove highly relevant to understanding the Mexican and Argentinian crises, as well as other currency crises.

9.2 A Brief Explanation of International Accounts

Here is a brief explanation of the way economists measure inflows and out-flows of foreign currencies in a country. Two key components of the 'balance of payments' are focused on here, the 'current account' and the 'capital account'. The current account primarily reflects the gap between imports and exports, and it may be out of balance, sometimes for many years. However, because the balance of payments must always be balanced, by accounting definitions, a surplus in the current account will largely be offset by a deficit in the capital account, and vice versa, a deficit in the current account will be offset by a surplus in the capital account.

Think of a home country, say Mexico, where its exporters are selling their goods to foreign countries. The exporters are paid in foreign currency for the goods they are selling (say dollars), but much of their expenses are denominated in the local currency, since payroll is paid in pesos, and various suppliers and taxes are paid in the local currency as well. To make those local payments exporters sell their dollars to the government and in exchange receive pesos. The number of pesos they receive for each US dollar is the exchange rate between those two currencies. Therefore, the primary source of foreign currency a country has comes from its export; the higher the demand foreign countries have for Mexican goods, the higher the inflow of foreign currency to Mexico. This inflow stems from trading activities and it is therefore recorded in the 'balance of trade' of a country, which is an important part of the current account.

On the other hand, Mexican importers need to pay for imported goods in foreign currencies. To conduct those deals they buy, say, US dollars from the government at the prevailing exchange rate, and import US goods. These transactions constitute an outflow of foreign currency, and because this outflow stems from trading activities, it is also recorded in the balance of trade. A surplus in the balance of trade occurs when more foreign currency is received than paid, i.e., the value of total exports is higher than total imports. A deficit in the trade balance occurs when imports are higher than exports. Notice a difference between surplus and deficit in the balance of trade: while the accumulation of surplus over many years can grow, theoretically without limit, a deficit depletes gradually the foreign currency reserves, possibly toward zero.

Furthermore, a surplus in the current account implies excess supply of foreign currency, while a deficit implies excess demand for it. *If* — and this is a big 'if' — the foreign currency trades freely and its price is determined by supply and demand, the same free-market rules apply: excess supply implies that the price of the foreign currency must decline, which means that Mexican citizens need to pay less pesos for one US dollar (e.g., instead of paying 13 pesos for one dollar, they will pay only 12). In this case we say that the dollar depreciated in value, and the Mexican peso appreciated against the US dollar. Some find it confusing because the exchange rate declined from 13 to 12, but the peso actually got 'stronger'. Obviously, the opposite occurs when there is excess demand for the foreign currency as a result of deficit in the current account. If the government adopts a flexible exchange rate policy, meaning it allows the exchange rate to be determined by supply and demand, a deficit will cause a devaluation of the local currency vs. the country's trading partners. If, however, the government adopts a fixed exchange rate policy, it effectively commits to buy or supply any excess supply or demand, respectively. Therefore, if there is excess demand for the foreign currency, which might happen for many reasons, the government is expected to supply this demand from its reserves at the fixed exchange rate to which it committed.

As noted, the current account is one of the two most important accounts in the balance of payments of a country. The other important account, the capital account, measures on one hand the flow of foreign currency abroad. This occurs as local investors invest in foreign assets, such as buying stocks, bonds, real estate or factories in other countries. On the other hand, the capital account measures the flow of foreign currency into the home country by foreign investors who buy local assets, such as local securities, real estate or factories. Therefore, the capital account can also be out of balance, but the sum of its imbalance with the imbalance of the current account must be zero for the balance of payments to be balanced.

9.3 Mexico

Source: By Radikian [Public domain], via Wikimedia Commons (accessed 18 November 2014).

Back to the Mexican haciendas. The meager wages and tough living conditions of millions of peones formed the backdrop to the Mexican revolution that broke out in 1910 and continued until 1917, destroying the economic infrastructure and at the same time completely changing the political system. The Institutional Revolutionary Party (PRI; Partido Revolucionario Institucional), which ruled Mexico after the civil war, adopted an inward-looking policy of encouraging local industry, and imposing high tariffs and obstacles to import. For over 40 years, from 1929 to 1972, the Mexican economy grew by an average annual average of 5.5%, a period that economists called the 'Mexican miracle'. At the same time, large income gaps prevailed between the *patróns* and the peones, although in a new form: Local industry was dominated by tycoons, who contributed generously to the PRI, and in return received import licenses and protection from competition. Extreme inequality existed within the working class: While the majority were paid measly wages, labor unions in profitable sectors, protected from competing imports, achieved much improved wage conditions for their members, thus creating what was known as the 'workers' aristocracy' (Krugman, 2009).

However, the oil crises of 1973 and 1979, which led to increased oil prices around the world, provided the incentive to explore for oil in Mexico. When large quantities of oil were in fact found, the government needed loans in order to develop the oil fields and prepare for export. At this time, interest rates in the international capital markets were low, creating the incentive to take out large loans, most of them denominated in US dollars. The vast oil fields that were discovered and developed made Mexico the fourth largest oil exporter in the world by 1981. When oil revenues began to fill the public coffers, the President of Mexico at the time, José López Portillo, announced that the time had come 'to manage prosperity'. He was referring to the fact that the revenue from the vast oil fields remaining in the government's hands would be directed to the country's social development.

This policy increased expenses in socially related budget items, and like in many other countries, the nature of government budgets is to grow and settle at the new level over time. Cutting any budget, and particularly social budgets, is a much harder move as it involves political struggles both inside the government, and between the government, the public and the media. When oil prices took a dive at the beginning of the 1980s, and the interest rates increased, Mexico found itself in trouble: The country's foreign currency income fell, while on the other hand repayment of its international debts rose.

Note that a country can print its local currency as it sees fit, but has only a limited 'inventory' of foreign currency. This is the foreign currency reserve, which is managed by the central bank. In Mexico's case, the main reserve currency was the US dollar. Rapid dilution of the reserves is dangerous because when the reserves run out completely the importers will not be able to pay for imported products, and more seriously, the government will not be able to repay foreign currency debts. When this happens, the country is declared bankrupt and is barred from the world capital markets. Unfortunately, this has happened to Mexico more than once. This time, the reserves ran out, and President Portillo, facing the end of his term, was left with no choice. He sent a delegation to Washington, explaining that Mexico was unable to repay its debts, or in other words, was bankrupt. The Mexican peso was devalued, the local banks were nationalized, and many industries faced severe hardships.

The devalued peso benefited Mexican exporters and made imported products more expensive. As a result, the Mexican consumer found local products to be cheaper than imports. At the same time, devaluation of the peso made foreign currency debts even more expensive, since it was necessary to convert large amounts of pesos to repay each dollar of loans. Foreign lenders were not willing to give Mexico new loans and it was forced to continue devaluing its currency. These devaluations created rapid inflation that continued for many years. The economy took a path of improvement when President Miguel de la Madrid, who replaced Portillo in 1982, implemented reforms and processes of liberalization, i.e., opening the Mexican economy to the world. He was followed by President Carlos Salinas, who continued to privatize many government companies and gradually remove obstacles to import, forcing inefficient local manufacturers to face up to competition. And yet, the burden of foreign debts still weighed down the Mexican economy.

In 1989, United States Secretary of the Treasury, Nicholas Brady, announced that it was clear that the countries of Latin America would not be able to repay their debts, and so he initiated a program to replace already existing debts with bonds of a lower face value. These were called Brady Bonds, and by issuing them, the United States took upon itself a 'haircut' in order to help these countries recover, where the bill was paid by US citizens. This measure increased the confidence of foreign investors in Mexico, and the interest rates required on its debts decreased rapidly. Within a year, the budget deficit was closed up and Mexico's situation improved. It should be noted that although the haircut, which came at the expense of the American taxpayer, helped Mexico and other countries in Latin America, it met with fierce resistance in Congress. At this time, President Salinas initiated the first steps for Mexico to join the North American Free Trade Agreement, NAFTA, together with the United States and Canada, a step that improved Mexico's standing. However, a number of serious mistakes were then made.

9.4 The Price of a Fixed Exchange Rate Policy

As noted, the high inflation rate continued throughout the 1980s, reaching a peak of 160% in 1987. President Salinas took decisive steps to reduce

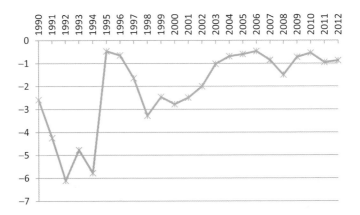

Figure 9.1   Mexico's current account balance (% of GDP)
Source: IMF, World Economic Outlook Database, September 2011.

inflation, and in fact succeeded to quite an impressive degree, but the exchange rate policy that he adopted was a fixed rate against the American dollar. Therefore, despite stability at the beginning of the 1990s, inflation, which was still high, caused the prices of local commodities to rise for Mexican residents, while imported products remained cheap (due to the fixed exchange rate). As a result imports increased, while exports declined, resulting in a deficit in Mexico's international trade balance. The deficit of imports over exports reached 7% of gross domestic profit (GDP) in 1994. This is considered an exceptionally high rate, and is risky in terms of economic stability because it shows an outflow of foreign currency from the country at a rapid pace (Figure 9.1).

Part of the large deficit was funded by exchanging short-term debt for special bonds called 'tesobonos', bonds whose face value was in pesos but linked to the US dollar. Mexico, which had already gone bankrupt in 1983, should have been aware of the dangers resulting from the depletion of foreign reserves, but the warning lights did not flash, because the economists thought that the deficit in the current account, that is, the import surplus, could actually be interpreted as a positive measure. Why positive? Here is the explanation.

Recall from Chapter 8 that the balance of payments that measures the total foreign currency coming in and going out of the country, is made up of two main parts, which together have to balance. The two components are the current account and the capital account. If one of them is in deficit, then according to accounting identity, the other will necessarily be in surplus. Mexico had a large deficit in its current account, which had to be funded from the capital account, that is, from a net flow of foreign investments into the Mexican economy. Many economists in Mexico and other places at the time held the opinion that the fact there was a surplus in the capital account was evidence that foreign investors had confidence in the local economy, and were therefore buying more Mexican assets than local investors purchased assets abroad. This process, they hypothesized, demonstrates trust in the local economy, creating a surplus in the capital account, and therefore the deficit in the current account conveyed no bad signal. Nobel Prize laureate in economics, Paul Krugman, thinks that the big mistake made by Mexican economists was to ignore the fact that, despite the large-scale foreign investments, the economy was growing too slowly. Between 1980 and 1989 average growth was 1.3% a year, and between 1990 and 1994 it was 2.8% a year, while the population was growing at a much faster rate. Therefore, per capita income was in fact decreasing. In other words, foreign investments were not producing the anticipated gains. Professor Rüdiger Dornbusch, who taught some of the Mexican economists, noted in 1993, on the eve of the tequila crisis, that Mexico should devalue its currency by about 30%. The reason is that the strong peso, which remained fixed relative to the dollar due to the fixed exchange rate policy, eroded the profits of Mexican exporters, who were unable to grow their businesses, recruit employees and reduce unemployment. Devaluation of the peso, according to Dornbusch, would speed up growth by allowing exporters to reap the fruits of investments made in the country, while making import more expensive.

The Mexican government rejected Dornbusch's suggestions and insisted on explaining that the economic situation was excellent and that it had no intention of devaluing its currency. One of the reasons for this was the battle in the US Congress at the time over final approval of Mexico joining NAFTA. This step faced strong opposition because of the haircut that American taxpayers suffered as a result of the Brady Bonds plan. Eventually, Mexico was admitted to NAFTA in spite of the difficulty that the Clinton administration faced. The agreement came into force on 1 January 1994.

9.5 The Tequila Crisis Unfolds

Soon after Mexico entered NAFTA, a number of things started to go wrong and the tequila crisis began to unfold. Signing the NAFTA agreement immediately caused the outbreak of a rebellion in the southern part of Mexico, in an area called Chiapas, by the Zapatista Army of National Liberation (EZLN).

Figure 9.2   Subcomandante Marcos, spokesman of EZLN

Source: By tj scenes/cesar bojorquez (flickr) [CC-BY-2.0 (http://creativecommons.org/licenses/by/2.0)], via Wikimedia Commons (accessed 18 November 2014).

This is an extreme left-wing movement based on Mayan tribal traditions, with elements of socialism, Marxism and anarchy. The movement, which is still active today, was protesting the unequal distribution of wealth in the country. The rebellion was wiped out within two weeks.

Several months later President Salinas' heir, Luis Donaldo Colosio, was assassinated, shaking up the political system. These events made many investors fear that Mexico was liable to be drawn once again into the internal battles that had previously undermined its economic development. Along with dilution of the currency reserves and the slow growth rate, investors felt that the economy could be facing recession. The local public's trust in the peso deteriorated as well, and foreign currency, primarily US dollars, was taken out of the country. The Mexican government understood that it had no choice but to devalue the peso (that is, make buyers of US dollars pay more for each dollar they bought). However, despite Dornbusch's recommendation, it carried out a devaluation of only 15%, half of what he had proposed. Moreover, it came to public attention that a number of business-people had received early warning of the devaluation, causing a serious loss of trust among foreign investors. The response was a massive withdrawal of foreign investments, and the devaluation of the peso continued apace. The government was forced to give up its policy of a fixed exchange rate, and the peso was quickly devalued by 80%, from 4 pesos to the dollar to 7.2. (Krugman, 2009).

This devaluation increased all foreign currency debts, including the tesobonos, further reducing investors' trust in the economy. Mexico asked for help from the international community, but Europe and Japan rolled the hot potato towards the United States, considered to be Mexico's main patron. The Clinton government had no choice. It tried to help by purchasing pesos, but this was not enough, and in the end it provided some $50 billion in securities for the loans. The peso exchange rate stabilized at 6 to the dollar, in other words, the depreciation stabilized at 50%. Note that some economists argue that the primary motivation for Clinton's administration to save Mexico was in fact to help US financial giants who lent to Mexico and faced a haircut.[1]

The currency crisis very quickly snowballed into a crisis in the real economy, causing the closure of many businesses and the firing of hundreds of thousands of workers. In 1995 alone, industrial sector output decreased by 15% and real GDP slumped by 7%. A collapse of this magnitude followed the crisis of the 1930s in the United States, and indicates the severity of the tequila crisis. The less pleasant surprise was the way the crisis rolled over into other countries in South America, and here we come to the story of Argentina.

9.6 Argentina's Bankruptcies

Let us open with a brief historical review that will prove to be important to understanding the events of the 1990s. During the decade between 1945 and 1955, the regime of Juan Perón nationalized many strategic industries and sealed the economy from foreign influences. This was the start of a long period of chronic inflation, at an average level of 26% a year, continuing for 30 years until 1974. Under the military dictatorship that ruled the country from 1976 until 1983 the economy shrunk, and government debt increased, causing mass bankruptcies and widening social inequality. This policy of high tariffs on imports, as well as blocking different imports, allowed inefficient businesses to continue operating in an oversized and inefficient public

---

[1] One good example is at EconTalk, where host Russ Roberts talks with Nobel laureate Joseph Stiglitz (9 July 2012, http://www.econtalk.org/archives/2012/07/stiglitz_on_ine.html, see 30:55).

sector. This is a recipe to suppress economic growth and to encourage corruption.

Following the Falklands War, democracy returned to Argentina in 1983, but attempts to stabilize the economy were unsuccessful. In 1989 inflation soared to a level of 5000% a year, eroding workers' salaries by 50%. Here it is seen that inflation can certainly be considered as the most serious haircut that citizens can endure from their own government. The public responded by avoiding paying taxes and smuggling foreign currency out of the country. Because the economy was seen by foreign investors as highly risky, they demanded a high interest rate on the debt, and as a result interest payments to foreign investors depleted foreign currency reserves.

In 1991, the Finance Minister, Domingo Cavallo, changed the exchange rate policy, replacing the Austral with the new Argentine peso, whose exchange rate against the US dollar was set to one. Argentina, which was a British colony, adopted a currency method that had been in use in the past in some colonies (Krugman, 2009). According to this method the local government determines the exchange rate for its currency against a hard currency such as pound sterling or the US dollar, and at the same time holds foreign currency reserves in an amount equal in value to its own local currency. This is supposed to prevent inflation, as the local currency has a fixed exchange rate against the hard currency. Foreign investors seemingly benefit from high safety since, at least in theory, all local currency can be replaced by the foreign currency reserves maintained in the vaults of the central bank. These rules mean that Argentina may only issue a new peso if it adds a dollar or a sterling pound to its foreign currency reserves. *But this arrangement also means that if foreign currency leaves the country, the central bank has to reduce the quantity of pesos in circulation.* When implemented, this policy indeed reduced the pace of inflation, and a rapid recovery started when in addition the government implemented aggressive privatization processes and projects for productivity improvement.

And so, when the tequila crisis erupted in Mexico in 1994, foreign investors decided to withdraw their investments from all the countries of Latin America, because those countries appeared to outside observers as a single unit. Withdrawal of foreign currency thus, by law, reduces the quantity of pesos, and the banking multiplier mechanism now started working in the opposite direction. If the ratio of the reserve is, say, one to ten, every peso that is printed generates deposits of 10 pesos, as described in Chapter 3. When the mechanism operates in the reverse direction, withdrawal of $1 from the Argentinian reserves causes 1 peso to be wiped out, thus reducing all the deposits in the banking system by 10 pesos. As a consequence, lines of credit to businesses and households shrink and the credit crunch causes the bankruptcy of many businesses, the dismissal of employees, and reduction of consumer spending. This resembles what was discussed regarding the 1930s crisis in the United States (Chapters 4 and 5).

In order to cope with 'bank runs', a government has to provide deposit insurance and convey a decisive and convincing message that it has the ability to serve as lender of last resort. But with the Mexican peso collapsing in the background, local and foreign investors suspected that the new Argentine peso would be devalued. Therefore, Argentinian residents and foreign investors alike sold local pesos to buy dollars; this high demand for the dollar increased its informal price (exchange rate), creating immense pressure for depreciation. At the same time, the central bank of Argentina was chained by its own law and unable to serve as lender of last resort because *it was not allowed* to print new pesos without increasing the number of dollars that it held. At the last moment, the International Monetary Fund (IMF) provided assistance to Argentina and the situation stabilized.

Argentina continued to maintain a fixed exchange rate of 1 peso $1, but not against other currencies, which normally change vis-à-vis the dollar. However, Argentina exported goods not only to the US, but also to Europe, and in particular, to Brazil. Therefore, when the exchange rate between the dollar and the other currencies changed, importers and exporters to Europe and Brazil experienced severe fluctuations in their profitability. Towards the end of the 1990s, Argentina's exports to Brazil, its biggest trading partner, were unprofitable and the country once again moved closer to recession. As usual in situations of this kind, foreign investors are fearful and withdraw their dollars, while fears of depreciation intensify. In 2001 the economy collapsed, and the peso depreciated by 70%.

This huge devaluation emphasized another problem, which economists refer to as 'currency exposure'. Because many debts were denominated in dollars, repayment required far more pesos than originally planned for, and Argentina effectively defaulted on its debt. The government reached an arrangement with some of its debtors by which it would pay only 30% of its debt. Once again, a 70% haircut. As the figure below shows, by 2002 real GDP had decreased by 20% and unemployment had shot up to a high of 25%. (This high unemployment rate had been experienced before, during the crisis of the 1930s, when the United States stopped purchasing raw materials from Argentina, primarily agricultural goods like cocoa and rubber. President Hoover did this in order to protect the US agricultural sector, but as aforementioned, it further intensified the crisis). Since then, the exchange rate has been allowed to fluctuate against the different currencies, and as of 2003, the economy has returned to reasonable growth rates. Another lesson learned was to link government debt to the rate of change of domestic product, and in this way the country was even able to survive the credit crisis of 2008 to 2010 without serious harm. In the summer of 2014, though, Argentina defaulted again on its debt after failing to renegotiate the terms of debt restructuring.

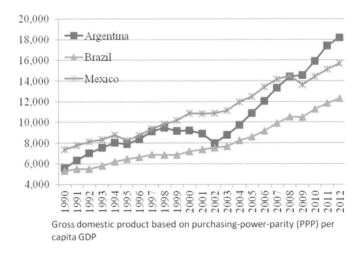

Gross domestic product based on purchasing-power-parity (PPP) per capita GDP

Figure 9.3   GDP per capita in Mexico, Argentina and Brazil

Source: http://www.imf.org/external/pubs/ft/weo/2011/02/weodata/index.aspx (accessed December 2012).

Additional Reading

Krugman, P. (2009). *The Return of Depression Economics and the Crisis of 2008.* New York: W. W. Norton & Company.

Mankiw, N.G. (2009). *Principles of Macroeconomics.* 5th edition. Boston, MA: Cengage Learning.

Mishkin, F.S. (1996). *Understanding Financial Crises: A Developing Country Perspective.* National Bureau of Economic Research Working Paper 5600, prepared for the World Bank Annual Conference on Development Economics, 25–26 April, World Bank, Washington, DC, pp. 29–62.

Mörner, M. (1973). 'The Spanish American Hacienda: A Survey of Recent Research and Debate,' *Hispanic American Historical Review*, 53, 2, 183–216.

10.

Japan and the East Asian Tigers

10.1 Japan: From Feudal Agriculture to a Global Industry Leader

Until the middle of the 19th century, Japan was an agricultural country with a feudal economic structure. Towards the end of the century, industrialization processes began to change the face of the economy, although the feudal structure remained: families like Mitsubishi, Mitsui and Sumitomo established industrial and financial corporations called 'zaibatsu', which literally means a centrally managed business group. These corporations included production and trading companies, often specializing in a few specific fields. Many had a shipping company (remember that Japan is an island involving much marine agriculture), a steel production company, a bank and a trading company. In business management terms the zaibatsu firms were 'vertically integrated', meaning that a given firm holds shares of its supplier firms, and/or shares of its clients. However, most of the shares of the group companies were held by a holding company that additionally held all the equity shares of the group's bank. The bank provided the other firms of the group with sources of long-term funding and its subsidiaries provided insurance and other financial services. The different zaibatsu competed with each other, captured market shares and grew. Following World War II, the legal status of the zaibatsu was revoked by General Douglas MacArthur under American military rule. Many zaibatsu conglomerates were forced to dismantle, and other holding companies were outlawed (Figure 10.1).

However, breaking the interlinkages between the group's firms was against local culture. The multilateral commitment between the different companies was perceived positively among Japanese business groups, employees and their families. Over time, the companies changed their

111

Figure 10.1   Seizure of zaibatsu assets, October 1946

Source: http://commons.wikimedia.org/wiki/File:Seizure_of_the_Zaibatsu_families_assets.JPG (accessed 14 October 2014).

holding structure in a way that reflected a more and more 'horizontal integration' structure, meaning that they held the shares of other companies of the group, not necessarily their suppliers or customers. Surely, the transformation was not clear-cut: many firms held shares vertically, and some features of the zaibatsu prevail today. The modified structure of Japanese business groups was called 'keiretsu' (i.e., subsidiary holdings), and the groups maintained their emphasis on a company's responsibility towards its customers, its suppliers, its employees and its creditors.

During the 1950s and 1960s, the Ministry for International Trade and Industry, known as MITI, initiated focused development programs for what were defined as 'strategic' industries. The government's goal was to provide those industries with supportive conditions for product development, proficient production and marketing experience. For example, MITI prevented the import of European and American products, and the finance ministry kept interest rates low and credit available for the preferred industries. In 1973, the first oil crisis increased production costs and slowed the growth rate of heavy industries. The impact on the overall economy was severe

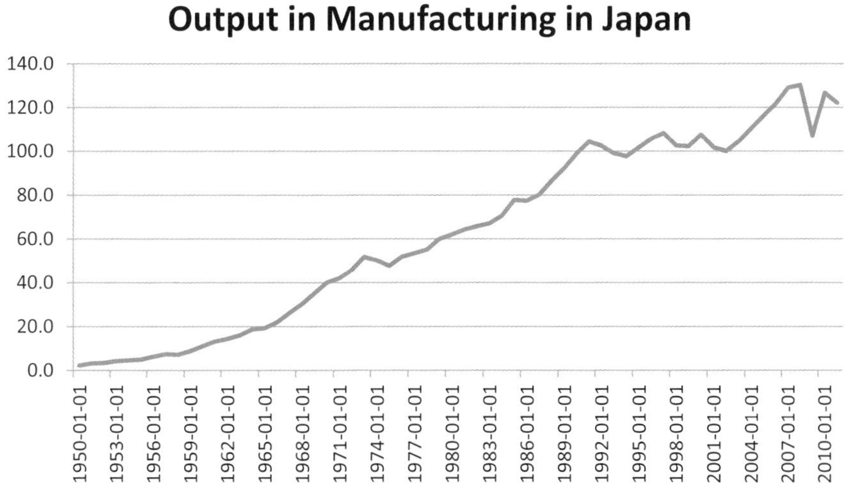

Output in Manufacturing in Japan

Figure 10.2   Industrial output in Japan 1950–2012

Source: Data Source: US Department of Labor: Bureau of Labour Statistics. Graph: by the author.

since Japan was, and still is, highly dependent on foreign energy supply. The response was to shift the industrial focus to electronics, where shrinking the printed circuit boards gradually into semiconductors generated high revenues with lower dependence on oil. This resulted in a rapidly growing consumer electronics industry, which further boosted the economy. When the second oil crisis hit world markets in 1979, Japan was well positioned and suffered less than the US and Western European countries. An interesting point to note is that unlike Western manufacturers, Japanese products were initially sold to the local market, and after a series of improvements, they were sold worldwide. The combined efforts, by the rapidly adopting keiretsu, the supportive government and the consuming public, turned Japan into a global leader in a range of industries, including optics, electronics, automobile, machine parts and more.

In 1985, Japan signed the Plaza Accord, an agreement with the leading Western economies (US, UK, West Germany, and France) aimed to depreciate the US dollar and the Deutsche Mark against the yen (¥). The motivation was to balance the favorable terms of trade that Japan had vs. its key trading partners. As a result of the joint actions of the key central banks, the yen appreciated from above ¥200 per $1 in 1985 to about ¥140 in the early 1990s (Figure 10.3). This, of course, resulted in tough trading conditions for Japanese exporters.

Average USD/JPY

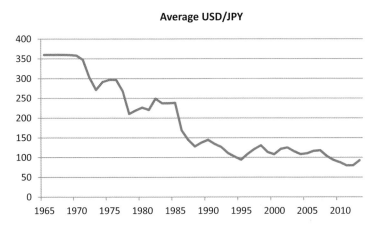

Figure 10.3   US dollar/Japanese yen exchange rate 1965–2012

10.2 Overheating with Easy Lending

Until the end of the 1980s, the growth rate of the Japanese economy was the fastest in the world, but this rapid growth in GDP was accompanied by an even more rapid increase in real estate prices and share prices. At the end of the 1980s, share prices on the Tokyo Stock Exchange (TSE) were so high that they could not be compared with share prices of similar companies operating in the same industries in other countries. For example, the shares of industrial companies were traded at a price earnings (P/E) ratio of 60 or more, while the average ratio was normally between 15 and 20; in other words, the share prices of stable companies in the economy were between three and four times higher than their historically average level.

A major part of the funds that were made available to the public in order to buy real estate and shares was loans given by keiretsu banks and non-bank financial corporations. One might think that since the sources of funding for the keiretsu companies came from the group's banks, these would avoid taking unnecessary risks. However, according to Paul Krugman (2008 Nobel Prize winner for economics), the loans were given very freely because there was an informal understanding among the bankers and the public that should there be a crisis then the government would serve as lender of last resort.

It is important to note the structure of incentives in such a situation: the public deposits money in the commercial bank and receives a low rate of interest; commercial banks play their traditional role and give long-term loans to businesses and entrepreneurs. As long as the banking system functions properly, the regulator makes sure that the bank is not exposed to a high level of risk. However, the Japanese regulators followed the worldwide approach that prevailed in the 1980s, of reducing financial regulation. In addition, the complicated structure of cross-holdings of the keiretsu made analysis of the overall risks particularly difficult, and the excessive proximity between the big corporations and the regulators was frequently manifested in the form of corruption, such as ignoring the increasing risks whenever convenient. While we have no proofs, this looks like regulatory capture, Japanese style.

As seen in prior cases, lax regulation and incentives to take on excess risks result in a motivation for borrowers to invest in increasingly riskier ventures. It was clear to all players that the risk in fact lay with the government, and not the investors or the banks. If the investment succeeded, all parties are happy, but if it failed, the government (using taxpayer funds) would rescue the banks, most of the depositors and some of the businesses. In the Japanese case, saving the keiretsu's bank implies saving most, if not the entire group.

According to Kindleberger, even though the growth rate of real estate prices in Tokyo had not been negative since the end of World War II, as of the mid-1980s real estate prices in Tokyo began to climb very rapidly (Figure 10.4). A worn-out story holds that the land value on which the

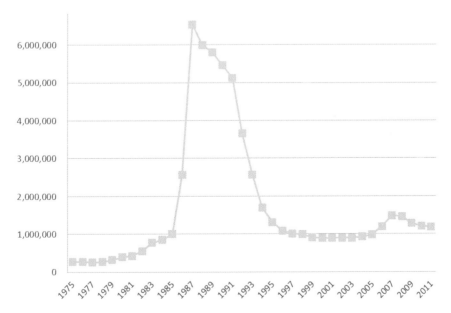

Figure 10.4   Residential land price Minato City (¥ per square meter)
Source: Housing Japan (2011).

Emperor's Palace stands in Tokyo was greater than the land value of the entire state of California. Because apartments were overly expensive, Japanese mortgage banks (primarily the big Nippon Mortgage and Japan Housing Loan) marketed mortgages repayable over an entire century ahead. A 100-year mortgage was necessary to enable families to buy homes, meaning that it would take three generations to pay off the mortgage for one apartment. Compare this with the 25- to 30-year mortgages banks normally issue, and see how overly optimistic the issuing banks were. On the other side of the mortgage contract were the buyers. Those century-long mortgages were very expensive, 8.9%–9.9%, which meant that repayments increased rapidly (Chun-Hao Chang *et al.*, 1995). Why would families be willing to commit to those terms? Partly because of the high inheritance tax, 70%, on all assets inherited, including the house. This meant that young families could not obtain an apartment in Tokyo even if they received an inheritance. To circumvent the problem they signed those century-long mortgages. These contracts allowed future generations to keep using the apartment and pay only a small fraction of the inheritance tax. These contracts had a number of adverse effects; for example, not only they did not achieve the ultimate goal, i.e., affordable housing for the middle class, they formed effectively a long-term tax haven for wealthy families, therefore increasing wealth inequality. Here is one more adverse effect: individuals who purchased properties at high prices as an investment, and rented them to others, found themselves paying large amounts to the bank every month while their rental income was lower than the repayments. This forced them to take out additional loans, which is not a sustainable strategy because it can only work as long as loans are available.

An additional source of demand for housing was foreign investors. The rapid growth in property prices led foreign investors to purchase shares and real estate in Japan for speculative gains. By doing so they were selling US dollars and European currencies and buying yen to finance their investments. In addition, the Japanese export surplus brought foreign currency into the local economy, and so its price decreased relative to the yen (excess supply of foreign currency). In other words, the yen was strengthened against Western currencies, which meant that imports to Japan became cheaper, while Japanese exports to the West became more expensive.

10.3 The Burst of the Bubble and its Cost

At the end of 1989, the governor of the Central Bank of Japan (BOJ) decided to cool down the overheated economy, mainly due to fear of inflation and concern that the nation's high housing costs would increase social gaps. The BOJ reduced money supply to mitigate both bubbles, and the stock market indeed responded quickly with rapid price drops. Stock market investors who purchased shares by means of loans had to repay them when share prices began to fall, after receiving margin calls from the banks. The stock exchange price crisis thus caused losses to the banks when borrowers could not repay their debts. As the stock market was sliding, the BOJ increased interest rates to address the housing market, where prices kept on increasing. This led to shrinking credit and caused difficulties for many real-economy firms. At the beginning of 1990 the Nikkei 225 index, which measures the value of the 225 largest firms on the TSE, stood at 40,000 points. Within two years, by the end of 1991, the index had fallen to 20,000 points, and for the rest of the 1990s it continued to stagnate between 13,000 and 20,000 points (Figure 10.5).

Among other things, the central bank restricted loans for buying real estate. The reduced supply of loans forced many real estate investors to sell their properties because they could not get those additional loans they needed to repay the mortgage, and so housing prices began to fall. In 1991, when both the real estate and the stock market bubbles were collapsing, the BOJ reversed its policy and started reducing interest rates: if long-term government bonds rates were about 7% in 1990, they dropped to 4%–5% by 1994 and to about 1%–2% since 1997 and until 2013 (Figure 10.6).

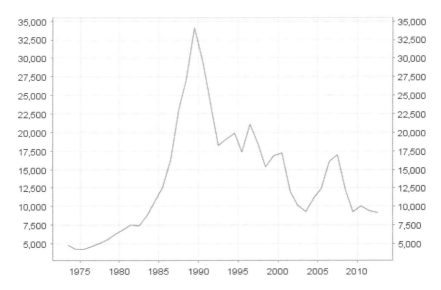

Figure 10.5   Nikkei 225 index (¥) 1970–2013
Source: ECB (2014).

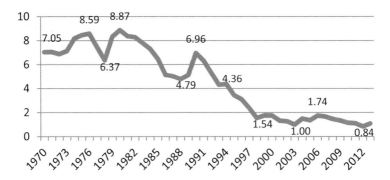

Figure 10.6 Japan: Benchmark interest rates 1972–2013
Source: Trading Economics, 2014.

From 1995, the government tried to stimulate the economy through fiscal policy, spending more than it collected in taxes, but GDP growth remained slow. The deficit was financed by issuing government bonds; therefore, over time the total government debt increased to 120% of GDP (in 2002), and in 2010 reached 200% (Figure 10.7). It is expected to decline to 160% of GDP in 2017.[1]

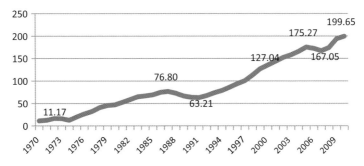

Figure 10.7 Japan: Government debt (% of GDP) 1970–2010

The collapse of both the housing and the stock market bubbles resulted in prolonged adverse effects on the Japanese economy. During two decades, 1990 to 2011, growth in Japan was only 0.9% per year. Compare this with average growth rates of 9.6% in the 1960s, 4.2% in the 1970s and 4.3% in the 1980s. Therefore, despite the fact that there was minimal growth, with a slow pace of job creation, these two decades were accompanied by high unemployment rates, a situation known as 'growth recession'. In 2003, the

---

[1] *Source*: IMF data, retrieved in December 2012.

Nikkei 225 index fell to a low of 8,000 points, after which the economy recovered slowly until the global credit crisis of 2008 again hit the Japanese economy.

10.4 The East Asian Tigers

One may wonder, how did events in Japan affect other countries in the region? The prosperity period of the 1980s and the availability of cheap credit enabled Japanese investors to purchase properties abroad, and contributed to a wave of overseas investment by Japanese conglomerates. Some of these investments were directed at the less developed countries of East Asia, in order to establish assembly and packaging plants. One of the key drivers for this trend was increasing production costs in Japan, which were no longer as cheap as they had been in the past. The main beneficiaries were South Korea, Indonesia, Malaysia, Singapore, China and Thailand. In a 1992 report, the World Bank referred to those countries as the 'East Asian miracle', since once they began to grow, they did so at remarkable annual rates of 5% to 10% (Figure 10.8). Their growth was accompanied by the migration of millions of poor farmers to the constantly growing cities, where they worked at more

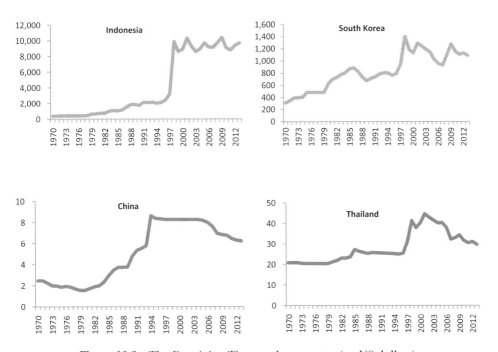

Figure 10.8   The East Asian Tiger exchange rates (vs. US dollars)

profitable occupations and acquired a profession, thus improving their standard of living.

The crisis in Japan mainly hit Thailand, South Korea and Indonesia.
Starting with Thailand, like its neighbors, stock prices there rose in the first
half of the 1990s by hundreds of percentage points, together with an
increase in real estate prices. Until the beginning of the 1990s, Thailand
financed its economic growth from its own sources, but the low interest
rates prevailing in Europe and the USA, together with the impressive price
rises in the East, caused an influx of foreign capital on an increasing scale.
Mutual funds specializing in the Asian tigers sprang up in Western countries
and in Japan, in order to invest in the local stock exchanges. Their motivation was to diversify their investments globally, and earn higher returns
from the exotic emerging markets. In addition, foreign investors brought
capital in for direct investments, purchasing real estate and investing in
factories and local businesses (foreign direct investment, or FDI). Further,
loans from the World Bank and the International Monetary Fund (IMF)
financed infrastructure and other country-level projects in countries of
the East.

A common negative aspect was corruption: Many entrepreneurs and
business people in the East, and particularly in Thailand, maintained tight
relationships with government officials (and semi-officials, like consult-
ants). In addition, as noted with Japan, the problem of moral hazard created an incentive for investments in ventures that were too risky, on the
assumption that the government would act as lender of last resort.

The flow of investment into Thailand until the mid-1990s caused a surplus of foreign currency, but unlike in the Japanese case, at that time the
exchange rate regime called for a fixed rate between the Thai baht and the
US dollar. Therefore, foreign currency coming into the country and being
converted into local currency (so that foreign investors and exporters can
purchase local goods with the local currency) meant that the central bank,
the Bank of Thailand (BOT), had to print more and more baht. If a central
bank prints lots of money, then the increasing amount of money circulating
in the local economy is spent to purchase goods, and the typical result is
inflation. In this case, in order to neutralize the effect of printing money,
the BOT issued bonds (which the public buys with the local currency),
thereby absorbing part of the increase in the quantity of money. The supply
of government bonds led to a decline in their prices, which, as discussed in
Chapter 2, meant an increase in the local interest rate. Thai business people
and entrepreneurs faced high interest when taking a loan from a local
bank, but at the same time a US-, Japanese- or European-based bank offered

lower interest rates when the loan was taken in the foreign currency. Therefore, business people and entrepreneurs may have considered taking a loan in US dollars rather favorably. In light of the prevailing fixed exchange rate regime, borrowers were not concerned by possible fluctuations in the exchange rate; therefore, they assumed that they would be able to repay the foreign loans at the fixed rate. Massive amounts of loans were taken in foreign currencies, but when the money came into Thailand, the BOT was again forced to print more baht, purchase the foreign currency and issue more bonds that were selling at lower prices (increasing interest rates).

Now, recall how the banking multiplier works: The increase that occurred in the quantity of local currency following a single transaction increased the deposits several-fold throughout the commercial banking system. This created far more credit that the local commercial banks had to offer to their clients. When competition intensifies across commercial banks, safety rules are often set aside and banks are willing to grant loans to increasingly riskier projects. Moreover, cheap and available credit supports the increase of real estate and share prices, sometimes through purely speculative investments. In Thailand, similar to the Japanese case, the sense of prosperity led to an increase in the level of consumption, both of local products and of imported products, together with an increase in Thailand's trade deficit.

During 1996 and the first half of 1997, real estate prices in Thailand began to fall. The IMF recommended to the Thai government that it devalue the baht against the US dollar, since this was the only way of stopping the spin in which the economy found itself — but the government refused. Foreign investors felt that the level of risk was increasing and therefore reduced the flow of loans into the country. Thailand's trade deficit with the rest of the world prevailed at this time; foreign funds stopped pouring in, and Japan hit rock bottom with its real estate crash, forcing some Japanese investors to liquidate their foreign investments and send the money home. This left the BOT with no alternative but to use its foreign currency reserves to finance the deficit.

Attentive investors know that a central bank's reserves are limited, so this policy cannot last very long. At this stage in Thailand, it was obvious to speculators and holders of local loans that, sooner or later, the reserves would run out and the government would be forced to devalue the baht significantly. Therefore, they bet against the baht by taking out loans in local currency and buying dollars. This is a reasonable speculative move because devaluation seems unavoidable, and if it occurs, their dollars will pay the original loan amount and leave them with some profit from the speculation. Here is a numerical example: Assume that a speculator takes a loan of 100,000 baht and for simplicity assume that the exchange rate is 10 baht/$. The investor converts the entire amount (ignore transaction costs) and now holds $10,000. Next, the devaluation event occurs, and the exchange rate now is 15 baht/$. Our speculator converts the $10,000 for 150,000 baht, pays out the loan of 100,000 baht, and keeps the gain of 50,000 baht.

This speculative trade by itself created additional demand for dollars, which the government was still selling at a fixed rate for baht. Therefore, the pace of dilution of reserves intensified and increased the pressure on government. On 2 July 1997 the dam broke and a devaluation, which started at 15%, increased to more than 20% by the end of the month. By December of that year, the devaluation had reached 55%, GDP dropped by more than 10% and the stock exchange collapsed by more than 80%. The IMF, together with other countries in the region, organized an initial aid package of $17 billion for Thailand.

The upheaval in Thailand quickly spread to other countries in the region, mainly because foreign investors withdrew their investments and stopped lending money to East Asian countries. What was wrong with the other countries? Nothing in particular was announced at that specific time, but as was the case with Mexico and Argentina, investors saw all countries of the region as being part of one family. The reason for the crisis spreading so quickly lies in a phenomenon discussed in previous chapters, the bank run. Here, too, foreign investors did not want to be the last in line, and therefore they rushed to withdraw their deposits and investments from stock exchanges in the region. Banks and other financial institutions, which were, for some part, brokers for the transactions held by cronies of the regime, had *borrowed* during the booming years considerable funds in Western currencies, therefore they found themselves with an opposite position of the transaction that the speculators did. Using the numbers of the earlier example: assume that a bank borrowed $10,000 and converted them to 100,000 baht before the devaluation. After a devaluation of 50% this bank has to pay 150,000 baht in order to buy $10,000 and close the loan contract. Therefore, just as the speculators gained from their position, these financial institutions lost on their positions once the depreciation occurred. These losses undermined their financial soundness and they needed government aid. Moreover, withdrawal of foreign deposits resulted in bankruptcy for many local banks, and so the supply of credit in these countries decreased as the banking multiplier now worked in reverse, resulting in liquidity crunch and pressure on otherwise stable businesses and the overall real economy.

Within days, the central bank of Malaysia, Bank Negara Malaysia, was forced to intervene in an attempt to protect local currency rates, and the Philippines asked for and received assistance from the IMF in order to protect their exchange rates. In August 1997, Indonesia understood that it had no choice but to devalue the rupee; although the first devaluation was 30%, by the end of the year the currency had declined 80% relative to the beginning of 1997. Indonesia closed 16 banks and received more than $40 billion in aid. The stock exchange fell by 86% during 1997, and GDP fell by 13%.

In October of that year, the crisis began to affect the relatively distant economy of South Korea, when the local currency, the won, began to weaken against the US dollar. In this way, the most advanced economy in East Asia outside Japan, three times the size of Thailand's economy, was dragged into crisis in the wake of the withdrawal of capital by foreign investors. As with the processes taking place in Thailand, Western investors stopped making loans to South Korea (for being a country of the troubled region), foreign currency reserves were quickly diluted, and there was a fear of bankruptcy to the government. South Korean banks operating abroad took energetic steps to attract deposits in Western currencies and bring them into South Korea, but these amounts were not sufficient and rumors began to spread that the foreign currency reserves were about to run out. The Bank of Korea (BOK), which tried to protect the won, had exhausted this measure and, in practice, faced one of two choices: to allow a number of financial institutions to go bankrupt and thus wipe out their debts, or to ask for assistance from the IMF. With the help of the United States and Japan, the IMF supported the move and South Korea received $57 billion in assistance. Once again, as in Thailand and Indonesia, 'crony capitalism' flourished and destroyed the incentive system. Financial companies belonging to the large business groups, the 'chaebol', that dominated not only the economy but also South Korean politics, invested in risky ventures on the assumption that the government, or their particular crony, would help out in the event of need.

10.5 The Lessons

10.5.1 *Financial liberalization*

Many economists consider that the reason for the crisis spreading so quickly across East Asia and affecting relatively advanced economies, such as that of

South Korea, as well as relatively less developed economies, such as that of Indonesia, lies in opening up their capital markets to the world. This openness, called 'financial liberalization', contributes on one hand to the local economy by allowing local industry to make use of foreign capital to develop at a faster rate than it could have done otherwise. On the other hand, liberalization requires the economic policy to be much more cautious, responsive and flexible than is necessary in a closed economy.

10.5.2 *Hedging and flexibility*

In the East Asian case, openness to world capital markets led to two serious mistakes: first, local investors borrowed considerable amounts of money in foreign currencies without proper hedging (i.e., protection[2]), and second the governments were trying to maintain a fixed exchange rate. As seen, depreciation makes foreign loans more costly and is liable to cause bankruptcies in the local economy upon a sharp and un-hedged devaluation. The attempt to maintain a fixed exchange rate when the country is exposed to changes in the global capital markets is almost hopeless in the short term, and completely hopeless in the long term.

10.5.3 *Speculators on the guard*

Changes in a country's import and export markets, in interest rates or in stock prices (which affect capital account transfers and FDI) can turn a surplus in the balance of trade into a deficit. When this occurs, the foreign currency reserves are diluted, and as seen both from the cases of Mexico and Argentina, and from the East Asian Tigers, reserves can and do run out. Speculators follow such trends, and when a government insists to avoid devaluation, and reserves deplete rapidly, they act. In many cases the country in question will be forced to devalue its exchange rate. In a certain sense, the movement of speculative capital across the globe can therefore be seen as the 'bad cop' of economic policy management. The fact that the possibility of a speculative attack exists means that governments have to act in a flexible, rapid and cautious manner in the global financial markets.

---

[2] There are ways to protect one's position from exposure to changes in foreign exchange rates. In this case, the downside would emerge from devaluation, therefore an example for a hedge would be holding an asset that would gain if devaluation occurs.

Additional Reading

Chang, C.-H., Dandapani, K. and Auster, A. (1995). 'The 100-Year Japanese Residential Mortgage: An Examination', *Journal of International Accounting, Auditing and Taxation*, 4, 1, 13–26.

Krugman, P. (2009). *The Return of Depression Economics and the Crisis of 2008*. New York: W. W. Norton & Company.

Smith, K. (2012). 'The Curious Case of Japan in the 21st Century,' Forbes, 8 June. Available at: http://www.forbes.com/sites/modeledbehavior/2012/08/06/the-curious-case-of-japan-in-the-21st-century/ (accessed 15 October 2014).

11.

The US Real Estate Bubble

11.1 Background

As in many events in history, the real estate crisis that started to roll in the US market in the summer of 2007 began with the best of intentions. American legislators responded to public need and changed the legal system and economic policy to make it easier for young families to buy a house. This chapter will focus on three changes made to the legal system: the first two, in 1938 and 1968, created a relatively stable system and resolved issues that the public had found oppressive. The third, in 1992, implemented as of 1999, changed this system, primarily through heavy lobbying activity that relaxed regulation. The new regulatory environment, which was far too lax in monitoring derivative assets and the complex interactions among different financial institutions, made the system highly unstable. This lack of stability was seen in the growth of a real estate price bubble, starting in the early years of the 2000s, until it burst between 2006 and 2008. The collapse of the real estate bubble swept the American economy and the economies of many other countries into a credit crisis. This crisis developed into the 'great recession', the most severe economic slowdown since the Great Depression of the 1930s, with severe global implications. For this reason the next three chapters are devoted to the real estate bubble and the consequences of its crash.

The chapter will start with 1938. Following the Great Depression that swept through the United States after the collapse of stock prices in October 1929, many homeowners, some of them unemployed, stopped making their monthly mortgage payments, or made irregular payments. As a result, mortgages were seen by mortgage banks, and by the private investors who used to make loans to these banks, as being relatively risky. Banks that gave mortgages charged a higher rate of interest than they used to in the past, rendering mortgages inaccessible to many people who were unable to buy houses. As part of the New Deal, President Roosevelt set up a company that was known by traders in the stock market as 'Fannie Mae', a name derived from the initial letters of its real name— the Federal National Mortgage Association (FNMA). Fannie Mae started out as a government company whose aim was to 'provide liquidity' to segments in the mortgage market.

11.2 Affordable Housing

In order to understand the meaning of providing liquidity, the following example will illustrate the way in which Fannie Mae operated. Think about a state in the US in which there are banks, or mortgage companies, generating mortgage loans. The sum of all the loans that those banks could make set, by aggregation, the total supply of mortgages for that state.[1] Now assume that in the state in question there is considerable demand for mortgages, and mortgage companies have exhausted their ability to generate mortgages. The excess demand for mortgages causes banks to increase the interest they charge for mortgages, therefore in this specific state, homebuyers struggle with expensive mortgages. At the same time, imagine that in another state the demand for mortgages is lower than the aggregate supply of mortgages, therefore the banks there are able to make loans, but because of the limited demand relative to supply, interest on mortgages is low. As a result, people living in different states in the US did not have an equal opportunity to purchase their own home and fulfill the American dream. This resulted in public pressure on the government.

Fannie Mae provided liquidity by purchasing large mortgage portfolios from those banks that had exhausted their ability to generate loans (i.e., the banks in the first state), so that they would be able to create new loans and offer lower interest rates. So, for example, a bank with a credit line (meaning ability to generate loans) of $1 billion would be able to sell $400 million of mortgages to Fannie Mae, and then be free to generate new mortgages up to $400 million for new borrowers. By reducing the excess demand for mortgages, Fannie Mae served to reduce the interest rate in the expensive mortgage states. In this way, people living in states where interest rates were

---

[1] In effect, their funding source is share capital, which is used to provide security against a line of credit given to them by institutional lenders. For example, against every dollar of share capital they can receive a line of credit in the amount of $9. From the moment the credit line is set up, the bank can generate mortgages on a scale equal to that of the credit line.

high had the opportunity of taking a mortgage at a lower rate of interest, and the government had solved a social problem.

But wait, where did the $400 million with which Fannie Mae purchased the portfolio of mortgages come from? Until 1968, Fannie Mae issued its own bonds, and with the money it received, purchased mortgage portfolios. Fannie Mae paid fixed interest to the bondholders on the bonds it issued. The interest rate that Fannie Mae paid on the bonds it issued was low because Fannie Mae was backed by the US government. Since interest payment was lower than the interest income from the mortgage portfolios, Fannie Mae was left with a profit with which to finance its operations. It is important to note that for the 30 years between 1938 and 1968, Fannie Mae kept the mortgage portfolios that it purchased in its possession, and so it both earned the difference between the interest rates, and it took upon itself the risks: If a particular mortgage portfolio yielded a low mortgage return in certain months (because some households did not make their mortgage repayments), Fannie Mae absorbed the loss. It should also be noted that until 1968, Fannie Mae was a monopoly in the commercialization of mortgage portfolios.

In 1968, in light of the budgetary difficulties that arose following the Vietnam War, the government preferred to reduce its involvement in Fannie Mae's activities, and in particular, wanted to remove its debts from the budget and turn it into a private company. And so, as of 1968 Fannie Mae was split up into two companies, one continuing as Fannie Mae, while the other was known by traders as Ginnie Mae (Government National Mortgage Association, GNMA). Starting in 1970, Fannie Mae was allowed to purchase mortgages that were *not* backed by the government, while only Ginnie Mae was permitted to operate in the government-backed mortgage market (such mortgages were issued mainly to veterans, or farmers in financial difficulty). In the same year, the government set up another company to compete with Fannie Mae, so as to limit its monopolistic power. The new company became known as Freddie Mac, again because of the initials of its name, Federal Home Loan Mortgage Corporation (FHLMC). The objective of the competition was to make the market more competitive and reduce mortgage interest rates.

It is important to note that despite the fact that both Fannie and Freddie had been made private, they were still considered as having government backing since they had a conditional access to a governmental line of credit, and so they were called government-sponsored enterprises (GSEs). They were exempt from paying state and Federal taxes, they were not required to show their audited financial statements (despite the fact that Fannie and

Freddie were traded among the 500 largest companies on the New York Stock Exchange), and they were also *not* subject to supervision by the Securities and Exchange Commission (SEC).

11.3 Securitization is Born

In 1968, Ginnie Mae developed an innovative financial product— mortgage-backed securities (MBS)— which, together with Fannie and Freddie, it developed and distributed on an increasingly large scale over the years. These securities are defined as debt products representing a claim on a mortgage portfolio and its cash flow. In practice, an investor purchasing an MBS holds a share of a mortgage portfolio. If the value of the mortgage portfolio is $100 million, and one million MBS units are issued against it, each unit is worth $100. If all the units afford an *equal right* to the cash flow produced by the mortgage portfolio, an investor holding one unit will receive 1/1,000,000 of the monthly income of the mortgage portfolio. Therefore, the cash-flow risk to the investor is the same as the cash-flow risk of the mortgage portfolio. As long as the cash-flow risk is reasonable, investors are willing to buy the MBS units, but in some cases the mortgage portfolio generates a cash flow that is too volatile: it sometimes pays as expected (when people adhere to their payment schedule), but too often too many borrowers do not pay as they were supposed to pay. And that will happen when many mortgages in the portfolio are held by households that cannot make payments. When the cash-flow risk is too high, rating companies such as Standard and Poor's (S&P) and Moody's would give it a low grade, for example 'B', which means that pension funds and other institutional investors are *not allowed* to hold such assets in their portfolios (the regulator wants them to avoid exposing our savings money to such assets). Any rating below BBB+ (as specified by S&P) is considered 'below investment grade', and not allowed for investment by those institutions. Rating and the rating companies will be elaborated upon in due course.

In those cases where the cash-flow risk is too high, individual investors are not enthusiastic about purchasing MBS units in the portfolio, and, as noted, institutional investors are not allowed to hold them. This creates an incentive for the MBS issuer to reduce the cash-flow risk. The method of creating assets that are less risky than the original mortgage portfolio is called 'credit enhancement'. The process of forming the MBS is called 'securitization', regardless of whether or not the MBS issuer has carried out credit enhancement. Such a process can be applied not only to mortgage-backed securities, but also to securities backed by pools (portfolios) of student loans, car loans, credit card loans and others. The name given to these

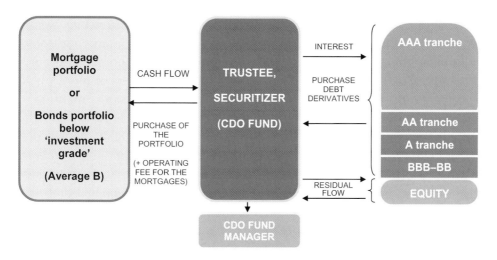

Figure 11.1   General structure of credit enhancement of a CDO
Source: Benmelech and Dlugosz (2009).

kinds of securities is 'collateralized debt obligation' (CDO). The trustee, or securitizer, usually creates a special legal entity to manage the CDO. This is often called a 'CDO fund'. Figure 11.1 shows the general process of creating a CDO.

Without going into unnecessary detail, the important aspects of the securitization process can be described according to the following three stages:

1. In the first stage, a mortgage portfolio is purchased from a mortgage bank and transferred to the trustee or securitizer. Focusing on the left-most box in Figure 11.1, you see that it resembles a mortgage portfolio or a portfolio of other loans or bonds that are below investment grade. In our example we assume that its weighted average rating is 'B'. The trustee (middle box) creates the CDO fund and infuses money into it, and the fund uses this money to pay and purchase the portfolio. The arrow pointing to the left resembles transfer of payment from the CDO fund to the bank that held the portfolio of mortgages or bonds. The CDO fund also pays the bank operations fee, since the bank has the dataset and the knowhow of handling the payment collection from the homeowners.
2. In the second stage, the trustee defines groups, or 'tranches', as seen on the right-hand side of Figure 11.1. The tranches are arranged from the safest to the riskiest. In order to illustrate how the tranches are arranged,

imagine a round pie dish with capacity of $1 million into which we are pouring a filling from three containers: the first contains chocolate cream, the second vanilla cream, and the third contains strawberry whip. The first container represents the initial amounts of money paid by the mortgage holders every month. Assume that it can contain up to $750,000. The second container can hold $200,000 at most, and the third container can hold the remaining amount, $50,000. This represents the assumption that the mortgage portfolio generates *an average* cash flow of $1 million a month. The first $750,000 that the mortgage holders pay will go into the first container, the next $200,000 that people pay will go into the second container, and an average of $50,000 will be placed into the third container.

Obviously, the first $750,000 and the second $200,000 are also averages, since there is a possibility, which statistical models can estimate, where the total collection in a given month will be lower than $950,000, or even less than $750,000.

In an average month, the MBS portfolio manager pours the $750,000 of chocolate cream into the pie dish. *Only then* does the manager add the $200,000 of vanilla cream, if it has actually been paid, and only at the end does the manager pour the remaining amount from the third container into the pie dish. As noted above, since certain households sometimes cannot pay their mortgage, while on the other hand others may decide to repay their entire mortgage ahead of time, the amount going into the third container is sometimes large, and sometimes small. If only, say, $900,000 is paid in a particular month, then in that month there is no strawberry whip and the vanilla cream layer is not $200,000 thick, but only $150,000.

Now that the entire amount, from all three containers, has been poured into the pie dish, the question is how does one distribute the pie to others, meaning what portion of cash flow does the MBS holder get. There are two primary ways to slice the pie. One way is to create 'equal tranches' (Figure 11.2) and the other is to apply 'credit enhancement' (Figure 11.3).

Securitization on the basis of equal tranches is different from securitization on the basis of credit enhancement, according to the specific way the pie is sliced. If the pie is sliced vertically, looking at it from the side we can see all three layers in each slice, one on top of the other — anyone holding these MBS tranches will share the same level of risk; everyone is liable not to taste the strawberry whip in a month when the mortgage payments are less than $950,000.

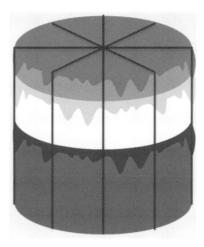

Figure 11.2   Securitization based on equal tranches

3. Alternatively, with credit enhancement the securitizing agent sells MBS tranches *from each layer separately.* This is how we get to the third stage, in which the trustee issues MBS units, by credit enhancement. As the previous example highlighted, the riskiest trench is the strawberry whip, the last one. An iron rule in the pricing of financial assets is that riskier assets must pay higher returns to the asset holder, or else, why would this investor be willing to tolerate the risk? As a result, the MBSs are sold to institutional or private investors at a price that corresponds with the level of risk. Credit-rating companies tag a risk level of the different MBS units, and the income from the mortgage portfolio is paid to the different segments according to the rating they received. The most secure will earn a low interest rate, and the riskiest will earn the highest interest rate. So, for example, a pension fund, which would not have been permitted to purchase the three-layer equal tranche MBS because it was too risky, can invest in MBSs under credit enhancement: They will simply purchase only the best-quality tranche, the chocolate cream, or the medium-quality tranche of vanilla cream.

Because the riskier the cash flow, the higher the returns demanded by investors, then the safest tranche will pay lowest yields, which is exactly what the CDO fund manager wants to achieve. The fund manager would prefer to pay as little as possible to the MBS holders, and therefore have an incentive to show that their portfolio has a very thick layer of top-rated MBSs. Average credit enhancement during 2005–2006 resulted in the fact that

Figure 11.3   Securitization based on credit enhancement

about 75% of the value of the portfolio of risky mortgages or bonds was turned into bonds with a *perfect AAA credit rating, like the credit rating of the US government.* About 20% became bonds with a mezzanine rating of between AA and BBB+, and 5% was turned into bonds with a level of risk similar to that of shares, often denoted the 'equity trench'.

Taking a bird's-eye view we may conclude that everyone was happy: households profit because mortgages become cheap and available. The mortgage producers profit from creating mortgages and servicing them before and after they are sold to the trustee. The trustee (the securitizer) profits from issuing the mortgage-backed securities and from commissions as long as the securities exist. The buyers of the mortgage-backed securities profit because they hold assets with a perfect credit rating that produce a higher yield than that paid by government or corporate bonds with a similar rating.

However, this mechanism opened up the possibility of financial alchemy: even if one considers a portfolio made of mostly risky mortgages, this portfolio transforms into MBSs with a lower risk rating, most of them tagged with the perfect AAA rating. Why alchemy? Because the risks have not really been cancelled out in this process, just concealed and reallocated. As long as the mortgages included in the portfolio are of good quality, the securitization process helps everyone involved and should not be ruled out. The problems develop when control mechanisms weaken and when the information on the real level of risk is unknown to the MBS holders.

11.4 NINJA Loans

The securitization process seems like a good option for everyone involved, and it indeed worked properly in the US until 1999. In 1992, President Bush signed a law requiring the government-sponsored agencies Fannie Mae and Freddie Mac, to meet quantitative targets for providing affordable housing for households with a low and medium income, but this law was not put into practice on a significant scale. In 1999, the Clinton administration put pressure on Fannie and Freddie to increase their support through loans for populations living in distressed areas, primarily in city centers. The social concept underlying these measures was that conferring ownerships on residents of distressed neighborhoods would help them escape the cycle of poverty that was perpetuated from one generation to the next. It was expected that homeowners would invest in their assets and neighborhoods, which would reduce violence level and improve residents' lives.

Clinton's administration altered certain rules, demanding banks to issue a specific amount of mortgages to those who may not have been able to get a loan. Banks were incentivized to follow since they received higher rating in accordance with the Community Reinvestment Act (CRA). Clinton's administration also used the Department of Housing and Urban Development (HUD) to make changes within Fannie Mae and Freddie Mac, entering into the subprime loan market. One change allows only 2.5% of capital to be kept on hand backing their investments as opposed to the regular 10%. Through the government-sponsored enterprises (GSEs), mortgage banks had the government implicitly backing their debt. With this guarantee, banks issued billions of dollars of loans to low-income districts with minimal requirement for a down payment. By 2007, the mortgage market consisted of $12 trillion, half of which was backed by Fannie and Freddie. Of new homeowners from 1995–2005, 49% consisted of minorities (Jones, 2008).

Because these populations were not able to meet the requirements set out by Fannie and Freddie to be granted prime mortgages, the mortgage bankers joined in to put pressure on the agencies to make the terms more flexible. The most binding terms were equity capital of 20% to 25% of the value of the property, and proof of income. Loans for these buyers were called 'subprime', because the borrowers were ranked below prime-rated borrowers (that is, good-quality borrowers). Table 11.1 shows the types of loan and the conditions required.

Notice that, from Table 11.1, categorization of households into groups based on their credit quality was more or less determined on the basis of several parameters, including the ratio between the value of the loan and

Table 11.1 Characteristics of different categories for rating the quality of mortgage borrowers

Characteristic / Borrower rating	Prime	Jumbo	Alt-A	Subprime
Ratio between loan to property value (LTV)	65–80%	65–80%	70–100%%	60–100%
Average LTV ratio	70–100%	70–75%	70–75%	80–85%
Credit rating (FICO)	700+	700+	640–730	500–660
Historic credit quality (meeting debt payments)	Impeccable	Impeccable	Impeccable	Deficient
Meeting criteria of mortgage agencies	In full	In full other than size of loan	Not met due to absence of documents or LTV ratio	Not met due to FICO, credit quality, or documents

Source: Gorton (2009).

the value of the property (LTV), such that the smaller the LTV, the safer the mortgage. This is why the bank was prepared to charge a lower interest rate. Further note that those people taking out mortgages who were rated 'Prime' were the ones who met all the requirements of the securitization agencies. Borrowers taking particularly large mortgages (over $417,000) were rated 'Jumbo' if they met all the other conditions. Borrowers who could not present documentation, such as salary income, or if their credit rating was low because at some time in the past they had failed to repay a loan on time, scored a lower rating. The lower the borrower rating, the higher the interest rate the borrower was required to pay, or they did not receive a mortgage at all. Subprime borrowers were defined as such if they took out loans that were high relative to the value of the property, and/or there were problems with the quality of their credit history, and/or they lacked documents. The characteristics of such borrowers who had no income, no job and no assets gave way to the term 'NINJA loans', which was commonly used in the market.

In order to deal with the pressure of the mortgage producers to create special securitization processes for subprime borrowers, Fannie and Freddie agreed, in around 2000, to consider securitization of mortgages that would price the risks characteristic of the subprime borrowers in an appropriate way. The mortgage producers concluded that one of the most important loan conditions for subprime borrowers, and for themselves, was to provide borrowers with the opportunity to increase their equity capital in the short term. The equity capital is defined as the difference between the value of the property and the value of the loan. For example, if the value of the property is $100,000 and the value of the loan is $80,000, the equity capital that the buyer is required to bring in is $20,000 (LTV = 80,000/100,000 = 80%). The basic idea was that if the value of the property increased in the short term, say two to three years after taking the mortgage, and during this period the value of the mortgage had not increased significantly, the borrower would increase their equity. Continuing with the same example, if after two years the value of the property has increased to $115,000, while the mortgage has increased to $85,000, the household's equity capital has increased to $30,000 (the difference between 115,000 and 85,000). In this situation, when the equity capital represents a little more than 26% of the home value (30,000/115,000 = 26.1%), this household could recycle the loan at the end of two or three years by proving to the bank that its equity capital has increased (in this case the new LTV is: 85,000/115,000 = 74%, lower than the original 80%). If, on top of the lower LTV, one or two in the household finds a stable job, this household will no longer be defined as subprime and the interest rate on the next mortgage will be lower, perhaps even rated as prime.

The most important change introduced by this new loan structure into the well-functioning system of the securitization processes was the establishment of linkage between households' ability to recycle the loan and the market price of the properties. This arrangement of increasing households' equity helps borrowers and mortgage producers only as long as house prices continue to rise: had the property price declined to say, $95,000, the household would find itself with a lower equity, $95,000 − $85,000 = $10,000, rather than the original $20,000 they invested. The entire plan aimed at improving subprime borrowers was therefore dependent on one key assumption: that residential asset prices would continue to rise. Moreover, from a macroeconomic perspective, so long as subprime borrowers made up a small share of the entire residential mortgage market, the risk they posed on the system was manageable. An important underlying assumption at the time was that the securitization process, which functioned more or less well for 30 years, was well regulated and its risks were transparent. Nevertheless, outside of the supervising eye several additional things developed.

Additional Reading

Fabozzi, F.J. and Modigliani, F. (1992). *Mortgage and Mortgage-Backed Securities Markets.* Boston, MA: Harvard Business School Press.

Financial Crisis Inquiry Commission (FCIC) (2011). *The Financial Crisis Inquiry Report, Authorized Edition: Final Report of the National Commission on the Causes of the Financial and Economic Crisis in the United States.* New York: PublicAffairs.

Krugman, P. (2009). *The Return of Depression Economics and the Crisis of 2008.* New York: W. W. Norton & Company.

Roubini, N. and Mihm, S. (2010). *Crisis Economics: A Crash Course in the Future of Finance.* New York: Penguin.

12.

Incentives, Regulatory Capture and Collapse

12.1 Introduction

House prices in the US rose between 2000 and 2006, a result of the expansionary monetary policy adopted by the mythological chairman of the Federal Reserve, Prof. Alan Greenspan. Greenspan's opinions and positions had a profound impact on economic policy, investor's expectations and hence on market prices, not only in the US but around the world. Therefore, a few words will be devoted here to describing the role of the Fed and in particular, Prof. Greenspan's responsibility for the crisis.

12.2 The Role of the Fed

Greenspan was appointed as chairman of the Board of Governors of the Federal Reserve in 1987 and served in this dignified position for 19 consecutive years, until January 2006 (Figure 12.1). He started reducing the interest rate that the Fed charges banks (which normally translates to interest reduction to borrowers) following the technology stock crisis in 2000. The Fed continued with this policy after the Twin Towers disaster of 11 September 2001, only to further continue this policy in light of the crisis of confidence in corporate America after the discovery of the accounting fraud between 2002 and 2004, with the resulting public deterrence of the stock market. The low-interest-rate policy continued until 2004, and it is considered by many as one of the main reasons for the emergence of the real estate bubble. The argument is that low interest rates paid by commercial banks to depositors,

Figure 12.1   Former Chairman of the Federal Reserve, Alan Greenspan, receiving a Presidential Medal of Freedom in 2005

Source: By White House photo by Shealah Craighead (Whitehouse.gov (link)) [Public domain], via Wikimedia Commons (accessed 18 November 2014).

and low yields that government bonds pay to their holders, made other investment opportunities more attractive and mortgages relatively cheap. Therefore, at the beginning of the 21st century, the two most common investment opportunities, the stock market and the bond market, were not attractive, and many people turned to what seemed to be a promising alternative: real estate investment.

Greenspan objected to implementing regulatory oversight on derivative financial instruments (details in Section 12.10), in spite of the rapid growth in credit derivatives like mortgage-backed securities (MBSs) and collateralized debt obligations (CDOs) of the securitization industry. The Fed and its chairman had data on the increasing turnover and widespread use of increasingly complex financial derivatives, including sharp increase in the activities of unregulated hedge funds, but the Fed did not rush to take action to monitor this industry. Nor did the Fed act on the increasing real estate prices. Apparently, the reason was that the overall loss of value of all subprime mortgages, should they evaporate entirely, was smaller than the loss of value on one bad trading day in the stock market (Bernanke, 2013).

In 1992, Representative Edward Markey asked the General Accounting Office (GAO) to study financial derivatives. The GAO reported that there are 'significant gaps and weaknesses' (Goodman, 2008). This view turned out to be predictive:

> The sudden failure of abrupt withdrawal from trading of any one of these large United States dealers could cause liquidity problems in the markets and could also pose risk to others, including federally insured banks and financial systems as a whole. In some cases intervention has and could result in a financial bailout paid for guaranteed for or guaranteed by tax payers. (GAO, 2004)

Markey introduced some derivative regulation, but did not gain enough support for the measures to be effective.

In 1994, Congress introduced a bipartisan bill called the Homeownership Opportunity and Equity Protection Act (HOEPA) to help control the regulation of the complex derivatives. The bill required standards, disclosures, accounting examinations and audits to regulate the mortgage companies. Greenspan overpowered Congress' legislation by testifying that the Federal Reserve had the money and the power to back up all the derivatives that were being sold and assuring the committee that the chances of a bailout were very minimal.

Professor Greenspan favored 'market regulation' over 'governmental regulation'. For example, he claimed that 'risks in financial markets, including derivatives markets, are being regulated by private parties [...] There is nothing involved in federal regulation *per se* which makes it superior to market regulation' (Cohen, 2013). There were many who opposed him, such as Warren Buffet, who said that 'derivatives were financial weapons of mass destruction' (Goodman, 2008). Yet once again, when a lawyer on the Commodity Futures Trading Commissions pushed to regulate derivatives in 1997, Alan Greenspan objected. In various speeches, Greenspan concluded that credit derivatives and other complex financial instruments have contributed to the 'development of a far more flexible, efficient, and hence resilient financial system that existed just a quarter-century ago' (Cohen, 2013). Apparently, Greenspan's belief that a drop in the value of subprime mortgages can be 'contained' by the Fed (there were no events of mass default in prime mortgage pools until then) was partially affected by his lesson in the stock market. Greenspan was the Fed chairperson during the largest Standard & Poor's 500 (S&P 500) drop in one day in history, an event known as 'Black Monday' (Figure 12.2). On Monday 19 October 1987 share prices collapsed 22.61% in a single day. A couple of investigation committees concluded that among

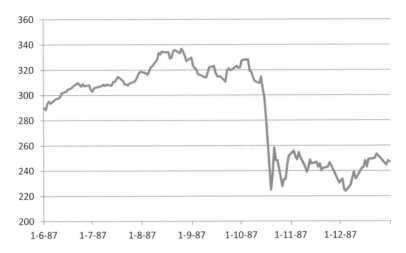

Figure 12.2   S&P500 Index: 1 June 1987–31 December 1987

Source: Author compilation.

the main reasons for the crash were program trading techniques, and particularly those known as 'portfolio insurance'. The latter indicate to a computer to buy more shares if the previous price increased, but sell if the price declined. Once implemented on a large scale (and even recommended to pension funds), these programed trades inflated a bubble that crashed on Black Monday, when all programs issued sell orders simultaneously.

In spite of the unprecedented price drop, the economy was not dragged into a recession, possibly due to the rapid response by the Fed, headed by Greenspan. Some argue, among them Nobel laureate Paul Krugman, that the expansionary monetary policy that Greenspan implemented, primarily by infusing cheap loans to the financial system, mitigated the impact of the crash, although other factors played important roles as well. Either way, there was a prevalent belief among Fed leaders that the age of financial crises had passed. The sustained growth period and the relative lack of severe declines in the real economy between the early 1980s and the end of the 1990s, is known as the 'great moderation', and Greenspan is considered its architect.

Greenspan was active in supporting financial deregulation and minimal intervention in the markets, which was promoted mainly by Republican

Figure 12.3 Alan Greenspan in testimony to Congress

Source: Wikimedia, public domain. Available at: http://commons.wikimedia.org/wiki/Alan_Greenspan#mediaviewer/File:Mvc-017x.jpg

members of Congress. Thus, for example, he did not intervene in the creation of subprime loans even though HOEPA enabled him to do so. In 1999 he strongly supported the final cancellation of the separation between commercial banking activities and investment banking, the restrictions that were imposed after the crisis of 1929 as part of the Glass–Steagall Act of 1933. For his support of deregulation, primarily opposing to regulate derivative assets, and his support for the repeal of the Glass–Steagall Act, some argue that the legendary chairman bears responsibility for causing or at least supporting the formation of the real estate bubble.

In his testimony to Congress in 2008, Greenspan admitted that the perspective he had held throughout his professional life collapsed before his eyes. An important part of this perspective was that a free market in which rational players behave according to their economic interests is preferable to a market directed by governmental regulation. In particular, he regretted the position by which financial institutions were allowed to decide on the *degree of regulation that they needed.* The claim was that rational judgment would mean that managers would not expose their organizations to unnecessary risks, because they would not want to endanger the organization or lose their jobs and their professional prestige. It turned out that dishonest norms, avarice and the possibility of rolling the risk over to someone else triumphed over rational judgment.

Prof. Greenspan was aware that generous mortgages were given to subprime borrowers, and knew of the risks arising from the widespread use of new and complex derivatives securities (far more complex than the MBSs and the CDOs mentioned in Chapter 11). He insisted on his professional opinion by which on the macroeconomic level, the resultant risk was not significant. Apparently, Greenspan, like many other economists, felt during the 1990s that a monetary policy that responds rapidly to crises could 'contain' them. It must be highlighted though, that unlike some executives in the financial industry during the bubble period, Prof. Greenspan was honest and acted according to his lifelong belief. To date, there is no evidence of any fraud or unethical stain in his actions.

12.3 Regulatory capture and the Gramm–Leach–Bliley Act

As explained in Chapter 4, the Glass–Steagall Act of 1934 separated commercial banking, which must remain safe and solid, and hence regulated by the Fed, from the market-sensitive and hence risky investment banking. The latter was not heavily regulated, therefore was allowed to engage in risky financial transactions that often yielded high average returns. Different aspects of this Act were deregulated during the 1990's, but its most important parts were formally repealed by the Gramm–Leach–Bliley Act (GLBA, also known as the Financial Services Modernization Act of 1999). By repealing the Glass–Steagall Act giant financial holding corporations were allowed to form, combining commercial banking, investment banking, insurance, and other financial activities. As a result, the power of those large financial holding companies increased dramatically, both politically and by eroding competition. In light of what appears to be beneficial to the financial sector at the expense of public interest, a key question emerges: *Were the regulators of the financial industry captured throughout the making of the Gramm–Leach–Bliley Act?* The short answer is 'yes', as the 'gold standard' of regulatory capture (by Carpenter and Moss (2013) definition) appears to hold in this case. Here is the longer answer.

As noted earlier, this question can be answered by following Carpenter and Moss's (2013) 'Golden Rule' to argue that capture indeed took place: First, show a defeasible model of public interest. Second, show that policy was shifted away from the public interest and toward industry interest; and third, show action and intent by the industry in pursuit of this policy shift that is material in making the shift.

The first and second of the three rules call for demonstrating how the financial industry gained at the expense of the public interest by changing regulations. This can be addressed in a number of ways. First, consider the motivation of firms to merge. A typical argument that is mentioned as a prime motivation for firms to merge is improved profitability. The merged firms may save different types of cost items, they may be more efficient in promoting sales, or improve technological synergies across the merged business activities. These will not necessarily draw from public interest. However, if all or most of the industry undergoes a wave of mergers, the previously competitive environment is replaced with an oligopolistic structure, where a few firms dominate the industry. In that case, the merged firms have asubstantial market power that enables them to reap oligopolistic rents, and so draw from the public interest. Another aspect that is especially important in the financial sector is increased risk for bank runs, banking crises, or even systemic banking crises. As explained in the first three chapters, a run on a small bank will normally not put the entire banking system at risk, but if a giant bank faces a run, the run might spread and sweep the other few giants as well. The merger of commercial banks and insurance firms together with investment banks exposes the former institutions, which must remain solid, to risks that emerge from swings in the stock, bond, or real-estate markets. Here is a quote from Nobel Prize-winner Joseph Stiglitz (2009):

> Commercial banks are not supposed to be high-risk ventures; they are supposed to manage other people's money very conservatively … It is with this understanding that the government agrees to pick up the tab should they fail. Investment banks, on the other hand, have traditionally managed rich people's money — people who can take bigger risks in order to get bigger returns. When repeal of Glass–Steagall brought investment and commercial banks together, the investment-bank culture came out on top. There was a demand for the kind of high returns that could be obtained only through high leverage and big risk-taking.

Knowing that they will be saved by taxpayer money, the familiar moral hazard problem, captains of the financial industry have an incentive to take on more risk and increase short-term profits. Therefore, by repealing the Glass–Steagall Act and instituting that Gramm–Leach–Bliley Act, the financial industry profits at the expense of public interest, satisfying Carpenter and Moss's first and second rules toward advocating that regulatory capture occurred in this case.

The third rule, which requires one to demonstrate action and intent by the industry toward making the regulatory (policy) shift, can be addressed by presenting evidence of intensive lobbying, campaign contributions and donations to politicians. In March 2008, in his campaign for presidency at Cooper Union for the Advancement of Science and Art, Senator Barack Obama said: *"By the time the Glass–Steagall Act was repealed in 1999, the $300 million lobbying effort that drove deregulation was more about facilitating mergers than creating an efficient regulatory framework."* Indeed, much evidence exists that big banks, insurance companies, and securities companies gave about $85 million to both the Democratic and Republican parties during 1997–1998, and about $150 million between 1999–2000.

In 1998, Citicorp and Travelers Group (which owned at that time the investment bank Salomon Smith Barney) merged and formed the world's largest financial services firm. They merged in spite of the fact that the Glass–Steagall Act and the Bank Holding Company Act, both forbid such mergers, were in effect. They did so by utilizing a loophole that allowed two years forbearance period, until a law that permits the merger had passed. Fearing that the law would not pass and the merger would have to be unwind, Citigroup's co-chairs Sandy Weill and John Reed led an aggressive lobbying campaign on Congress. They hired Robert Rubin, who recently stepped down as Treasury Secretary, to promote the legislation.[1] Former Texas Senator Phillip Gramm (Democrat who turned Republican), who served as chairperson of the Senate Committee on Banking, Housing and Urban Affairs (often abbreviated as the 'Banking Committee'), led the new act. He was a key supporter of deregulation and advocated tax-cuts. Gramm was an ideal match for Weill and Reed, both ideologically, and as chair of the Banking Committee, therefore their lobbying activities were highly effective.[2] After service, Gramm opened a lobbying firm, Gramm Partners.

---

[1] Together and without notifying the public, Rubin negotiated with Weill and Reed the terms for his hiring as an 'executive without portfolio' at Citigroup. In fact, Rubin joined Citigroup as a board member and as a participant 'in strategic managerial and operational matters of the Company, but [...] no line responsibilities' (*Wall Street Journal*, 2008). *The Wall Street Journal* called this 'murky'. Robert Rubin received over $17 million in compensation from Citigroup and an additional $33 million in stock options as of 2008. His total compensation from Citigroup between 1999 and 2009 was $126 million. During those years, Citigroup shareholders have suffered losses of more than 70%.

[2] In 1996 he spent $20 million trying to be elected as the Republican Party presidential nominee, but failed. Among his top contributors, one can find accounting, insurance and securities companies, as well as Enron and other gas and oil companies. His wife, Wendy, served on the board of Enron before it collapsed.

Phil Gramm, chairman of the Senate Banking Committee from 1995 to 2000, was mentioned by *Time* magazine as one of the 25 people to blame for the financial crisis. *Time* writes: 'Gramm was Washington's most prominent and outspoken champion of financial deregulation. He played a leading role in writing and pushing through Congress the 1999 repeal of the Depression-era Glass–Steagall Act, which separated commercial banks from Wall Street. He also inserted a key provision into the 2000 Commodity Futures Modernization Act that exempted over-the-counter derivatives like credit-default swaps from regulation by the Commodity Futures Trading Commission. Credit-default swaps took down AIG (*Time*, 2014a).

Picture by RickK at en.wikipedia (Transferred from en.wikipedia) [Public domain], from Wikimedia Commons (accessed 2 December 2014).

To summarize, the third rule proposed by Carpenter and Moss's (2013) 'Golden Rule' appears to have been met throughout the process of repealing the Glass–Steagall Act and replacing it with GLBA. There was action and intent in changing the law. The financial industry played an important role in changing prevailing policy. Therefore, I trust it would be reasonable to conclude that regulators were captured by the financial industry, who extracted value from the public for its own benefit.

12.4 Private-Label MBS

Until 2003, most securitization processes were carried out by Fannie Mae and Freddie Mac, and a minority by private trustees (private label). Yet, the securitization process, which included the purchase of mortgage portfolios from the banks that had produced them, reorganizing them and selling them to investors through MBSs can be implemented by others as well.

As of 2004, the private trustees working for investment banks that were not under the supervision of the central bank took over the market and produced mortgages for subprime borrowers on an increasingly large scale. Chief of them was Lehman Brothers, headed by Dick Fuld. This takeover of the market was carried out through the aggressive marketing of mortgages by sales agents who went from door to door in the less desirable areas of the cities, mainly in the US and in England, but also in Spain

and other European countries. Since the regulator permitted the marketing of loans to households that could not produce documented evidence
of income or employment, and since supervision of the documents was
lax, the sales agents were signing people who had never owned a home
and did not understand the financial implications of their signature on
risky mortgages. These activities expanded even further the unsupervised
banking system into tremendous proportions, which grew from the beginning of the 1980s and which came to be known as 'shadow banking'. The
evolution of the shadow banking system and its role will be expanded
upon in Chapter 13.

Dick Fuld, denoted by Time magazine as the 'Gorilla
of Wall Street', is considered the one who headed
Lehman into the private-label business of subprime
mortgages. For his excellent services to the firm, he
was paid about $500 million, until the firm collapsed
(*Time*, 2014b).

Picture by World Resources Institute Staff (http://flickr.com/photos/
wricontest/369118382/) [CC-BY-2.0 (http://creativecommons.org/
licenses/by/2.0)], via Wikimedia Commons (accessed 2 December 2014).

Not only the private-label securitizing firms grew in relative market
share, they also took upon themselves higher risks. While Fannie and
Freddie provided a guarantee to the MBS securities that they sold, the private trustees were not prepared to give any form of guarantee. Fannie and
Freddie kept a significant part of the risk in house, while the private trustees
kept only a small part of the risk. As a result, the greater part of the risk was
rolled over to the MBS buyers.

The aggressive marketing activities of the private trustees also affected
the behavior of the banks and the companies that produced the mortgages. As private labels' dominance in the market grew, Fannie and
Freddie lost their ability to supervise and control the activities of the
banks that produced the mortgages. Therefore, their ability to oversee the
quality of the securitization processes weakened. Shareholders in Fannie
and Freddie saw how competition erodes their companies' profitability,
and in an effort to retain market share, the managers of the two companies were forced to ease the requirements for supervision and control of
the securitization processes. Because of the fierce and unsupervised competition, in 2006 and at the beginning of 2007 subprime borrowers were

able to obtain mortgages at 100% of the value of the property, and even
more.

12.5 Incentives

The changes that began in 1999 therefore caused the system of incentives and
supervision of the securitization processes to malfunction. Taking a bird's-eye
view of the system, finds the following processes:

- Households that were previously unable to allow themselves property
  ownership discover that they can be homeowners although they are
  defined as NINJA borrowers (no income, no job, no assets). In other
  words, they have no documentation of salary income, no significant
  equity capital, and the quality of their credit history is problematic.
- Households meet the shrewd agent of the mortgage bank, who makes a
  profit on every agreement that they bring to the bank. As a result, the
  agent and the household's joint incentive is to sign the mortgage papers.
  If the borrowers purchase the property just with loans, then there is
  some probability that in a few years they will have some equity as the
  value of the property rises. The household paints a rosy picture of a
  home of their own... However, they also think of the possibility that the
  value of the property might fall: 'Don't worry,' says the agent, 'in that
  case let the bank have the asset and you will return to your original
  status.' The situation of those who invested their meager savings was
  obviously more risky, but evidently, many were willing to bet on increasing
  future prices.
- The mortgage bank, in its turn, knows that it profits from producing
  mortgages, and servicing them for a fee (that is, sending invoices,
  collection and dealing with customers). More importantly, the bank
  knows that before the end of the first two years of the loan, it will sell the
  mortgage portfolio for securitization. In other words, from the outset
  the mortgage bank has no incentive to keep holding the risky mortgages.
  This bank is probably among the few who know the risks involved with
  the mortgagor, and does not want to lose if they will be unable to meet
  the mortgage payments. Knowing that these mortgages will be tossed
  away for securitization shortly after issuance, the mortgage bank now has
  no incentive to examine the quality of the borrower, the quality of the
  document, and verification of the sales agent's report.
- The trustee, whether it is Fannie or Freddie, or a private trustee, knows
  that it will make a profit by repackaging and selling uniform MBSs, or by

applying credit enhancement and creating MBSs of different credit risk, and selling them to investors all over the globe.

- Credit-rating agencies such as S&P or Fitch and Moody's, which carried out the credit assessments of the different tranches for the MBS units, had an incentive to give AAA ratings. Like the cat that gets the cream, if they rate a large fraction of the portfolio AAA, they receive fat commissions and additional business. However, if they give a lower rating, the trustee will turn to a different agency that will give them the desired AAA rating. Therefore, whether credit quality was high or not, the agencies gave the desired AAA stamp of approval. On the eve of the crisis, 50% of the rating companies' income came from MBS ratings.

- The investors purchasing the MBS units know that they are purchasing assets with a perfect credit rating, producing a yield that is higher than US government bonds or their European equivalent. These investors are the largest institutional investors in the world, among them the government of China, insurance companies, pension funds or trust funds from all over the world. What the investors do not know is the level of risk of the original assets — that is, the level of risk of the mortgages. Still, these investors know that there is no free lunch in financial markets: if a AAA MBS pays a higher yield than a US government bond, there must be an additional risk factor to justify it.

- Since mortgages to subprime borrowers were relatively new and there was no significant historical information about the level of risk of their mortgage derivatives, the risk assessment was carried out using mathematical models based on various assumptions. Only a few financial engineers understood what the input and output from these models actually meant. Managers, however, used those obscure outputs to justify additional business and additional risk taking.

- Overall, the cheap money from Greenspan's economy was aggressively marketed by other entities within the financial system, primarily a sector known as 'home equity loans'. These loans were given to anyone who could demonstrate having equity against their home. In other words, these are the 20% of the property value that the mortgage bank demanded against the 80% mortgage it granted to a household. In this way the commercial bank in which the household's checking account was managed supplemented the basket of loans given against that property to the sum of 100% or higher. Thus, the commercial banks were also exposed to risks resulting from the housing market.

An important outcome of the changes in the securitization process for subprime borrowers was opacity: MBS buyers were unable to assess the risks involved with holding the specific trench they bought, and therefore the real level of risk was not fully expressed in the prices of the mortgage derivatives. As mentioned in Chapter 2, financial assets should pay higher yields to their holders the riskier they are. In this case, the AAA MBSs indeed paid higher returns, suggesting that investors recognized that these derivatives were not as safe as US government bonds, but at least toward 2007 this gap should have been even higher.

Almost all of the participants in this process were under *moral hazard*. Many had an incentive to expose themselves to higher risks because they rolled these risks over to someone else in the system. The problem was that a significant portion of those risks eventually funneled into one huge insurer, AIG Financial Products. The role of AIG in the crisis will be expanded upon later, but ultimately some of its managers had no knowledge and no desire to know just how much risk the company was undertaking. In this fog of ignorance, the risk was concealed and business appeared cheerful, so long as house prices continued to rise.

12.6 The Role of Hybrid Loans

The mechanism that links rising housing prices and subprime borrowers lies in the special structure of the mortgages created for them. The subprime loans have different structures to the standard residential loans in order to meet the special needs of this segment of the population. Regular loans have either fixed interest or variable interest for 30 years. While many different loans were tailored to meet the needs of subprime borrowers, the two most popular ones will be focused on here.

The majority of subprime loans are a combination of the abovementioned two types of standard loans — they consist of loans at a fixed, relatively low, interest rate for two or three years, and variable — and much higher — variable interest for the remaining 28 or 27 years of the loan, respectively. This is why they are referred to as 'hybrid loans'. For example, in 2006 it was possible to receive fixed interest of about 8.64% for two years on a 2/28 (two years fixed rate + 28 years variable rate) loan, and at the end of the two years the rate went up to LIBOR + 6.22%. The LIBOR rate at that time was 5.4%, so that the variable interest rate started at 11.62% and varied as the LIBOR rate changed semiannually. A household that thinks it can meet its mortgage payments when interest rates are low might face difficulties when interest rates increase. Clearly, this is merely a generalized description while the particular loan agreement consisted of various different terms.

One of the important conditions of hybrid loans was a high exit fee before the end of the fixed-rate term (the first two or three years of the loan). From the household's perspective, the structure of the subprime loans created an incentive to take the cheap teaser-interest rate loans and to refinance (recycle) them at the end of the first two or three years. This would enable them to avoid sharp increases in the interest. And so, once two or three years had passed from the date the mortgage was received, many subprime borrowers approached their mortgage bank asking to have the loan rolled over, but often their equity was not sufficiently high (remember, many took home equity loans and by 2005/2007 mortgage banks subtracted those loans from the household's total equity). When increasing numbers of homeowners that found themselves declined for refinancing could not pay the higher monthly payments, they were forced to sell or abandon their homes, and the bubble started to deflate.

12.7 The Crash Unfolds

In April 2006, statistical reports started indicating that real estate prices in Florida had stopped increasing, followed by California, and then joined by other states as time went on. Consider what happens in a neighborhood where a particular household is unable to meet its mortgage repayments: The US law permits the bank to seize the property if the borrower has not paid a number of mortgage payments. Now assume that the bank has seized one property in one neighborhood, and wants to sell it. Sale of the property by the bank is different from sale by the homeowner because the bank will reduce the price by a considerable percentage, say 10%. Neighbors living near the property (some of them may have also taken out a mortgage of 80% to 100% of the value of the property) understand that the value of their home cannot be higher than the value of the home for sale by the bank. Whether they are 'above the water' or 'below the water', that is, whether the value of their property is higher than the value of the mortgage or below it, the neighbors will also prefer to sell their property immediately before market prices continue to decline. These decisions lead to an increase in the supply of homes, and therefore house prices throughout the entire neighborhood start to fall.

When the fall in prices brings the value of many properties in the neighborhood down below the value of the loan, an increasing number of tenants stop paying the mortgage (after all, the property is worth less than the mortgage). Mortgage banks are now forced to sell many more homes, but the increasing pressure to sell implies more painful concessions over the price and so the fall in prices not only continues, it is even accelerated. A sense of panic takes hold among both mortgagors and banks.

Because this process occurs at the same time in many towns and many states, all those involved in the process start bearing significant losses. At some point, banks stop offering foreclosed assets for sale first because they know there are no buyers around, and because they do not want to push prices even lower. While, initially, banks forced tenants out if mortgage payments were not made fully or timely, this turned out to be a losing strategy because empty houses were easily robbed and deteriorated physically. Moreover, banks had to write those houses off their balance sheets or acknowledge a significant loss of value that further jeopardized their financial stability. As a result, many banks allowed tenants to stay. As of the end of 2011, around 35% of people with mortgages in the United States lived in homes whose value was lower than the value of the mortgage.

12.8 Should the Government Have Stepped In?

To conceive the magnitude of the impact of falling house prices consider these two numbers: In December 2007, Fannie and Freddie together backed around $6 trillion of debt obligations. At the same time, their joint equity capital totaled $83.2 billion. This may sound a lot, but $83.2 billion is *less than 1.5% of $6 trillion*. The meaning is that it would take merely a loss of 1.5% of the debt obligations to wipe out the entire equity capital of the two companies, and bring them down.

If Fannie and Freddie had collapsed, that would have been enough to cause the collapse of other financial giants not only in the US, but also on a global scale. Now, consider the money multiplier of commercial banks. If commercial banks collapse it leads to the evaporation of credit and therefore to the bankruptcy of many real-economy businesses, which in turn increases unemployment and is likely to result in recession. The collapse of pension funds would doom many pensioners to an impoverished old age. The collapse of insurance companies would paralyze business activities, because most businesses are not permitted to operate without insurance. Without insurance, planes would not take off, ships would not set sail and factories would not open their gates.

One may argue that financial institutions that adopted ill practices should have been left to their own fortune and collapse. This would have mitigated the moral hazard problem. But apparently, decision makers thought that the message could be delivered at a significantly lower public cost. The US administration under President George W. Bush, together with the Fed (chaired since 1/2006 by Prof. Ben Bernanke) and regulators concluded that the outcome of letting those financial giants fall was far too painful to the public and the rest of the economy.

The government decided to step in and act as a lender of last resort. To that end the Bush administration established a few rescue programs, the biggest being a $700 billion program named TARP (Troubled Assets Relief Program). Its primary mandate was to purchase with taxpayer money those MBSs and other credit derivatives that were later coined 'toxic' as their true level of risk was then unknown. The sequence of events leading to that decision will be discussed in Chapter 13, but those interested in further detail may want to listen to an interesting podcast at EconTalk[3] with Neil Barofsky, author of *Bailout* and the former Special Inspector General for the TARP program. In an interview with Prof. Russell Roberts, Barofsky describes the decision-making processes and ill incentives, and offers an insider's reservations on the way the TARP program was formed and executed. Among other reservations, Barofsky criticizes the decision to give away incredible amounts without creating incentives for the receiving financial institutions to roll over the government money to their clients in order to ease the widespread credit crunch. Moreover, in spite of the harsh criticism on credit rating agencies, the TARP program effectively granted them further roles in assessing the quality of toxic assets. Above all, the decision-making process in formulating TARP, so argue both Barofsky and Roberts, was biased in favor of the financial industry by politicians, who in turn were influenced by leaders of the financial industry.

In July 2008, the government publicly declared its willingness to extend its assistance to Fannie and Freddie. In August 2008, their share prices had dropped by 90% relative to the previous year. Henry Paulson, treasury secretary in the Bush administration, and White House sources issued announcements to the press stating that the government believed in the financial soundness of Fannie Mae, with the aim of preventing panic in the

---

[3] EconTalk (http://www.econtalk.org/) is part of the Library of Economics and Liberty. Hosted by Russell Roberts, it releases weekly podcasts on a variety of economic issues. The series on the recent financial crisis is highly recommended. The talk with Mr. Barofsky is found here: http://www.econtalk.org/archives/2012/09/barofsky_on_bai.html.

entire financial system. However, press releases cannot save such a complex system. In a period of increasing panic, it was now clear that backed mortgages to subprime borrowers were a broken reed. Even though they were but a small portion of the losses caused during the crisis, their importance stemmed from the fact that they led to losses in other areas of a financial system that was in a very fragile state. The two companies were incapable of coping with the required bailout.

Henry Paulson also knew of the difficulties at Lehman Brothers, which was among the leading private trustees in the roaring MBS market, and he was not able to devote his attention to and take the time to deal with Fannie and Freddie. He therefore decided to take the two companies through a limited default process called 'conservatorship' on an immediate basis. He described his assessment of the anticipated speed of collapse of the two companies to President George W. Bush as follows: 'The first sound that the companies will hear is their heads smashing on the floor' (Paulson, 2011). On 7 September 2008 the two companies were taken into Federal Government ownership. Eight days later, on 15 September, the Lehman Brothers investment bank collapsed, an event that marked the start of the credit crisis that was a direct result of the real estate crisis. On 16 June 2010 the shares of Fannie and Freddie were delisted from the New York Stock Exchange because their price fell below $1.

12.9 Conclusions of the Inquiry Commission

The National Financial Crisis Inquiry Commission headed by Phil Angelides stated that the securitizing trustees were careless in examining the quality of the mortgages and deliberately ignored underwriting rules; they also failed to inform investors of the real risks involved in some of the mortgage derivatives. Similar and additional conclusions are reported by Crouhy *et al.* (2008).

The committee concluded that the most important regulator, the Securities and Exchange Commission (SEC), *failed in its enforcement* of its own due diligence regulations. It exempted from examination assets that should have been examined and prevented states that requested this supervision from supervising the quality and properties underlying some MBSs to be sold within their borders. Thus, the SEC failed to comply with its principal goal, that of protecting the investing public. The SEC further stated that the Federal Reserve Bank failed to foresee the risks of the housing prices bubble and refused to act toward moderating the bubble. The Federal Reserve erred when it believed that it could contain the bursting of the real estate bubble.

12.10 Were the Regulators Captured by the Industry?

Against the claims made against Greenspan and other regulators of the US financial system, one may wonder whether the Fed and the other regulators were captured. Most interesting is the Federal Reserve Bank of New York (NY Fed), which is one of 12 Federal Reserve Banks of the United States. The NY Fed is considered the most influential of the Federal Reserve Banking System, partly because it is the regulator of Wall Street. Unfortunately, however, its president is selected by and reports to a board dominated by the chief executives of some of the financial institutions the NY Fed oversees. One might argue that the Fed must work with other regulators, like the Treasury and SEC, therefore they must collaborate in a way that would safeguard overall investor protection through regulations and minimize capture. Well, that is true, but as described in the Preface, it might as well lead to regulatory capture. The table of chapter 16 shows that indeed Carpenter and Moss's (2013) 'gold standard' of regulatory capture applied here.

In 1997, Robert Rubin, then treasury secretary, and Federal Reserve chairman Alan Greenspan strongly opposed giving the Commodity Futures Trading Commission (CFTC) oversight of over-the-counter credit derivatives. Chris Cox, SEC chairman, also adopted a lax approach toward regulation. The request for regulation came from Brooksley Born, the head of the CFTC. Arthur Levitt, Jr., the former chairman of the SEC (mentioned in Chapter 6) has said in explaining Rubin's strong opposition to the regulations proposed by Born that Greenspan and Rubin were 'joined at the hip on this. They were certainly very fiercely opposed to this and persuaded me

 **Chris Cox**, chairman of the SEC adopted lax enforcement policy against financial giants. To defend his actions Cox said that the SEC 'lacked authority' to limit the massive leveraging of US financial institutions. *Time* magazine included Cox among the 25 people to blame for the financial crisis, arguing that he had plenty of power to go after big investment banks like Lehman Brothers and Merrill Lynch for better disclosure, but chose not to. Cox oversaw the dwindling SEC staff and a sharp drop in action against some traders (*Time*, 2014c).

Picture by Alamar2000 at en.wikipedia (Transferred from en.wikipedia) [Public domain], from Wikimedia Commons (accessed 2 December 2014).

that this would cause chaos' (Goodman, 2008). However, in Rubin's autobiography, he notes that *he believed derivatives could pose significant problems* and that many people who used derivatives did not fully understand the risks they were taking (Rubin, 2003). Why, then, did Rubin act against his own belief? Moreover, when Born attempted to advance increased regulation of derivatives in a way consistent with a 1994 General Accounting Office report, Rubin went public in June 1998 to denounce Born and her proposal, urging that the CFTC be stripped of its regulatory authority (Taibbi, 2010).

Michael Kirk (2009) reported in the TV series 'Frontline' that because of heavy pressure from the financial industry, primarily through lobbying, legislation was passed by the Congress prohibiting regulation of derivatives by Born's agency. On June 1, 1999 Born resigned. Later in 2009 Born, together with Sheila Bair of the FDIC, was awarded the John F. Kennedy Profiles in Courage Award, recognizing the 'political courage she demonstrated in sounding early warnings about conditions that contributed to the current global financial crisis.' According to Caroline Kennedy, the daughter of former US President John F. Kennedy, '... Brooksley Born recognized that the financial security of all Americans was being put at risk by the greed, negligence and opposition of powerful and well connected interests ... The catastrophic financial events of recent months have proved them [Born and Sheila Bair] right (Kirk, 2009).'

Additional Reading

Acharya, V., Cooley, T.F., Richardson, M. and Walter, I. (2011). *Regulating Wall Street, The Dodd–Frank Act and the New Architecture of Global Finance.* New York: John Wiley & Sons.

Barofsky, N. (2012). *Bailout: An Inside Account of How Washington Abandoned Main Street While Rescuing Wall Street.* New York: Free Press.

Bernanke, B.S. (2013). *The Federal Reserve and the Financial Crisis.* Princeton, NJ: Princeton University Press.

Financial Crisis Inquiry Commission (FCIC) (2011). *The Financial Crisis Inquiry Report, Authorized Edition: Final Report of the National Commission on the Causes of the Financial and Economic Crisis in the United States.* New York: Public Affairs.

Paulson, H.M. (2011). *On the Brink: Inside the Race to Stop the Collapse of the Global Financial System.* New York: Grand Central Publishing.

13.

Shadow Banking, the Collapse of Investment Banking and the Rescue of AIG

13.1 Introduction

Chapter 12 made it clear that although subprime mortgages were the risky assets that caused the initial losses of 2007, the collapse of the American financial system was due to a much broader failure. How then was the US financial system, which is among the most advanced systems in the world, so severely challenged, and why did its collapse echo around the globe?

13.2 The Increasing Size and Complexity of the Financial System

Let us begin by examining changes in the magnitude and complexity of the US financial system in the 30 years that preceded the crisis. If in 1978, aggregate debt in the US financial sector amounted to approximately $3 trillion, in 2007 total debt stood at $36 trillion, *doubling its ratio to gross domestic profit (GDP)*. At the end of the 1970s, financial companies consisted mainly of private *partnerships*, who essentially assumed the risks of their businesses. However, at the beginning of this century they turned into giant *public companies*, where some of the risk is shared by the public and moral hazard issues ended with effective risk transfer to the general public. In the 1970s, commercial banks did commercial banking and investment banks did investment banking, each familiar with its business environment and its' risks. Thirty years later the boundaries blurred, partly because of mergers and acquisitions, and the resulting giant financial institutions were exposed to a broad

159

variety of risks, as the complexity of financial instruments grew tremendously. Throughout this process the financial industry became more and more centralized.

The weight of the financial sector grew from 15% of GDP in 1980 to 27% on the eve of the crisis (FCIC, pp. xvi–xvii). The free-market capitalist paradigm had changed its character: It became a system that saw the financial sector grow not only in size but in political power, capturing the legal and regulatory systems. It created celebrities and new millionaires, attracting young talented graduates while the weight of the manufacturing and technology development sectors on GDP shrank gradually. The US transferred its technological innovations and manufacturing plants to Japan and China, and consumed their products beyond its own means; that is, consuming through borrowing. Furthermore, financial markets had become global and more closely connected than ever before. Technology had accelerated information flow and transaction speed. Financial instruments, which had made it possible to sell risk created a sense of no risk for the seller, but at the same time facilitated excess risk taking by the buyer.

13.3 The Shadow Banking System

The Financial Crisis Inquiry Commission (FCIC), which published its final report in 2011, enumerated four main factors that undermined stability of the financial system. The first factor was the refinement of the securitization process, described in Chapter 11. Securitization created a false appearance of safe credit ratings for extremely risky financial products. This factor was the background of the subprime crisis. The second factor was the placing of excessively high hopes on the Fed's ability to 'contain' financial bubbles and crises. The belief was that the Fed had learned how to mitigate crises and contain bubbles without causing painful damage to the real economy. The third factor was the introduction of financial products so complex and sophisticated that no one could truly evaluate their macroeconomic impact, particularly when interactions between players in the financial system were both unknown and unpredictable. All these have been discussed. This chapter will expand on the fourth and final factor, the rapid development of the 'shadow banking system'.

In order to understand what shadow banking is, it is important to clarify what sets it apart from non-shadow banking. Commercial banking and insurance, for example, which receive deposits and extend loans, operates under a spotlight, i.e., is kept under regulatory supervision. Outside the perimeters of this spotlight is shadow banking: financial institutions that are not subject to supervision, but interact with supervised institutions. The reason why some financial institutions are supervised while others are not originates with the supervisory institutions, which were established following the crisis of the 1930s. The Glass–Steagall Act separated commercial banking and investment banking: The SEC (Securities and Exchange Commission) was established in order to supervise information relayed to investors; the Federal Deposit Insurance Corporation (FDIC) was established in order to provide security to depositors and reduce their concerns over a bank run. If despite depositors' insurance, a bank run did develop, the understanding was that the government, through the Fed, would assume the role of lender of last resort, and thus prevent the supervised commercial bank from collapsing. Investment banks, which were involved in the domain of securities trading and financial intermediation were not subject to supervision nor to the restrictions imposed on commercial banks; thus they were not meant to receive assistance from the government as the lender of last resort. Since provision of assistance to commercial banks implied the use of taxpayer money, Congress demanded that commercial banks not get involved in risky financial activities. Such activities were left in the courtyard of the investment banks.

13.4 Money Market Funds and Repos

One of the important restrictions imposed on commercial banks, known as Regulation Q, set an upper limit of 6% interest that a commercial bank could pay its depositors. The goal was to prevent competition that might endanger the banks. In 1975, safe traded assets were yielding returns higher than 6%, thus investment banks applied pressure to Congress, which allowed them to establish funds for investing in highly liquid and highly secure assets. This led to the creation of one of the most important institutions of shadow banking: money market mutual funds (MMMF). In the beginning, the funds invested in short-term government bonds such as Treasury Bills. With a bit of added political pressure on Congress, checks were allowed against the MMMF accounts. By so doing, investment bank clients could gain safe returns, higher than 6%. Moreover, large financial institutions, like pension funds or insurance companies, that often end a typical business day with tens of millions of dollars in cash, had almost no protection if the cash was deposited in a commercial bank. Assume, for example, that a pension fund has $20 million to 'park' overnight. The FDIC insures only a small fraction of this amount, about $100,000, in a commercial bank, therefore the pension fund is exposed to a risk of losing $19,900,000 of its cash if the commercial bank defaults.

The risk is small but real. Because MMMFs invested in ultra-safe highly liquid assets, they offered indirect insurance to institutional investors. As a result, competition emerged between investment banking and commercial banking, and the borders between them grew fuzzy. In 2000, some $1.8 trillion were deposited in such accounts in investment banks. Prior to the collapse of September 2008, the funds were managing approximately $4 trillion, one-third of short-term funding sources for businesses (Schapiro, 2012).

The two primary types of assets in which MMMFs invested were 'commercial paper' and 'repo' (short for 'repurchase agreement') transactions. Commercial paper securities are nothing more than short-term loans, with terms of one day to nine months. The loans were granted to large and solid companies such as IBM, General Electric or Caterpillar, which were authorized to issue such securities. In time, financial institutions were also allowed to issue commercial paper. Since these companies were perceived as very stable, the investment was considered safe despite the fact that the issuing company did not provide any collateral. Instead, the company provided a line of credit from an FDIC-protected banking institution.

Note the intricacy of this situation: MMMFs and commercial paper are not eligible for assistance in the event of insolvency because they reside in the domain of shadow banking; however, the bank extending the line of credit is regulated and therefore eligible for assistance. In the event of a failure among one of the three players, the incentive mechanism amongst the three is to kick the problem over to the commercial bank. As a result, the taxpayer's money assists in extricating shadow banking from possible default. A precedent did indeed occur in 1970 when the Penn Central Transportation Company went bankrupt. The sense of danger froze all other transactions in the market, which created a credit squeeze among the largest firms in the US economy. The Fed extended assistance to commercial banks and thereby saved the shadow market of commercial paper. The message received by players in the shadow banking sector generated the familiar problem, none other than *moral hazard*. Why? Because despite not being formally insured by FDIC, non-formal insurance did exist for shadow banking. Recall that the moral hazard problem arises when a party that purchases insurance, or knows that it will be made whole in the event of damage, has an incentive to take more risk. Knowing that the Fed would save them with taxpayer money, MMMFs had an incentive to take more risk and make a profit until the damage occured.

The repo market is similar in certain aspects to the commercial paper market. However, in the repo market, security traders in need of cash sell low-risk bonds to banks, with the promise to repurchase them back within a few days at a slightly higher price. Before the crisis, such assets consisted of assorted debt derivatives including mortgaged-based derivatives (Garbade, 2006). Just to get an indication of the magnitude: Before the crisis of 2008, the extent of daily trading in the repo market totaled $2.8 trillion (FCIC, p. 284).

An important characteristic of these two financial instruments of shadow banking is rapid debt rollover. Since the loans have terms of several days or months, many companies paid out loans by issuing new similar loans, also with durations of several days or months. Any problem with debt rollover was bound to affect the ability of the large companies in the US economy to conduct their routine business operations.

13.5 Unclear Boundaries

As shadow banking continued to develop it competed against the regulated commercial banking while biting away at its market share, profitability and growth. As a result, the regulated banking industry applied heavy pressure on Congress to allow it to expand its fields of operation, obviously toward the unregulated activities of investment banking. This pressure won the support of Alan Greenspan, Chairman of the Fed, and steadily eroded the laws created in the 1930s (as described in Chapter 12). Thus, financial institutions outside the purview of supervision shifted their business toward commercial banking; however, not too close, in order to avoid getting under the wings of supervision. At the same time, commercial banks were approaching the other side of the fence — they gradually drew closer to investment banking activity, although making sure they did not step out of the supervision perimeter in order not to lose the Fed's protection. In 1999, the separation between investment banking and commercial banking was removed altogether, thus leading to the creation of giant corporations, like Citigroup and J.P. Morgan-Chase, that included investment banking, commercial banking, insurance and more.

13.6 Bear Stearns and BNP Paribas

This is the setting against which investment bank Bear Stearns descended into an ever-worsening situation during 2007 and at the beginning of 2008. Losses accumulated due to the inability of subprime borrowers to meet their payments in the face of falling real estate prices. The bank received margin calls from its commercial partners and its equity eroded rapidly; the rumor spread and its customers began running to withdraw their investments and deposits. Repo traders avoided lending the bank monies and on 16 March 2008 the bank was acquired by JP Morgan with the assistance of the Fed.

The FCIC concluded that the bank collapsed for the following reasons: it held numerous mortgaged-based derivatives; it depended on the rapid rollover of short-term loans; it utilized loans in a radical manner, i.e., with high leveraging; it had an incentives system in place for its employees and managers that encouraged taking excessive short-term risks. All this is supposed to work nicely when skies are clear and the market is rising; however, it is a recipe for disaster when skies darken and the market falls.

The losses from mortgage derivatives impacted financial institutions outside the US as well. One of the banks affected was the French giant BNP Paribas. Three of its investment funds, which managed some $2.2 billion in good quality (rated AA and better) subprime derivatives, lost 20% of their value within two weeks. On 9 August 2008, the bank announced it was abstaining from calculating the value of those three funds because illiquidity in the US securitization market prevented the calculation of credit derivatives.

This event was viewed by many as the turning point in the evolution of the credit crisis because it revealed the naked truth — holders of subprime derivatives *did not know* just how risky the assets they held were. The panic began to spread. This illiquidity was also expressed by the money market funds, which were invested in subprime mortgage derivatives.[1] With its unknown risk level, MMMFs were not willing to invest in those assets and thus totally stopped the commercial paper and repo market from being able to roll over short-term debt. The decreasing value of mortgage derivatives also caused several MMMFs to 'break the buck' and return the money to depositors. The funds, whose investment units were always valued at one dollar each, found themselves with a diminishing total asset value, therefore they were only able to return less than one full dollar to investors for each dollar invested. According to regulatory rules, if the value of a fund's investment unit goes lower than 99.5 cents for each dollar, it is considered to be 'breaking the buck'.[2]

---

[1] In fact, they invested a portion of their accumulated sums in complex products (SIVs — structured investment vehicles), sorts of financial asset packages that included, among others, mortgage derivatives.

[2] One example is the fund of the giant General Electric Company, which managed the pension fund of company employees. The company had losses of some $200 million out of a portfolio of $5 billion; thus, when it 'broke the buck' the fund was closed and the company returned 99.5 cents on the dollar to its employees.

Once the MMMF halted, the entire shadow banking system halted as well, which in turn halted the regulated commercial banks, because it wasn't clear what was the exposure of trading partners to those 'toxic assets'. The implication of a halt in the banking system is lack of financing, not only for financial companies but also for industrial firms, and the beginning of a credit crunch in the real economy. Fearing further deterioration, the central banks of the US and Europe announced that immediately upon the next day, 10 August 2008, they would supply banks with almost unlimited funds. The task was to reassure depositors all over the world that their deposits were safe; otherwise, the central banks dreaded, there would be a worldwide bank run.

13.7 Lehman Brothers and Merrill Lynch

Following the collapse of Bear Stearns, many investors were convinced that the collapse of the investment house nearest in size to it, Lehman Brothers, was only a matter of time. That opinion took root in the US Fed, the SEC and the Department of the Treasury. As of the end of March 2008, Lehman Brothers held approximately $8 billion in commercial securities, $197 billion in repos and some 900,000 contracts in derivative assets with counterparties in the US and abroad. Regulators closely followed the bank's situation as they continuously examined its liquidity, i.e., its ability to handle a bank run, and its equity capital, which determines the bank's value. If MMMFs, hedge funds and other investment banks believed that the bank was on the verge of bankruptcy, they would not lend to it and it would indeed collapse. As fears grew, more and more of Lehman's commercial partners demanded higher guarantees, supplied it with shorter-term loans, and demanded higher interest rates for the loans that they did grant the shaky bank. The assessment in the market was that saving Lehman Brothers would cost the taxpayer double what it cost to assist Bear Stearns. Senior officials in the Fed were determined to send a message to the shadow banking sector, or the prevailing moral hazard problem would be intensified. They wanted uninsured institutions (stakeholders in those firms) to pay the price, rather than roll it over to the general public. In other words, the Fed wanted to convey a message that it would not use taxpayer money to save shadow banking. On 14 September 2008, Lehman Brothers, among the leaders of the US financial industry for 157 years, filed for bankruptcy.

At the same time, the managers of Merrill Lynch deduced that if Lehman collapsed their bank would collapse immediately after it; thus, they turned to Bank of America with a proposal for it to acquire the company.

The deal was devised on the same week of Lehman's collapse. By the end of September, the two remaining investment banks, Morgan Stanley and Goldman Sachs, asked to be brought under the wings of regulation and thus became bank holding companies. As a result they gained lender of last resort protection and, in fact, closed a chapter in the long history of Wall Street investment banks.

Should these giants be allowed to fail as well? The answer is overly complex because one must account for the fact that on the go, decision makers were convinced that if they did not save those 'too big to fail' institutions, their collapse would take under not only the US financial system, but that of many other countries as well. Was the decision-making process transparent? No, it was not. Decisions were made among a handful of people who led the administrative and regulatory systems, like the Fed, the SEC and the Treasury, together with industry leaders. The involvement of industry leaders was probably the most problematic because they were in a severe conflict of interest and had very strong political and professional leverage. The remaining question — What would constitute a better resolution mechanism for such instances? — is addressed in the next section.

13.8 AIG

Lehman's collapse immediately raised fears concerning the stability of the world's largest insurance company, American International Group (AIG). As of 2004 the company had assets worth $850 billion, 116,000 employees in 130 countries, and 223 subsidiaries. Yet fears over AIG's collapse did not stem from the company's classical insurance activities (that were regulated) but from the activity of its subsidiary, AIG Financial Products (AIGFP), in insuring credit derivatives.[3] Since the parent company had a perfect AAA credit rating, the subsidiary made use of it in order to execute commercial activities in derivative assets, until the volume of activity reached $2.7 trillion. Among other things, the company sold insurance against mortgage derivatives and other debt derivatives through a vehicle called CDS (credit default swap). Without going into detail, this financial instrument is designed to compensate holders of debt derivatives should losses be incurred. The first CDS that

---

[3] AIGFP is a subsidiary of AIG that was founded in January 1987 and is headquartered in Fairfield, CT. The purpose of the subsidiary was for AIG to be able to branch off its core business, insurance, and to generate revenue from complex derivate transactions. By 1990 it had opened offices in Paris, Tokyo and London.

AIGFP executed was in 1998 when JP Morgan approached AIGFP and asked them to insure corporate debt that the company had accumulated. After running some models, AIG believed that the chance of AIG ever having to pay out would be 0.15%. After internal discussions, AIGFP decided it would insure the debt for a handsome fee. With that transaction, CDSs were born. While seemingly this is the selling of insurance, unlike a regular insurance contract issued by an insurance company, here the insuring company is not required to place guarantees against the CDS that it issues because it is not under supervision. This insurance is provided in the shadow banking system.

When looking at the emergence of AIGFP, the deals it did with JP Morgan and others were low risk. In the beginning, AIGFP was insuring banks that had given loans out to IBM and General Electric. At the turn of the decade, banks started adding other forms of debt to the packages. These included car and student loans, credit card debt and prime mortgages. All of these would now be included in the debt pile to be insured by AIGFP. The whole idea of credit default swaps was relatively new and many of the parties involved were not well informed. One trader from AIGFP mentioned that although the type of debt being insured changed, the way both parties viewed the transactions did not. To both parties, debt was debt, and neither analyzed how types of debt differ and whether the risks are different.

This type of insurance was sold by AIGFP to large banks in Europe and the US, mainly to Goldman Sachs. Over time, deals between Goldman Sachs and AIGFP were rampant. Each side believed they were taking advantage of the other— AIGFP kept running models on the chance they would never have to pay out, and began to realize that it was 'virtually impossible', so that insuring these piles of debt was practically free money. They figured that even if the people that owed Goldman Sachs or JP Morgan defaulted on their obligations, the chance that AIGFP would have to pay was still minimal because at that point the financial system would be 'near collapse' and it's obligation to cover the debt they insured would be a 'non-issue' in a rock-bottom economy.

The culture in AIGFP changed when a man named Joseph Cassano took over operations in 2000. Cassano, by all accounts, did not have a head for numbers and certainly not the background needed to assess the correct amount of risk that was involved in these transactions. He was an operations man and was promoted from being the chief operating officer (COO) to the chief executive officer (CEO) (Lewis, 2009; Voreacos and Smith, 2008).

> **Joe Cassano**, the son of a Brooklyn cop, was known as a rough character and ran AIGFP as a 'dictator'. Traders later testified that the fear level at AIGFP was so high, that no matter what the stakes, you had to keep your responsibility to continue to bring in deals (*Time*, 2014d).

Among the 400 people that worked at AIGFP, no one dared to confront Cassano on how he managed the group. Those that did usually ended up leaving. Cassano's greed and narrow focus on generating revenue led to his reputation in AIGFP as having a rubber approvals stamp ready to go. Under his tenure at AIGFP, any deal that led to a commission was approved (Dennis and O'Harrow, 2009). The amount of money being made by AIGFP employees was astronomical. A typical lawyer received a $25 million bonus one year. Cassano himself made $300 million from 2000 to 2008. After he 'stepped down' he received a monthly consulting fee of $1 million.[4]

The banks bought the CDS insurance from AIGFP enthusiastically since it neutralized the credit risks to which the banks were exposed. This implies that from the perspective of the CDS buyer, its exposure to credit risk, i.e., the risk that its creditors will not pay a loan, was zero. Having zero risk in the balance sheet implies that the bank can issue more risky loans and insure them too. As long as the transactions are profitable, there is no incentive to stop issuing more loans and insuring them. The banks that insured their loans with CDS were required to place much less of their own capital against credit, only 1.6% instead of 8%. And so, if in 2005 AIGFP wrote $107 billion of CDS contracts, in 2007 that sum reached $379 billion. In addition, AIGFP sold insurance against the fall in value of commercial paper[5] by committing itself to buy the security if no other party wanted to buy it. The total insurance sold by the company against credit risks reached a record of more than half a trillion dollars ($533 billion) in 2007.

Following months of continued and growing losses, AIG was starved for cash on the eve of Lehman's collapse. Although it had assets worth more than a trillion dollars, they could not be used because they represented guarantees against regulated insurance activity. On Friday 9 September 2008, AIG needed to roll over short-term debt beyond its capabilities: It had to roll over commercial paper worth $1.4 billion, but money market investment funds were not willing to lend to the company, because of their

---

[4] Cassano's retirement agreement via House Committee on Oversight and Government Reform.
[5] A product called an AIG Put option.

suspicion that AIG was in trouble. Lenders in the repo market who gave cash to AIG against $9.7 billion of debt contracts feared its situation and the quality of assets given, which in part were mortgage derivatives. To these were added CDS insurance payments in the amount of $4.5 billion, which needed to be paid within a week, and it seemed that further losses should be expected.[6] Above all, the credit-rating companies threatened to downgrade the company's perfect credit rating, a move that would necessitate the infusion of another $10 billion as guarantees, plus another $4 billion for purchasing commercial paper. To sum up, in the coming two or three weeks AIG was expected to pay out more than $30 billion, while it only had $9 billion in cash.

During the weekend of 10–11 September feverish consultations took place among senior officials in the economic system in an attempt to decide whether or not to rescue AIG. On Monday 12 September, following Lehman's bankruptcy announcement, the Fed decided to try to persuade JP Morgan and Goldman Sachs to rescue the company. They refused, however, claiming they had to rescue their own companies first. On Tuesday, the Fed decided to lend AIG $85 billion in order to meet its urgent financing needs. The loan's guarantee would consist of all of the parent company's assets and its shadow banking subsidiaries along with all stock of its supervised insurance companies. The rationale for rescuing AIG and not Lehman was that the collapse of AIG would lead to high public losses, an additional jolt to an already fragile financial system, and impact to the economy. AIG was considered to be 'too big to fail', that is, too important for the stability of the US, and perhaps the world's financial stability, for the administration to allow it to fail. The problem was that by supporting it, the government exacerbated the moral hazard problem in shadow banking. Chapter 14 will examine the global implications of the crisis and the moves taken in order to correct the impairment of the financial system.

Additional Reading

Dennis, B. and O'Harrow, Jr., R. (2009). '1998–2005: AIG & the Anatomy of the Crash,' *The Washington Post*, 5 January.

Financial Crisis Inquiry Commission (FCIC) (2011). *The Financial Crisis Inquiry Report, Authorized Edition: Final Report of the National Commission on the Causes of the Financial and Economic Crisis in the United States*. New York: PublicAffairs.

---

[6] The losses caused due to CDS insurance reached $23.4 billion out of which the company paid out only $18.9 billion; thus as of 12 September, it had to pay more than $4.5 billion.

Garbade, K.D. (2006). 'The Evolution of Repo Contracting Conventions in the 1980s,' *FRBNY Economic Policy Review*, 12, 1. Available at: http://www.newyork-fed.org/research/epr/06v12n1/0605garb.html (accessed 14 October 2014).

Lewis, M. (2009). 'The Man Who Crashed the World,' *Vanity Fair*, August.

Voreacos, D. and Blair Smith, E. (2008). 'Statements on AIG Probed by Prosecutors, People Say.' 26 November, Bloomberg. Available at: http://www.bloomberg.com/apps/news?pid=newsarchive&sid=a6m_BOe9Ftk4 (accessed 14 October 2014).

14.

New Regulations

14.1 The US Financial Crisis Inquiry Commission

In January 2011, the report of the US Financial Crisis Inquiry Commission (FCIC) headed by Phil Angelides was published. The Commission investigated the crisis, including how and why things developed. In its opening remarks, the Commission determined that the crisis did not stem from an unforeseeable external shock — an aberrant event that people like Nassim Taleb (2010) compare to the appearance of a black swan. To the contrary, maintained the Commission. The crisis was the result of certain actions and failures. The heads of the financial system ignored the overt warning signs and should have alerted the FCIC to the continually rising levels of risk in the system they managed. This wasn't merely a lapse, as Wall Street and Washington officials would like to claim, but a major error. In addition, the Commission determined that the failure primarily rested with the supervisory system; the regulators failed to curb the greed of many leaders in the financial industry. The Commission determined that those leaders exploited their political power, among other things with the assistance of contributions to both parties, in order to reduce regulation while assuming short-term risks without weighing the long-term considerations. The Commission highlighted ill codes conduct in numerous financial institutions, their risk management methods and their offhand attitude to credit derivatives. For example, in reference to the statement of the Citigroup chief executive officer (CEO) to the Commission — that he invested only a fraction of 1% of his time managing those assets — the Commission concluded that in this case, 'too big to fail' meant 'too big to manage', hinting at the need to dismantle such large corporations.

14.2 The Dodd–Frank Act

The legal response was enacted by a pair of legislators, Christopher Dodd and Barney Frank, who passed a law that was signed by President Obama in July 2010. The reform they suggested must be understood in light of the relaxed, captured regulation, which repealed the Glass–Steagall Act, and was blamed on facilitating the evolution of shadow banking. Moreover, the reform had to account for the great complexity of modern financial markets and the instruments traded in them.

This is a brief review of the highlights of the reform that followed from Dodd–Frank Act:

- First, regulatory supervision must be formulated and applied towards 'systemic risk', i.e., risk that threatens the financial system's stability. For this purpose, a Systemic Risk Council must be established and have the power to determine that a specific financial institution is important for systemic stability and therefore be subject to supervision. Moreover, that institution will be subject to dismantling should the need arise, even if it is not a banking institution. Additionally, a unit will be established in the Department of the Treasury to gather and analyze information in order to identify anticipated crises.
- Second, an end will be put to the concept known as 'too big to fail'. The law requires that there be orderly procedures for dissolving giant companies that threaten the system's stability. The law prohibits the use of taxpayer money in executing the dissolution. Instead, the management of the dissolved body is fired while shareholders and debtors will bear the cost of the dissolution. If costs exceed the value of shares and debt, taxes will be imposed on similar large companies that survive in order to finance the dissolution. The implication of the law is increased cost in managing giant corporations. Thus, practically speaking, a tax is imposed on the corporation's complexity, an outcome that would be expected to help reduce systemic risk.
- Third, expanded responsibility and authority of the Federal Reserve. The Fed was granted responsibility for all institutions defined as important from a systemic perspective, as well as having the role of reviewing financial stability. Restrictions over Federal assistance to specific companies were also imposed.
- Fourth, the law resurrects in a sense the Glass–Steagall Act in what is known as the Volcker Rule, named after Greenspan's predecessor Paul Volcker It restricts bank holding companies from investing in particular assets, such as hedge funds, and prohibits them from assisting those funds

should they run into trouble. By doing so, the law directs high-risk investing to those funds and averts the problem of moral hazard, to some extent.

- The fifth point refers to expanding the regulatory scope such that it includes numerous derivative assets that do not serve for commercial hedging. Let us point out that although most derivative assets are meant for hedging against business risks (thus serving an important need of farmers, importers, exporters, manufacturers and others) they can also be used for risk taking and speculation. It is upon the last uses that the law imposes mandatory supervision.

Beyond the above, the law imposes control and various accountabilities on credit-rating firms, hedge funds, mortgage producers, securitization dealers, money market funds and other entities. Finally, the law requires banks and non-banking institutions to elaborate the terms and conditions on various financial products to the public via the Bureau of Consumer Financial Protection (BCFP). This is perhaps the law's most popular step even if it is less important for preventing crises.

14.3 Criticism and Alternatives

Even before the ink was dry on the Dodd–Frank Act, academics analyzed it and concluded that the US government still provides excessive protection to large corporations, mainly those in the shadow domain. The reason is that it does not impose a fine on damages they cause upon their fall to other firms in the economy. If those damages would also be imposed on large corporations in the form of a tax, the remaining moral hazard problem would reduce even further. Academics attack the law particularly because it imposes fines on surviving companies, even if they played no part in the damage created by other companies that collapsed.

The Act does not refer to another problem, which is the incentive mechanism shareholders of financial companies have when exposing their firm to high risk. Apparently, shareholders are supposed to monitor risks to which managers expose the company when seeking high profits. However, it is possible that the shareholders themselves have no incentive to mitigate long-term risk. This is because, as in the case of Bear Stearns and Lehman Brothers, they have invested only a little of their equity in the company and rely on the government to act as the lender of last resort. Moral hazard — again.

Given the deficient reform proposed by the Dodd–Frank Act, one might conclude that a comprehensive solution is either highly complex or nonexistent. However, a rather simple and effective alternative has been proposed. In an influential book, Anat Admati and Martin Hellwig (2013a) argue that if financial institutions held more equity, hence putting at highest risk a substantial bank's shareholders capital, much of the incentives mechanisms would have changed. As seen from Chapter 2, equity shares are more risky than bonds since shareholders receive the *residual pay*, both as long as the firm (here, the bank) is operating normally, and upon bankruptcy, when the firm assets are sold to repay claim holders. Because they are first to lose their investment, bank shareholders would be more cautious the greater the amount they jeopardize by investing in their bank. This notion, also known as having 'skin in the game', is a fundamental one in economics and taught in every business school. Why did this fundamental concept escape the financial industry while it is effective in every other industry? The short answer is the weakness of politicians and regulators when facing donations, future employment opportunities and other rewards that the financial industry offers.[1]

In their book, Admati and Hellwig debunk, one by one, various arguments that executives in the financial industry raise against their proposal. They do so by showing that some of the arguments have no economic content, and some are nothing but lies aimed to frighten policymakers. Surely, leaders of the financial industry have an incentive to oppose reforms aimed to restrict their ability to gain from excess risk and roll over the risk to taxpayers. This is conflict of interest in action. Unfortunately, the action takes place by paying lobbying firms to pay, not necessarily in cash, politicians and regulators that should have reshuffled the financial industry after the crisis. Lessig (2011) proposes that in its current corrupt form, the US financial industry is the most severe problem facing the US as a nation, not only as an economic and political global leader.

Perhaps more disappointing is the finding that tough lobbying on politicians and regulators, primarily in Washington, DC, and a silent academic environment reduced the impact of post-crisis reforms. Why more disappointing? Because one may expect the academic community to honor its contract with society and use the protection it receives in the form of 'tenure' to express its criticism more clearly. Why primarily in Washington, DC? Because if Washington legislators had forced US financial institutions to bear the costs of their excess risk taking, for example by financing banks

---

[1] For a longer answer and description of the heavy toll that a fragile and corrupt financial industry imposes on the US economy, the reader may want to read Lessig (2011).

with more equity, it is rather probable that Western European legislators would follow suit, one way or another.

The fact that legislators, regulators and academics were unable to leverage the crisis toward substantial reform after the most disastrous financial crisis since the 1930s implies that the corrupt financial industry won. Nevertheless, this might prove to be a Pyrrhic victory since the US, and many Western European financial systems, are still highly fragile and will pay a heavy toll when the next crisis arrives. Lacking public support to save financial institutions, governments and central banks will be able to offer limited support to the financial industry when they would need it most. As seen throughout the book, in all financial crises, a healthy financial sector is vital to real-sector recovery. In that sense, the legislation post the 2008–2010 financial crisis has been a waste of a rare opportunity for reforms. One may pray that the next crisis, that will surely come, would hit *after* the world economy fully recovers from the 2008–2010 crisis, merely because its impact on a fragile world economy would find the global financial system with poor ability to avoid a severe impact on the real economy.

14.4 Executive Pay

Another issue addressed by the Dodd–Frank Act is the exceptional salary levels and bonuses paid out to managers and employees in the financial industry. To illustrate, the total salary paid to senior managers of 25 hedge funds in 2008 exceeded the total salary paid to the senior managers of all 500 companies in the Standard & Poor's (S&P) 500 (Roubini and Mihm, 2010, p. 175). Most economists would agree that management remuneration amounts were not a direct factor in the crisis, but some argue that the method of remuneration generated an incentive for high risk-taking among investment managers. For the most part, traders and managers receive high bonuses in the same year in which they produce profits. Yet, it seems more reasonable and fair to design mechanisms for depositing those bonuses in trust for several years and offset 'negative bonuses' against them insofar as losses from the same trader or manager indeed accumulate. Moreover, it should be possible to delay bonus payments for several years in order to make sure that profit has not been produced because of business activities that turn out to be profitable in the short term, but loss-making in the medium or long term.

The Dodd–Frank Act stipulates: that shareholders can express their opinion on the level of remuneration; that remuneration committees are established with external directors only; that companies will be required to publicize the linkage between remuneration and performance;

that remuneration be under regulatory supervision; and the recall of past mistaken payments. All these do not constitute a substantial change relative to the previous prevailing approach in the US because what they do is impose 'market discipline'; in other words, relying on the fact that shareholders and investors will punish companies that deviate from the rules by not investing in their stocks. Notwithstanding, the law grants directors the option to act insofar as they find fit (Carpenter *et al.*, 2011).

14.5 About Ideology

These recommendations of increased regulation tie in with a question that arose after the crisis and during the wave of social protests in the US, Europe and other countries. Is the free market system to be blame for causing the crisis and if so, what can be done to avoid additional crises?

Blaming the free-market system is easy, but wrong. While radical left elements accused the free-market system of precipitating the crisis, the real culprits are bad incentive schemes, improper regulation, and yes, some corrupt people and systems. The alternative to free-market economy, a centralized market regime, proved to be a barrier to economic growth. The highly inefficient central planning of the Soviet Union failed and resulted in its breakup. Observing the fortunes of the communist Soviet Union, Chinese leaders are transforming gradually their economic system into a controlled market economy. This transition has resulted thus far in unprecedented growth rates. While Western economies experienced crises in the course of growth, centralized market systems did not generate growth and ended up in deep ideological and economic rift. Assuming that a market economy is the least inferior method, the relevant question is: To what extent should the economy be free, and in which areas should the state intervene? The Scandinavian model is one of a highly involved government, but history proves that is not immune from such crises. Such a question of ideology, politics and political economics is certainly beyond the scope of this book.

Additional Reading

Acharya, V., Cooley, T.F., Richardson, M. and Walter, I. (eds.) (2011). *Regulating Wall Street, The Dodd–Frank Act and the New Architecture of Global Finance*. New York: John Wiley & Sons.

Financial Crisis Inquiry Commission (FCIC) (2011). *The Financial Crisis Inquiry Report, Authorized Edition: Final Report of the National Commission on the Causes of the Financial and Economic Crisis in the United States*. New York: PublicAffairs.

Garbade, K.D. (2006). 'The Evolution of Repo Contracting Conventions in the 1980s,' *FRBNY Economic Policy Review*, 12, 1. Available at: http://www.newyork-fed.org/research/epr/06v12n1/0605garb.html (accessed 14 October 2014).

Lessig, L. (2011). *Republic, Lost: How Money Corrupts Congress — and a Plan to Stop It.* New York: Twelve.

Roubini, N. and Mihm, S. (2010). *Crisis Economics: A Crash Course in the Future of Finance.* New York: Penguin.

Schapiro, M.L. (2012). 'Testimony on "Perspectives on Money Market Mutual Fund Reforms,'" Before the Committee on Banking, Housing, and Urban Affairs of the United States Senate, 21 June. Available at: http://www.sec.gov/news/testimony/2012/ts062112mls.htm (accessed: 16 December 2012).

15.

Global Implications of the Credit Crisis

15.1 Introduction

In a testimony before the Financial Crisis Inquiry Commission (FCIC), the chairman of the Federal Reserve, Professor Ben Bernanke, said that the crisis of September and October 2008 was the largest financial crisis in world history, including the Great Depression. During those months, 12 out of the 13 largest financial firms in the world were on the verge of collapse within a couple of weeks. Had they gone bankrupt, their global business partners and clients would have suffered severe losses and the fear was that the broader impact would result in a global financial meltdown. How exactly does such a chain of events spreads globally? Who is more at risk, and who should be saved — the individual, innocent depositors; commercial banks; investment banks; insurance companies; pension funds? If countries and foreign institutions are prone to collapse, should a rescue plan financed by the US taxpayer save them? This chapter will describe along general lines the reasons and ways the US crisis spread across the globe, who was affected by the crisis, and how the rescue plan worked. Chapter 16 will discuss some moral implications of financial crises.

15.2 Global Linkages

Lehman Brothers' collapse erased billions of dollars of commercial paper held by other institutions. Money market mutual funds (MMMFs) that held much of this debt suffered losses and some funds collapsed. A case in point is the Reserve Primary Fund that held $785 million, and did not liquidate it until it was too late. On 16 September 2008, only one day after Lehman collapsed, this fund 'broke the buck' as it could not pay investors $1 for their shares. This event initiated a 'run' on MMMFs, and in a matter of days, institutional investors (and less so individual investors, an important distinction addressed later in this chapter) withdrew some $450 billion. This brought the repo market to a near halt, thus withholding a vital source of overnight funding for securities dealers (Duffie, 2011, Ch. 1). Moreover, real-economy businesses that desperately needed an infusion of short-term debt could not fund operations, a situation known as 'liquidity crunch'. The Bush administration acted as lender of last resort by infusing $700 billion to ease liquidity and panic.

The US administration rescued insurance firm AIG, presumably because it insured a large portion of that debt but lacked the cash to compensate the insured parties for their losses. The collapse of AIG also resonated across the world because it held contracts and executed transactions with a large number of banks, insurance companies, pension funds, hedge funds and investment firms in the majority of developed and developing countries. At that time, financial institutions feared that they were dealing with others that might be at high risk. As a result, the market for interbank lending froze and with it, so did the entire financial sector.

Fear over counter-party credit quality was expressed in a sharp rise in interbank interest rates and credit risk premiums, not only in the US, but around the world. Several days after AIG's rescue, the European financial system tumbled towards the abyss, despite the fact that in the months before the Lehman Brothers collapse, the Europeans regarded the crisis as if it was an internal US problem. The governments of Ireland, Germany, the UK and even Canada were forced to extend 'last resort' assistance to larger and smaller banks in order to curb bank runs.

European manufacturing companies primarily used bank loans to finance their operations, unlike US companies that relied mainly on the capital markets to solicit debt. Therefore, when European banks absorbed losses due to the falling value of subprime mortgage derivatives, which at this stage had already infected prime mortgage derivatives as well, they cut back loans to the real sector. Facing limited credit, businesses impeded their normal operations; this was expressed by the lowering of purchase of raw materials, reducing production costs and cutting payroll expenditure. In this way the credit crisis began to impact real-economy activity.

However, how *exactly* did the crisis spread to the rest of the world? For one, the large European banks held subsidiaries in Eastern Europe, which were forced to limit exposure to third parties as part of corporate-wide decisions. The limited availability of funds therefore introduced liquidity constraints to local businesses, and so in fact the liquidity crunch was exported to peripheral countries as well. A second channel was international trade. As described in Chapter 5 when presenting Kindleberger's explanations for the 1930s' global crisis, reduced demand in developed countries spread the crisis into countries that were considered the engines of world growth, i.e., Brazil, Russia, India and China. Those countries exported their products to Western countries, while producing them by buying raw materials and hiring employees from poorer countries. And so, when the exporting countries faced low Western demand, their economic activity slowed down as well. This immediately reduced demand for raw materials and foreign employees, thereby transferring the crisis to the weaker economies. As a result, there was also decreased demand for commodities, and the prices of oil, gas and wheat fell.

As a direct result of all of the above, and primarily the shrinking demand for goods and services coupled with higher uncertainty about many firms' future profitability, affected stock prices around the globe. As seen in Chapter 2, the value of a stock today is determined by the firm's *expected* profitability and riskiness. As real-economy firms were not expected to be as profitable as they were, and coupled with higher expected risk, stock prices plummeted worldwide. Since household savings are invested in stocks and bonds, and both shrank in value, the eroding public wealth further reduced the public's demand for goods.

15.3 Financial Fragility

Shocks to the financial sector were not uniform across countries. These shocks caused severe damage to the real economy in those countries in which the government or the business sector acted irresponsibly, primarily via excessive borrowing. For example, Israel and India have better-supervised banking systems and debt levels in the financial sector and in most of real-economy firms were relatively low. Thus, in these countries the impact of the crisis was relatively mild. In particular, the crisis affected particular sectors that were excessively leveraged and invested in risky assets. For example, the impact of declining real estate prices did affect highly levered Israeli real-estate holding companies who invested in Eastern European real estate assets.

During the years of prosperity, many Western and Eastern European countries could not resist the temptation of low interest rates. Political pressure to increase government spending and raise salaries in sectors that had felt discriminated resulted in increasing government deficits. Put simply, these deficits are expenses today that are financed by long-term loans the government takes from its own citizens or from foreign lenders. Greece, for example, presented a falsely optimistic picture of its true financial status in order to gain acceptance to the European Union (EU) in 2001. This enabled Greece to finance, through massive debt, showcase projects like the 2004 Olympic Games in Athens. But loans must be repaid, and when interest and principal payments burden a country's budget, government responsibility implies reducing other, less rigid expense items. Often, cutting those expense items include cutting governmental services, salaries to public sector employees and the like. The people in Greece demonstrated against those budget cuts. But eventually a bitter pill had to be swollen to heal the economy. Moreover, high debt levels weaken government's ability to function as the lender of last resort in crisis times, and this is what happened to the Greek government. Because it could not act as the lender of last resort, and because it could not print euros or devalue the euro, Greece resorted to the aid of foreign countries.

In the years preceding the financial crisis, cheap money flowed into the private sector and created real estate bubbles in numerous countries. The US real estate bubble was expressed in a 73% increase in residential home prices in the ten years preceding 2007. This sounds like a lot, but in Spain prices during the same period rose by 145%. Real estate bubbles also occurred in Ireland, Iceland, New Zealand, Vietnam, Thailand, China, South Africa, Singapore and others (Roubini and Mihm, 2010, Ch. 5).

The fever of cheap credit also blinded governments that until then were considered sensible and cautious, from Britain to Dubai and even to Iceland. For example, the Labour government in Britain adopted a liberal financial policy, striving to turn London into a financial center of comparable importance to New York. The mortgage securitization industry flourished, mainly in Britain, Spain and Holland, as mortgages to problematic borrowers were packaged and sold to pension funds, insurance companies and banks all over the world. In 2007 alone, mortgages valued at about half a trillion euros were securitized due to a lax regulatory system. Even though this seems like a high amount, note that as of the last quarter of 2009, the total amount of securitized assets stood at $11.6 trillion, about one-third of all American debt securities (Acharya *et al.*, 2011).

15.4 Dubai

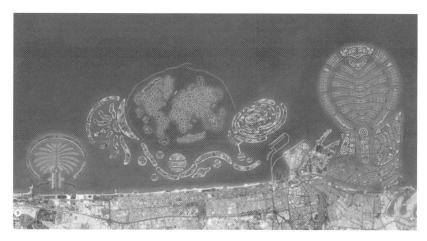

Source: By Tobias Karlhuber (Own work) [Public domain], via Wikimedia Commons (accessed 18 November 2014).

Dubai has established huge real estate projects, premier among them the highest building in the world, Burj Khalifa.[1] Luxury apartments

---

[1] Dubai is a city within an emirate of the same name. The emirate of Dubai is one of seven emirates that make the United Arab Emirates. Dubai is the largest in terms of population and it is the second largest, after Abu Dhabi, in terms of land territory. Dubai and Abu Dhabi have veto power over nationally critical matters.

constructed on artificial islands have been sold at a pace of $1 billion *per day* to investors from around the world. Most of those investors had no intention of living in the apartments, but rather selling them to other buyers at higher prices — pure speculation. Funding for these speculative purchases was made possible thanks to available cheap money in Tokyo, Europe and the US. When the crisis expanded, the flow of speculative dollars to Dubai stopped almost entirely and the investment company Dubai World, a large portion of whose stock was held by Mohammed bin Rashid Al Maktoum (Vice President of the United Arab Emirates and monarch of Dubai), could not meet its debt payments of some $59 billion. Dubai's economy verged on a major collapse until it received assistance from Abu Dhabi and arrived at a debt arrangement with its creditors in May 2010.

15.5 Iceland

Davíð (pronounced 'David') Oddsson was Mayor of Reykjavík from 1982 to 1991, the longest-serving prime minister of Iceland between 1991 and 2004, and commissioner of the Central Bank of Iceland between 2005 and 2009. In 2009, he was appointed editor of newspaper *Morgunblaðið*, an act that caused rage and cancellation of one-third of all subscriptions. A special investigation commission found that the appointment was motivated by intensions to manipulate political decisions through the media.

Davíð Oddsson was included in *Time* magazine's list of the 25 people to blame for the financial crisis. In 2010, Reuters reported that an official investigation committee found Oddsson, together with other high-ranked officials, responsible for acting with 'gross negligence' during the period preceding Iceland's financial collapse (*Time*, 2014e).

Picture by Lennart Perlenhem ministerrådet/rådet/norden.org [CC-BY-2.5-dk (http://creativecommons.org/licenses/by/2.5/dk/deed.en)], via Wikimedia Commons (accessed 2 December 2014).

Oddsson wanted to transform Iceland from a tranquil country of fishermen to a modern financial center. Note that Iceland is a remote island in the North Atlantic and the Arctic oceans, just south of the Arctic Circle, with 320,000 residents and three banks, which are big by local standards but

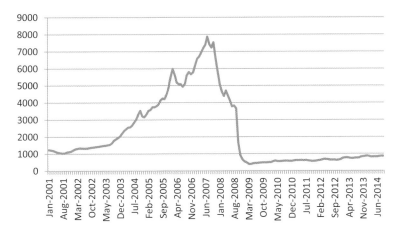

Figure 15.1   Iceland All-shares index; Total Stock Market Index 1/2001–6/2014

Data Source: OECD Statistical Database. Monthly Monetary and Financial Statistics. Chart by the author.

small by EU or US standards, thus surely incapable of making an infrastructure for a financial center. Oddsson privatized the main income source for
the island's inhabitants, the fishing industry, via one of the country's largest
banks. The country's banks extended short-term loans to each other while
promising investors, primarily in Britain and Holland, high long-term
returns. When the crisis arrived, a run developed for Icelandic deposits in
England and Holland. However, the three major Icelandic banks were
unable to meet the high cash demands. Those banks collapsed and were
nationalized. The banking collapse in Iceland was the largest relative to
gross domestic profit (GDP) when compared with any other country worldwide, at any time in history. The index of Iceland's major stocks plummeted
from a level of almost 8,000 in mid-2007 to less than 400 April 2009, a drop
of about 95%.

Additional Reading

Acharya, V., Cooley, T.F., Richardson, M. and Walter, I. (eds) (2011). *Regulating Wall
   Street, The Dodd–Frank Act and the New Architecture of Global Finance*. New York:
   John Wiley & Sons.
Duffie, D. (2011). *How Big Banks Fail, And What To Do About It*. Princeton, NJ:
   Princeton University Press.
Financial Crisis Inquiry Commission (FCIC) (2011). *The Financial Crisis Inquiry
   Report, Authorized Edition: Final Report of the National Commission on the Causes of
   the Financial and Economic Crisis in the United States*. New York: PublicAffairs.

16.

Regulatory Capture and Corruption vs. Integrity and Stability

16.1 Introduction

This book has made clear that some financial crises result from bad decisions, like refusing to depreciate a currency under a fixed exchange rate regime even when indicators and experts are clear about it (e.g., Mexico, Argentina, and Thailand). However, in many other cases bubbles evolve in asset prices because of short-term manipulation (e.g., US in 1929; Israel in 1983), or due to abuse of loopholes in law or regulations (e.g., the US accounting scandals and the subprime real estate bubble). In some cases, those entrusted with the public's savings use their power to tilt the law or regulation to their favor, thereby shifting wealth from the public to their constituents. These cases do not mean, of course, that all people or all actions in the financial industry are corrupt, but they do raise many questions about the levels of morality and ethics in the industry.

Arguing that a particular action is unequivocally moral or ethical, or that it is not so, appears to be difficult, if not impossible. One reason is that an action or behavior that is considered moral or ethical in one society might be considered otherwise in a different society. Moreover, within a given society, an action that once was considered immoral or unethical may be acceptable today. Compare those notions with the simpler notion of illegal behavior: An action is illegal if it violates the country's law, but it may be legal in another country. Therefore, one cannot make an absolute cross-country statement about the legality of this action. While the legal environment changes and evolves in a documented manner (i.e., the book of laws), morality and ethics change with the accepted norms in society, and these are not formally documented, thus impossible to formulate in universal terms.[1]

An important term that relates morality and ethics to actual behavior is 'integrity'. Erhard *et al.* (2010) define the integrity of a person (or an organization or system, such as the legal system) based on the consistency between what the person is saying and doing. A person or organization that acts under the moral constraints of society and keeps its word is in a state of integrity. Perhaps the most important assertion of the Erhard *et al.* theory is that integrity is as important to organizations as a factor of production, like know how, patents or commercial data. As such, integrity adds value to a firm and if integrity is destroyed, value is lost as well. Erhard and Jensen (2012) argue that an organization operating with integrity can be much more productive than a non-integrity benchmark. The following section offers a brief review of lack of integrity throughout the financial crises that are covered in this book, their implications for regulatory capture, immoral or unethical behavior, and the loss of value that such actions caused.

16.2 Regulatory Capture, Loss of Integrity and Loss of Value through Financial Crises

As seen in Chapter 1, Hyman Minsky considered economic expansion and shrinkage throughout the business cycle as given and pointed at the role of excess debt and credit as key drivers of default. Minsky argued that in periods of expansion, businesses will take loans and banks will be happy to give out those loans, as the future looks promising. However, ideally, regulators and policy makers (like the central bank) would step in and limit banks' loan-making activity because they would know that excess credit leads to defaults, and possibly to financial crises. The question then is: What motivates regulators and policy makers to allow financial institutions to extend excess loans to businesses knowing that when the business cycle shrinks, the likelihood of financial crises increases?[2]

There is no doubt that financial institutions have an incentive to give excess loans due to moral hazard considerations. The discussion that follows argues that those moral hazard considerations motivate some financial institutions to capture financial regulation. But motivation alone

---

[1] Morality, ethics, and legality are extremely important notions for social order, but there is much ambiguity in their use. Interested readers may want to read Erhard *et al.* (2010).
[2] The term 'excess loans' refers to loans granted beyond the long-run safe level of lending that a particular financial institution normally gives away.

is not enough to prove capture, as Carpenter and Moss (2013) argue. The following table (Table 16.1) outlines the three criteria that Carpenter and Moss consider important in determining whether regulatory capture indeed occurred. When all three criterions are met, they are denoted the 'gold standard' of regulatory capture by Carpenter and Moss's criteria.

The table shows that among the cases described in this book, four cases meet the gold standard. The four cases are (1) the accounting scandals of the late 1990s in the US; (2) the manipulation of Israeli banks share prices; (3) the inability of passing CFTC regulation on derivative assets; and (4) enacting the Gramm–Leach–Bliley Act in 1999. Reading through the table shows in what ways public interest was damaged; it shows that indeed, there has been a policy shift that favored the financial industry; and in the right-most column it shows that the financial industry played an effective role, both action and intent, toward making the policy shift.

As one can read from the table, once captured, financial institutions often gains twice: first, by extending excess loans or otherwise increasing their business activities, and second they shift downside risks to taxpayers, knowing that the government will step in to save them when the crisis occurs.

Chapters 4 and 5 highlighted that during the 1929 bubble and the early 1930s speculators were buying and selling stocks based on rumor. Often, the speculators themselves initiated those rumors or bid up prices, as explained in Section 1.2.[3] Small and large investment banks issued and sold to the public securities of firms that were void of reasonable economic value, while promising, implicitly or explicitly, high future returns. Put simply, they were lying and therefore not acting with integrity. These trading patterns seem to have played important roles in creating and sustaining the bubble of 1920s that, like all bubbles, had to crash. When the party ended, the massive market meltdown of October 1929 took down many financial institutions that would have otherwise been solvent and so resulted in a massive loss of value for many in society. The lesson is that absent or weak regulations increase

[3] A lack of rules and regulations, which facilitated speculative trading, prevailed prior to the first documented crises of the Dutch Tulip Bubble (1636–1637), and the South Sea Bubble (1720), among others not discussed in this book. See Kindleberger and Aliber (2005). Because there were no regulations, one cannot argue that there was regulatory capture in those, and the 1929 crises, because there was no policy shift. However, Carpenter and Moss (2013) consider 'cultural capture', which changes '… the assumptions, lenses and vocabularies…' in public discourse. The latter may have prevailed prior to financial crises in the pre-regulation era, but proof is more difficult.

Table 16.1 Diagnosis of regulatory capture using the 'gold standard' of Carpenter & Moss (2013)

Case	Show a defeasible model of public interest	Show policy shift from public interest and toward industry	Show sufficiently effective action and intent by industry in making policy shift
Cendant, Enron, WorldCom, and similar corporate America Scandals (Chapter 6)	One or more of the following: 1. Overvalued assets in the balance sheet. 2. Undervalued debt and liabilities in the balance sheet (by abusing Special Purpose Entities). As a result: a) Financial risk was under represented. b) Traded stocks were overvalued, thus crushed when true information disclosed.	1. Managers pressure accountants to relax accounting standards in order to present the company better than it really is. 2. Accounting firms pressure politicians to reduce the power of SEC.	By opposing reforms that were suggested between 1978–1979 by the Cohen committee recommendations, by the John E. Moss bill, and by the SEC, the big accounting firms preserved their power on auditing practices. In particular, the efforts of SEC chairman Levitt between 1997–2000 to improve audit quality were strongly opposed by the big accounting firms who employed pressure on Congress people.
Israeli bank-stock manipulation (Chapter 8)	1. Overvaluation of stocks. 2. False representation of low risk of bank stocks.	1. Started manipulation in late 1970's secretly. 2. Regulators learned about it but were pressured by the banks to allow the manipulation. 3. The Commission found that in 1980, the Ministry of Finance had approved 12 stock issues and therefore was supposed to understand the risk entailed by the manipulation activities and the necessity to act against them.	Official meetings with Ministry of Finance officials. Dr. Heth told the Commission that the fact that the banks controlled the board of directors of the exchange prevented him from passing decisions to prevent or reduce the use of 'leaders' for the purpose of manipulation. ISA demanded that the banks reveal some facts concerning the manipulation in their prospectuses, but the banks opposed it arguing that: 'The public will notice that the king is naked.'

Inability to pass CFTC regulation of over-the-counter credit derivatives by CFTC head, Mrs. Brooksley Born Section 12.10	Public interest was hurt by increased risk that stems from excessive use of unregulated credit derivatives. Some institutions misused credit derivatives to leverage their own institutions to levels that were not acceptable had they been regulated.	Industry profits by creating and using credit derivatives to hedge transactions between different financial institutions. In most cases (predominantly SWAP contracts), the exposure and risk were known only to the parties involved. Born's initiative was aimed at imposing oversight on those unregulated transactions.	Because of heavy pressure from the financial industry, primarily through lobbying, legislation was passed by the Congress prohibiting regulation of derivatives by Born's agency.
Gramm–Leach–Biley Act 1999 (GLBA) (Section 12.3)	Deregulation enabled the formation of giant financial institutions that became "too big to fail". As a result, the competitive environment changed into an oligopolistic one, transferring value from the public to the industry. Moral hazard created an incentive for those giant institutions to take excessive risks, trusting they will be saved by taxpayer money if failed.	GLBA was the peak of deregulation efforts by the financial industry. It effectively repealed the Glass–Steagall Act of 1933. GLBA extracted regulatory oversight of the SEC on large investment bank holding companies.	Citigroup's co-chairs Sandy Weill and John Reed led an aggressive lobbying campaign on Congress. They hired Robert Rubin, who recently stepped down as Treasury Secretary, to promote the legislation. They worked energetically with Phil Gramm, chair of the Banking Committee in lobbying and promoting the change in policy. The change in policy, from the Glass–Steagall Act to GLBA was a radical shift in policy, which later was partly rewind by the Dodd–Frank Act.

the likelihood of deterioration of morality and ethics, which lead to loss of integrity, as exemplified by the creation of bubbles.

The US political and legal systems reacted in the early 1930s to the 1929 meltdown by creating new laws, most notably the Glass–Steagall Act (1934) and the Securities Act (1933), and it created new institutions like the Securities and Exchange Commission (SEC) and Federal Deposit Insurance Corporation (FDIC). Comparable laws and institutions soon were established in other countries, suggesting of their necessity. The understanding that international trade and financial cooperation in times of distress are important for economic growth and financial stability motivated the creation of a number of international agencies and collaborative agreements. Most notable are the International Monetary Fund (IMF) founded in July 1944, the World Bank founded in December 1945, and the gradual reduction of barriers to trade through GATT (General Agreement on Tariffs and Trade) and WTO (World Trade Organization) agreements since 1947. On the surface, it seemed like financial crises were tamed, in spite of the eruption of inflation in the 1970s and other short-term shocks to the global financial system.

However, beneath the surface ill symbiosis developed in corporate America and threatened its moral standards. As seen in Chapter 6, the big US accounting firms' desire to increase revenues motivated them to reduce the power of the SEC as the 'watch dog' of traded corporations. They did so by lobbying and donating to political representatives, who were implicitly or explicitly expected to cut budgets from the SEC and reduce its staff and its ability to promote effective supervision. At the same time, the Big Eight merged amongst themselves, increased their cartel power, and were the rule-makers for almost all firms traded in the New York Stock Exchange (NYSE). Their consulting services to those public firms exposed them to conflicts of interest and moral hazard that resulted with firm-level corruption.

Evidently, the numbers and words that were printed in the financial statements of NYSE firms prior to the scandals of early 2000s were out of integrity. Unfortunately, this was the information that the accounting firms signed on and the public relied on. By so doing, the accounting firms contributed to the deteriorating moral standards of the US business community. Immoral and unethical norms prevailed and resulted in a crisis of confidence. Enron and WorldCom were the first to collapse, followed by dozens of others, imposing on society a loss of value in a variety of ways: loss of jobs, savings, pensions, trust, hope and prosperity.

16.3 Executive Pay

Starting from the 1990s some top managers at established, as well as young, new-technology firms favored short-term growth in the stock market over long-term, fundamental growth in real business. One motivation to do so was their desire to gain from stock options that those managers received as part of their compensation packages. Thus, while most members of society lost value when the dot-com bubble crashed, a few gained value. Erhard and Jensen (2012) argue that many of these compensation packages were based on lies, and because they were lacking integrity, they were immoral and non-ethical. The primary reason for those compensation schemes to be classified as such is that they were based on 'under promise and over deliver'. You see, if a manager is generously compensated based on achievements, but the bar is set rather low, both the board of directors and the manager know that the bonus will be most likely paid. Such a compensation plan is lacking integrity because it is a simple lie: both parties know in advance that the true plan is to pay the manager under almost any future scenario, whether the manager is indeed skilled or not. This is one way through which value was shifted from the firm, which belongs to *all* shareholders, to a few shareholders.

A second way through which value was transferred from all shareholders to top executives is known as the 'dilution' effect. Consider a firm that used to be 100% owned by its original shareholders, but then issued stock options to its top executives that if exercised would amount to 10% of the shares outstanding. This means, for example, that if the firm has 100 (possibly million) original shares, 10 more shares are issued to top executives. Once the executives hold those 10 shares out of the now 110 outstanding shares, they will receive about 9.1% (=10/110) of all future dividends, payable forever, while all of the original shareholders receive 90.9% of the company's profits. This second effect of options plans has long-lasting effects on the allocation of value among shareholders, and income distribution across groups in society.

In the 1970s accountants agreed that paying managers through stock options was part of the payroll expense of the firm. However, when this remuneration technique gained popularity, primarily throughout the dot-com bubble (1995–2000), and up until 2006, they changed their mind. Pressured by the same managers that hired them, accounting firms no longer deemed the compensation through stock options as an expense. There are a number of reasons for this. First, if remuneration through options is an expense, the business presents lower profits and the manager's compensation shrinks. Second, payroll differentials between top executives and other employees grow, with ill implications on the public standing of the firm. While academics and independent professionals insisted that stock options should be expensed (Bodie *et al.*, 2003), the big accounting firms objected. Alan Greenspan (2002) described those compensation plans as: 'perversely created incentives to artificially inflate reported earnings in order to keep stock prices high and rising'. These practices motivated managers to capture accountants, urging them to increase short-term reported earnings (as described in Chapters 6 and 7), and by doing so, they caused loss of value in the long term.

Notice that the issue is not whether compensating managers with options is right or wrong, for it surely was meant to solve the agency problem between shareholders and management. Unfortunately, in those years, codes of conduct were broken toward maximizing executives' short-term gains. The ways by which the parameters of the options plans were determined were corrupt; for one, chief executive officers (CEOs) were dominant in boards of their colleagues, and they knew that if they approved a friend's bonus plan, their plan was likely to be approved as well. For that, and other reasons, the Sarbanes–Oxley Act increased the power of independent directors in remuneration committees. Only in 2006, after the accounting scandals mitigated the Big Four's power to object, and with the International Accounting Standards Board (IASB) requiring that options be expensed, the US rule changed and options are now expensed again.

A common denominator across these examples is that information was available, at least in professional outlets (normally, academics and the media are expected to digest the information and make it accessible to the public). Therefore, it is conceivable that at least some of the information must have been known, albeit not necessarily to the finest details, to decision makers of the financial system. Still, in the early 2000s Mr. Greenspan's low interest rates policy, coupled with the Homeownership Opportunity and Equity Protection Act, motivated households to buy houses they could not afford, and a new bubble thus emerged. Apparently, Mr. Greenspan's policy was based on genuine professional belief that low interest rates were necessary to stimulate the economy. Similarly, his decision to avoid tighter supervision of credit derivatives was not a result of greed or expectation for future personal gain. Therefore, it does not seem right to consider Mr. Greenspan as a person that was not acting with integrity. As described in Section 12.3, Robert Rubin, Phil Gramm and others were backed by Greenspan-promoted deregulation. Some of the people involved were captured by the big financial institutions, while the Gramm–Leach–Bliley Financial Services Modernization Act of 1999 effectively repealed the

Glass–Steagall Act and the separation between commercial and investment banking (Baram, 2008).

Poor integrity among top managers of financial corporations, coupled with easy-to-buy politicians, resulted in aggressive lobbying and regulatory capture that changed the rules of the game in favor of the financial sector. In particular, the financial sector demanded and received a greater share of the American pie at the expense of the public. This low integrity of top management sank in to many within their organizations, and initiated the slippery slope of moral norms. Peter Forstmoser, chairman of the insurance giant Swiss Re, delivered in 2006 a speech entitled 'Integrity in Finance' to the Swiss Banking Institute. Forstmoser lists explicit phrases that were in use in financial organizations, presumably to justify unethical behavior:

- Everybody else is doing it.
- We've always done it. That's the way this business works.
- If we don't do it, somebody else will.
- Nobody's hurt by it.
- It doesn't matter how it gets done, as long as it gets done.
- It works, so let's not ask for too many questions.
- No one's going to notice.
- It's legal, but …

Evidently, decision makers in the financial industry figured that if they would 'round a corner' by a bit, told only 'part of the truth' or used a white lie, they would gain while others would not lose. Of course, things do not work that way and the proof came when the real estate bubble crashed and swept the corrupt US financial industry away with it, together with many ill European financial systems.

16.4 Incentives

As detailed in Chapters 11 to 14, the incentives according to which players acted throughout the real estate bubble highlighted short-term personal gain over integrity. Subprime households signed papers testifying they could meet their financial obligations, while in fact they were unable to commit to those payments. Yes, they might have been naïve and less informed than profession-als of the field, but this is the role of the mortgage bank agent, who was sup-posed to balance their optimism and minimize risk for the bank. Unfortunately, this agent also preferred the short-term personal gain and presented the household with unrealistic dreams of homeownership. The mortgage bank managers knew that these new loans to subprime borrowers were riskier than mortgages they had issued in the past to prime borrowers. However, knowing they would package and sell those mortgages to Fannie, Freddie or Lehman Brothers, they favored the short-term gain over maintaining integrity with their business partners.

As part of the production process of toxic credit derivatives, the securitizing agency paid rating companies to rate as large a proportion as possible of the mortgage-backed securities (MBSs) as AAA. By accepting those terms and knowing that the pooled assets are riskier than prime pools, the rating agencies also act without integrity, taking part in the corrupt process. Institutional investors from around the globe had a clue that the subprime-based MBSs were more risky than the US government AAA bonds. The clue was the higher return those AAA MBS trenches paid above the US government bonds. The writing was on the wall, but all players in the financial system had the incentive to ignore it.

Apparently, financial crises are more likely to evolve when organizational, and often political, norms have deteriorated to a point where a loss of integrity and immoral behavior become the *acceptable norm*. Managers, for example, might not understand why earning hundreds of millions of dollars a year could be immoral if their performance is mediocre. The emphasis is on *organizational* and not *personal* norms because it takes more than the activities of one person to transform the moral standards of an organization. If that happens, many employees and executives draw from the 'public good' and reduce the value the organization generates to its stakeholders. For a financial institution, this means that lenders hold bonds that are more likely to default, depositors might not receive the full value of their deposits and shareholders might end up losing their investment.

16.5 Lobbying, Politicians, and Regulation

Is the financial industry more corrupt than other industries? Is it the complexity of the financial industry that makes it more prone to run into crisis? Why has the US financial system run into so many financial crises, while Canada has faced not even one?[4]

The financial industry has grown more complex over time and consequently recruited employees that are more educated. However, as seen in

---

[4] An interesting and relevant EconTalk about this subject was held on 16 September 2013 between host Russ Roberts and David Laidler (http://www.econtalk.org/archives/2013/09/david_laidler_o.html).

Chapter 4, even in its infancy, when most traders were not financial engineers or bright mathematicians, fraud and manipulation prevailed. By Wall Street jargon, many traders are motivated by 'fear and greed', but this is not enough to explain the recent crises of the dot-com bubble, the accounting scandals, the real estate bubble and the credit crisis of 2008 to 2010, for these went beyond individuals' behavior, effectively involving much broader organizations and systems.

Compare, for example, the financial industry to a high-technology industry like telecommunication. Both are complex and recruit many highly educated and highly motivated employees. In both industries, the average pay is rather high, and bonuses and stock options are widely used to increase motivation. One key difference however is the *measurability of outcomes*. A telecommunication system will work better or worse depending on physically measurable criteria. The performance of one system can be compared with the performance of a competitor's system, and problems can often be traced down to specific teams, or even specific individuals. As such, it is difficult for an individual, a team, a system or an organization to diverge away from integrity. In the financial industry, however, many variables and asset values are subject to professional judgment, as seen in the statement of analyst Lise Buyer who was involved in the valuation of Netscape (*The Wall Street Journal*, 1995).

> Everyone is using their own set of growth rates based on current net-related products and a little crystal-ball gazing and fairy dust,' says Ms. Buyer. 'I don't know how to put a value on it — you pick a price you're willing to pay and you find a way to rationalize it.

In such an environment, it is far easier to act without integrity, as the individual, team, organization or system can disguise their performance by the vagueness of outcomes.

Moreover, in the financial industry individuals manage huge amounts of money, while the telecommunications industry puts in the hands of high-ranked employees' valuable hardware and software. The relative ease by which one can diverge away from integrity and still be paid fairly, and the high temptation to tilt the numbers in one's favor, puts many honest employees in tough situations. Some individuals might not fully comprehend the responsibility that lies in their hands and the implications of unethical behavior. To cope with this problem, financial institutions must incorporate sound ethical codes of conduct as an immanent aspect of their organizational culture and norms. Integrity and ethical behavior must be clearly visible through each and every action taken by all employees, at all levels. While a financial institution can post a page on its website in which an ethical plan is described by using high language, this act is void of content as long as ethical and moral values are not present in the daily routines of that organization.

On top of the personal level, there exist macro-level incentives for financial institutions to act without integrity and draw from the public's wealth. Zingales (2012) argues that the major adverse impact of abandoning the separation between commercial and investment banking (by undoing the Glass–Steagall Act in 1999), was that the interests of large financial institutions became rather uniform. Before the repeal of the Glass–Steagall Act, commercial banks and investment banks lobbied to mitigate the impact of new regulations and laws on their businesses. By representing two rather different types of financial institutions each party verified that the other party does not receive too much power or benefits. However, once the Glass–Steagall Act was gone, most influential financial institutions lobbied for greater power for the financial industry as a whole. Zingales argues that this immense power, which was earned by donations to Congress people and political parties, tilted many rules to be pro-business, rather than pro-market. The two differ materially since a law that is pro-business favors a specific business or industry (here, the financial industry, but this is not the only case), hence transfers value from the public to the business. Conversely, a pro-market law promotes efficiency by improving competition, an act that forces businesses to improve and so transfer value *to* the public, and not *from* the public.

When talking about his book with Russ Roberts, host of EconTalk,[5] Prof. Zingales argues that while lobbying is a legitimate business in a free society as it is consistent with the principles of freedom of speech and freedom of occupation, this particular profession changed over the past several years. While in the past lobbying primarily served industries to mitigate the impact of legislation on their businesses, over the last several years lobbying has transformed to focus on changing or creating laws and regulations in order to transfer value from the public to the business sector. This kind of lobbying, argues Roberts, is unethical and immoral, in spite of being legal.

To put those notions in perspective, one must acknowledge that regulation indeed imposes heavy costs on the financial industry. To make the point that pro-business lobbying is not the route the financial sector should

---

[5] Listen to Russ Roberts's talk with Prof. Zingales here: http://www.econtalk.org/archives/2012/07/zingales_on_cap.html.

have taken, Zingales presents the case where the financial industry lobbied to grant super-seniority for derivative asset holders in the event of default, as part of the changes discussed in Chapters 7 and 13 to the Bankruptcy Law of 2005. Arguably, this was one of the motivations in 2005 for the financial sector to start making and holding derivative assets, hence causing the acceleration of the real estate bubble.

Additional Reading

Erhard, W. and Jensen, M.C. (2012). 'Putting Integrity into Finance: A Purely Positive Approach.' Harvard Business School Working Paper, No. 12-074, April.

Erhard, W.H., Jensen, M.C. and Zaffron, S. (2010). 'Integrity: A Positive Model That Incorporates the Normative Phenomena of Morality, Ethics, and Legality Abridged.' Harvard Business School Working Paper, No. 10-061, February.

Kindleberger, C.P. and Aliber, R.Z. (2005). *Manias, Panics, and Crashes: A History of Financial Crises*. 5th edition. New York: John Wiley and Sons.

Rajan, R. and Zingales, L. (2003). *Saving Capitalism from the Capitalists*. New York: Random House.

Zingales, L. (2012). *A Capitalism for the People: Recapturing the Lost Genius of American Prosperity*. New York: Basic Books.

Bibliography

Abreu, D. and Brunnermeier, M.K. (2003). 'Bubbles and Crashes,' *Econometrica*, 71, 173–204.

Acharya, V., Cooley, T.F., Richardson, M. and Walter, I. (eds.) (2011). *Regulating Wall Street, The Dodd–Frank Act and the New Architecture of Global Finance*. New York: John Wiley & Sons.

Admati, A. and Hellwig, M. (2013). *The Bankers' New Clothes: What's Wrong with Banking and What to Do About It*. Princeton, NJ: Princeton University Press.

Arrow, K.J. (1951). *Social Choice and Individual Values*. New York: Wiley.

Bagehot, W. (1999). *Lombard Street: A Description of the Money Market*. New York: Wiley.

Baram, M. (2008). 'Who's Whining Now? Gramm Slammed By Economists,' *ABC News*. Available at: http://abcnews.go.com/Politics/story?id=5835269 (accessed 7 January 2015).

Benmelech, E. and Dlugosz, J. (2009). 'The Alchemy of CDO Credit Ratings.' NBER Working Paper #14878.

Bernanke, B.S. (2013). *The Federal Reserve and the Financial Crisis*. Princeton, NJ: Princeton University Press.

Bodie, Z., Kaplan, R.S. and Merton, R.C. (2003). 'For the Last Time: Stock Options Are an Expense,' *Harvard Business Review*, 81, 3, 62–71.

Berton, L. (2003). 'Advertising has Hurt Accounting's Ethics: Critics,' *Chicago Sun-Times*, January 13, 2003.

Carpenter, J., Cooley, T. and Walter, I. (2011). 'Reforming Compensation and Corporate Governance,' in Acharya *et al.*, *Op. Cit.*, pp. 493–509.

Carpenter, D. and Moss, D. (2013). *Preventing Regulatory Capture: Special Interest Influence and How to Limit it*. Cambridge: Cambridge University Press.

Chang, C.-H., Dandapani, K. and Auster, A. (1995). 'The 100-Year Japanese Residential Mortgage: An Examination,' *Journal of International Accounting, Auditing and Taxation*, 4, 1, 13–26.

Cohen, D. (2013). 'The Education of Alan Greenspan,' *Huffington Post*. Available at: http://able2know.org/topic/124756-1 (accessed 14 October 2013).

Commission on Auditors' Responsibilities (1978). 'AICPA Commission on Auditors' Responsibilities: Report, Conclusions, and Recommendations. An independent Commission established by the American Institute of Certified Public Accountants.' Available at: http://documents.routledge-interactive.s3.amazonaws.com/9780415508117/articles/commission.pdf (accessed 14 October 2014).

Cramer, J. (2003). 'Netscape's IPO Sparks a Boom,' *The New York Times*, 31 March. Available at: http://www.time.com/time/specials/packages/article/0,28804,1977881_1977895_1979084,00.html (accessed 14 October 2014).

Crouhy, M.G., Galai, M. and Mark, R. (2013). *The Essentials of Risk Management.* New York: McGraw Hill.

Crouhy, M.G., Jarrow, J.A. and Turnbull, S.M. (2008). 'The Subprime Credit Crisis of 2007,' *The Journal of Derivatives*, Fall 2008, 16, 1, 81–110.

Dal Bo, E. (2006). 'Regulatory Capture: A Review,' *Oxford Review of Economic Policy*, 22, 2, 203–225.

Dennis, B. and O'Harrow, Jr., R. (2009). '1998–2005: AIG & the Anatomy of the Crash,' *The Washington Post*, 5 January.

Duffie, D. (2011). *How Big Banks Fail, and What To Do About It.* Princeton, NJ: Princeton University Press.

Erhard, W.H., Jensen, M.C. and Zaffron, S. (2010). 'Integrity: A Positive Model that Incorporates the Normative Phenomena of Morality, Ethics, and Legality Abridged.' Harvard Business School Working Paper No. 10-061, February.

Erhard, W. and Jensen, M.C. (2012). 'Putting Integrity into Finance: A Purely Positive Approach.' Harvard Business School Working Paper No. 12-074, April.

European Central Bank (ECB) (2014). 'Japan — Equity/index — Nikkei 225 Stock Average Index – Historical close, average of observations through period — Japanese yen.' Available at: http://sdw.ecb.europa.eu/quickview.do?SERIES_KEY=143.FM.A.JP.JPY.DS.EI.JAPDOWA.HSTA (accessed 14 October 2014).

Financial Crisis Inquiry Commission (FCIC) (2011). *The Financial Crisis Inquiry Report, Authorized Edition: Final Report of the National Commission on the Causes of the Financial and Economic Crisis in the United States.* New York: PublicAffairs.

Forstmoser, P. (2006). 'Integrity in Finance — Theory and Practice: A Positive Approach.' Presentation before the Swiss Banking Institute, 15 November.

GAO (2004). 'Financial Derivatives: Actions Needed to Protect the Financial System,' Testimony, 05/19/94, GAO/T-GGD-94-150.

Galbraith, J.K. (1954). *The Great Crash of 1929.* New York: Penguin.

Garbade, K.D. (2006). 'The Evolution of Repo Contracting Conventions in the 1980s,' *FRBNY Economic Policy Review*, 12, 1. Available at: http://www.newyork-fed.org/research/epr/06v12n1/0605garb.html (accessed 14 October 2014).

Goldfarb, B. Kirscha, D. and Millerb, D.A. (2007). 'Was there too little entry during the DotComEra?' *Journal of Financial Economics*, 86, 1, 100–144.

Goldston, R.C. (1981). *The Great Depression: The United States in the Thirties.* New York: Fawcett Books.

Goodman, P.S. (2008). 'Taking Hard New Look at a Greenspan Legacy.' *The New York Times*, 8 October. Available at: http://www.nytimes.com/2008/10/09/

business/economy/09greenspan.html?pagewanted=all&_r=0 (accessed 14 October 2014).

Gorton, G. (2009). 'The Subprime Panic,' *European Financial Management*, 15, 10–46.

Graham, B. and Dodd, D. (1996). *The Memoirs of the Dean of Wall Street*. New York: McGraw-Hill.

Graham, B. and Dodd, D. (2008). *Security Analysis*. 5th edition. New York: McGraw-Hill.

Greenspan, A. (1996). 'The Challenge of Central Banking in a Democratic Society. Remarks by Chairman Alan Greenspan at the Annual Dinner and Francis Boyer Lecture of The American Enterprise Institute for Public Policy Research,' Washington, D.C., 5 December. Available at: http://www.federalreserve.gov/boarddocs/speeches/1996/19961205.htm (accessed 13 October 2014).

Greenspan, A. (2002). Testimony of Alan Greenspan before the Committee on Banking, Housing, and Urban Affairs, U.S. Senate, 16 July.

Higgins, M. and Osler, C. (1997). 'Asset Market Hangovers and Economic Growth: The OECD During 1984–93,' *Oxford Review of Economic Policy*, 13, 110–134.

Hilzenrath, D.S. (2010). 'Commodity Futures Trading Commission judge says colleague biased against complainants,' *Washington Post*, 19 October.

Housing Japan (2011). 'The History of Tokyo Real-Estate Prices.' Available at: http://housingjapan.com/2011/11/10/a-history-of-tokyo-real-estate-prices (accessed 13 October 2014).

Jones, T. (2008). 'How A Clinton-Era Rule Rewrite Made Subprime Crisis Inevitable,' *Investors Business Daily*, 25 September.

Kaminsky, G. and Reinhart, C. (1996). 'Banking and Balance-of-Payments Crises: Models and Evidence.' Working Paper, Board of Governors of the Federal Reserve, Washington, D.C.

Kaminsky, G. and Reinhart, C. (1999). 'The Twin Crises: The Causes of Banking and Balance of-Payments Problems,' *American Economic Review*, 89, 473–500.

Kindleberger, C.P. and Aliber, R.Z. (2005). *Manias, Panics, and Crashes: A History of Financial Crises*. 5th edition. New York: John Wiley and Sons.

Kirk, M. (ed.) (2009). 'The Warning: Interviews-Arthur Levitt,' Frontline (U.S. TV series).

Krugman, P. (2009). *The Return of Depression Economics and the Crisis of 2008*. New York: W. W. Norton & Company.

Lessig, L. (2011). *Republic, Lost. How Money Corrupts Congress – and a Plan to Stop It*. New York: Twelve.

Levine, M.E. and Plott, C.R. (1977). 'Agenda Influence and Its Implications,' *Virginia Law Review*, 63, 561–604.

Levitt, A. (2000). 'Speech by SEC Chairman: A Profession at the Crossroads,' 18 September. Available at: http://www.sec.gov/news/speech/spch399.htm (accessed 3 October 2013).

Lewis, M. (2009). 'The Man Who Crashed the World,' *Vanity Fair*, August.

Mariathasan, M. and Merrouche, O. (2014). 'The Manipulation of Basel Risk-weights,' *Journal of Financial Intermediation*, 23, 3, 300–321.

Mörner, M. (1973). 'The Spanish American Hacienda: A Survey of Recent Research and Debate,' *Hispanic American Historical Review*, 53, 2, 183–216.

Nofsinger, J.R. (2013). *The Psychology of Investing*. 5th edition. Upper Saddle River, NJ: Prentice Hall.

Patsuris, P. (2002). 'The Corporate Scandal Sheet,' Forbes, 26 August.

Paulson, H.M. (2011). *On the Brink: Inside the Race to Stop the Collapse of the Global Financial System*. New York: Grand Central Publishing.

Valdimarsson, O. (2010). 'Iceland probe accuses former PM and ex-central bank head,' Reuters, 12 April.

Rubin, R. (2003). *In An Uncertain World*. New York: Random House.

Roubini, N. and Mihm, S. (2010). *Crisis Economics: A Crash Course in the Future of Finance*. New York: Penguin.

Schapiro, M.L. (2012). 'Testimony on "Perspectives on Money Market Mutual Fund Reforms,"' Before the Committee on Banking, Housing, and Urban Affairs of the United States Senate, 21 June. Available at: http://www.sec.gov/news/testimony/2012/ts062112mls.htm (accessed 16 December 2012).

SEC (2001). 'Human Capital Challenges Require Management Attention (GAO-01-947)', September. Available at: http://www.gao.gov/products/GAO-01-947 (accessed 14 October 2014).

SEC (2002). SEC Operations: Increased Workload Creates Challenges (GAO-02-302)'. March. Available at: http://www.gao.gov/products/GAO-02-302 (accessed 14 October 2014).

SEC (2004). SEC News Digest, 9 August. Available at: http://www.sec.gov/news/digest/dig080904.txt (accessed 3 October 2013).

SEC (2005). SEC Charges Deloitte & Touche For Adelphia Audit, 26 April. Available at: http://www.sec.gov/news/press/2005-65.htm (accessed 3 October 2013).

Smith, K. (2012). 'The Curious Case of Japan in the 21st Century,' Forbes, 8 June. Available at: http://www.forbes.com/sites/modeledbehavior/2012/08/06/the-curious-case-of-japan-in-the-21st-century/ (accessed 15 October 2014).

Stevens, M. (1981). *The Big Eight*. New York: Macmillan.

Stiglitz, J. (2009). 'Capitalist Fools,' *Vanity Fair*, January 2009.

Taibbi, M. (2009). 'The Great American Bubble Machine,' *Rolling Stone*, 9–23 July.

Taleb, N. (2010). *The Black Swan: The Impact of the Highly Improbable*. New York: Penguin.

The Wall Street Journal (1995). 'Lise Buyer Netscape,' 8 August, p. C7.

The Wall Street Journal (2008). 'No Line Responsibilities,' 3 December.

Time (2014a). '25 People to Blame for the Financial Crisis: Gramm,' *Time*, November 2014. Available at: http://content.time.com/time/specials/packages/article/0,28804,1877351_1877350_1877330,00.html (accessed 18 November 2014).

Time (2014b). '25 People to Blame for the Financial Crisis: Fuld,' *Time*, November 2014. Available at: http://content.time.com/time/specials/packages/article/0,28804,1877351_1877350_1877326,00.html (accessed 18 November 2014).

Time (2014c). '25 People to Blame for the Financial Crisis: Cox,' *Time*, November 2014. Available at: http://content.time.com/time/specials/packages/article/0,28804,1877351_1877350_1877323,00.html (accessed 18 November 2014).

Time (2014d). '25 People to Blame for the Financial Crisis: Cassano,' *Time*, November 2014. Available at: http://content.time.com/time/specials/packages/article/0,28804,1877351_1877350_1877321,00.html (accessed 18 November 2014).

Time (2014e). '25 People to Blame for the Financial Crisis: Oddsson,' *Time*, November 2014. Available at: http://content.time.com/time/specials/packages/article/0,28804,1877351_1877350_1877340,00.html (accessed 18 November 2014).

Trading Economics (2014). 'Japan Interest Rate 1972–2014.' Available at: http://www.tradingeconomics.com/japan/interest-rate (accessed 14 October 2014).

United States History (n.d.1). 'Richard Whitney.' Available at: http://www.u-s-history.com/pages/h1808.html (accessed 14 October 2014).

United States History (n.d.2). 'The New Deal.' Available at: http://www.u-s-history.com/pages/h1851.html (accessed 14 October 2014).

Voreacos, D. and Blair Smith, E. (2008). 'Statements on AIG Probed by Prosecutors, People Say.' 26 November, Bloomberg. Available at: http://www.bloomberg.com/apps/news?pid=newsarchive&sid=a6m_BOe9Ftk4 (accessed 14 October 2014).

Weiss, M. (2002). *The Worsening Crisis of Confidence on Wall Street: The Role of Auditing Firms.* Palm Beach Gardens, FL: Weiss Ratings, Inc.

Womack K. (1996). 'Do Brokerage Analysts Recommendations Have Invested Values?' *Journal of Finance*, 51, 1, 137–167.

Zingales, L. (2012). *A Capitalism for the People: Recapturing the Lost Genius of American Prosperity.* New York: Basic Books.

Index